David G

SELECTED PLAYS
1999–2009

David Greig was born in Edinburgh. His plays include
Europe, *The Architect*, *The Speculator*, *The Cosmonaut's
Last Message to the Woman He Once Loved in the
Former Soviet Union*, *Outlying Islands*, *San Diego*,
Pyrenees, *The American Pilot*, *Yellow Moon: The Ballad
of Leila and Lee*, *Damascus*, *Midsummer* (*a Play with
Songs*) and *Dunsinane*. In 1990 he co-founded Suspect
Culture to produce collaborative, experimental theatre
work. His translations and adaptations include Camus's
Caligula, Euripides' *The Bacchae*, Strindberg's *Creditors*
and *Peter Pan*.

DAVID GREIG

Selected Plays
1999–2009

San Diego

Outlying Islands

Pyrenees

The American Pilot

Being Norwegian

Kyoto

Brewers Fayre

faber and faber

First published in 2010
by Faber and Faber Limited
74–77 Great Russell Street, London WC1B 3DA

Typeset by Country Setting, Kingsdown, Kent CT14 8ES
Printed in England by CPI Bookmarque, Croydon, Surrey

A CIP record for this book
is available from the British Library

ISBN 978–0–571–23415–8

2 4 6 8 10 9 7 5 3 1

For Lucie

This is no other place
Than where I am, between
This word and the next.

W. S. Graham, 'The Dark Dialogues'

Contents

Introduction

Most days I look at my desk and I see chaos. Today, for example, I see annotated drafts of two scripts, coffee cups, three different notebooks, a sheet of scrap paper with a list and four sub-lists on it, index cards, a pile of books, a paper bag and a lucky stone: the accumulated unplaceable detritus of the script I am presently writing. This, it occurs to me, is what a play looks like.

When a writer says they are 'working on' a play, it might sound as if this is a sculptural process. Perhaps the writer approaches a mass of material and chips away until its shape is satisfactory. If so, the metaphor is deceptive. Whatever it is I am working on, it has no substantial existence. It is without mass. If it exists at all, it exists as a ghost somewhere in between the lists, cards, laptop, drafts and books on my desk. When someone asks me, 'What are you writing just now?' I say, 'A new play for the Traverse.' But if they ask, '*Where* is the play?' I would be lost. I could only point vaguely at the desk and mumble, 'Somewhere there.'

The uncertainty continues on my shelves. Box files bulge with different versions of each text. On my computer it's the same. If I search my hard drive for a recent script, *Damascus*, for example, my computer asks if I want *Damascus First Draft A.doc*, *Second Draft C.doc,* or *Second Draft D.doc*, or maybe *Damascus NYC Draft A.doc*, *B.doc*, *D (Final).doc.* Each contains changes: some, tiny tweaks to dialogue and others, a radical reworking of the play's ending. Which is the real *Damascus*?

Nowadays a play is usually published in book form to coincide with its first production for the very good reason that the scripts can then be sold to the audience at the theatre. But this modern process also freezes the script at a point a week or so into rehearsals. That moment – like a passport photograph – becomes the defining moment of the play's existence, the version performed in perpetuity.

In perpetuity, that is, until the author is given the enormous privilege of drawing his work together in a volume like this. This is a chance to tidy up my desk, to tidy up my plays, to tidy up my writing life and bring forth from its chaos some kind of order.

The choice of plays was made by a process of elimination. The texts I have produced for Suspect Culture since 1990 seem to exist as a unit and to belong in a separate volume. I have also written a fair number of plays for children and young people which, again, seemed to belong together. Once I discounted adaptations and translations, and those too recent to include, that left the plays collected here. *Being Norwegian*, *Kyoto* and *Brewers Fayre* were conceived as a trilogy to be performed by the same company of actors. They have had separate productions but, as yet, there has been no staging of all three together. For that reason I've kept them as separate works.

The plays are presented in the order they were written rather than the order they were performed. If anyone cares to read the collection from start to finish, perhaps some narrative of becoming might reveal itself. They amount to the work of a decade, from 1999 to 2009. Rereading, I found that some work went counter to approaches I might take now. I shouldn't be surprised. What kind of writer would I be if I hadn't changed over the last ten years? What kind of human being would I be if I didn't think I had grown up a little? Looking at my younger writing self, I had a powerful temptation to cut and rewrite and alter. But touching up the past to suit the present is like Stalin attempting to paint Trotsky out of the photographs of the May Day parade. The gap will always somehow echo. A play is not a static object, it is a process of arranging words in pursuit of something else, an event. The overriding event in a play's life is its first night. So, in the end, I decided to present the texts pretty much as they were then.

The Scottish poet W. S. Graham was once lost on Rannoch Moor during a snowstorm. He had struck out of Glencoe hoping for a lift which never came. For some time he wandered lost in the great white blankness of the moor, alone. He was cold. He began to fade. He thought he might die until eventually he was rescued by a shepherd who took him back to his croft and gave him brandy. Out of this experience Graham conjured up a whole mythology of writing. For him, the aloneness and the emptiness and the whiteness of the snow became an echo of the aloneness and the emptiness and whiteness of the blank page: a landscape across which the author moves, stumbling and searching and leaving behind traces.

That story holds a special place for me partly because the metaphor of the man in the snow is one I have used in *Pyrenees* but also because most of these plays were written in a cottage on Rannoch Moor sitting at a kitchen table and looking out at the very same vast wasted moor across which W. S. Graham was trying to walk that night.

Creating a play happens for me when, driven by some mad impulse, I strike out into the chaotic snowstorm of my heart and mind in search of a lift home. Looking at these plays now, I can't discern myself behind the words. I don't know what I was searching for in their writing and I don't know whether I ever found it. I have, in fact, no memory of actually writing any of these plays at all. It is as if each play has had its writer and each writer has vanished in the snow. Perhaps by reading these plays, you will be able retrace his steps and in doing so make contact with the someone, or the something, that wrote them, and perhaps experience a sharing of the same mad impulse that caused them to be written.

David Greig, July 2010

SAN DIEGO

For Annie

San Diego was first produced by the Tron Theatre Company in a co-production with the Edinburgh International Festival at the Royal Lyceum Theatre, Edinburgh, in August 2003. The cast was as follows:

David Greig Billy Boyd
Pious/David in Consultancy Callum Cuthbertson
Laura Abigail Davies
David the Patient Huss Garbiya
Counsellor/Woman on Phone/Mother Superior/Patience Tamzin Griffin
The Pilot Tony Guilfoyle
Innocent/The Bedouin Tribesman/David in Consultancy Paul Thomas Hickey
Marie/San Diego Cop Vicki Liddelle
Daniel Milton Lopes
Andrew/San Diego Cop/David in Consultancy Nicholas Pinnock
Stewardess/Amy (Hooker)/Sarah Gabriel Quigley

Directors Marisa Zanotti and David Greig
Designer Simon Vincenzi
Lighting Designer Chahine Yavroyan
Sound Designer Graeme Miller

Characters

David Greig
the author

The Stewardess

The Pilot

Andrew

Marie

Daniel/Grey Lag
an illegal immigrant

The Woman
a telephone receptionist

Laura
a patient

The Counsellor

Pious
an illegal immigrant

Innocent
an illegal immigrant

Amy
a hooker

David
a patient

San Diego Cop 1

San Diego Cop 2

David A
someone who works in conceptual consultancy

David B
someone who works in conceptual consultancy

David C
someone who works in conceptual consultancy

Sarah
someone who works in conceptual consultancy

The Bedouin Tribesman

The Mother Superior

Patience / Amy
a real estate agent

Setting

The summer of the year 2000

Prologue

David Greig is sitting in an aeroplane seat.

David Greig It's the summer of 2000. I'm flying to San Diego, California. It will be the first time I have ever visited the American continent. I have been in transit for some eighteen hours now and for almost all that time I have been awake and drinking alcohol. When I left Scotland it was early morning and now, as I approach San Diego airport, it is early afternoon on the same day: June 10th 2000. On the plane I've been reading the *Blue Guide to San Diego*, and I've been particularly struck by two facts that it mentions. First: that San Diego has the highest quality of life of any city in the United States; and second: that despite being such a great place to live, San Diego has featured in almost no fictions, films, novels or plays, but it has, and I quote, 'served as the un-named backdrop for several episodes of *America's Missing Children*.'

I always like to know the facts about a place.

Here comes the Stewardess, she's called Amy.

The Stewardess passes and David stops her.

Excuse me, I couldn't possibly have another whisky by any chance?

Stewardess Of course, sir, one moment.

David I spent a ten-hour hiatus in Toronto Airport, drinking Molson in the tiny glass-fronted smoking lounge. During that period I watched a Filipino woman refuelling a 747, a tiny figure standing on the huge wing.

7

The aeroplane tailfin had a picture of a greylag goose painted on it. Almost simultaneously I read in a two-day-old British newspaper about a Quebecois biologist who had heroically saved a flock of baby geese from extinction. The geese had been orphaned by some calamitous pollution event. Now the season was changing and the goslings were filled with an instinctive urge to migrate, but being motherless they didn't know where to go or what to do in order to satisfy their longing. The biologist knew that, at a certain stage in its development, the gosling's brain is a wet clay ready to imprint the image of its mother. He also knew that when a goose is at that stage, again I quote, 'any sufficiently large object which emits a rythmical sound' will become imprinted as the mother and the goslings will instinctively follow it. The heroic biologist stood before the lost goslings and made the calls of a mother until the geese learned to follow him. And then he got into a microlight aircraft and led the orphans, at the head of an elegant V, all the way to their summer breeding grounds in the Arctic. It has just, at this precise moment – 3.17 p.m. San Diego Time, 11.17 p.m. London time – occurred to me that *America's Missing Children* are perhaps drawn to San Diego because it is sufficiently large and emits a rhythmical sound.

The Stewardess brings David a whisky.

Thank you.

David drinks the whisky in one gulp.
   A flock of geese, in a V-shape, rise from a marsh and fly north.
   David rises from his seat.
   The stage transforms.

Act One

ONE

David In the cockpit, the Pilot is preparing to land. The Pilot, Kevin, is very experienced. He'll soon be ready to retire, but right now he's at the top of his game. I'm not at all concerned about the landing. He has a voice that tells me he knows where he's going.

In the cockpit.

Pilot Ladies and gentlemen, good evening, this is your Captain speaking. You may have appreciated we have now started our descent into San Diego. If we don't get any air-traffic-control delays we should be landing in approximately twenty-five minutes from now, well ahead of schedule. If you haven't reset your watches from the time in the UK, it's a matter of winding back eight hours, weather in San Diego is fine, a very warm afternoon, 31 degrees Celsius, that's 82 degrees Fahrenheit. Thank you.

. . .

One to go
San Diego, Speedbird seven november level two-six-zero descending to level two-four-zero.

David Speedbird seven november, San Diego Centre roger, resume normal speed and maintain one-three thousand, two-five-zero knots, no holding. San Diego altimeter two-niner-eight-three.

A young couple, Andrew and Marie, are sitting in loungers by a pool.

This is Andrew, the Pilot's son, he's staying in a motel in the desert near San Diego. He's an actor in a film they're

9

doing out there. This is his wife, Marie. They've got a kid, about nine months. Lovely kid, prone to allergies.

Marie Andrew.

Andrew Yes, love?

Marie Did you check on the boy?

Andrew Yeah.

Marie How was he?

Andrew Still asleep.

Marie How's he sleeping?

Andrew Soundly.

Marie How was his breathing?

Andrew It was regular, love.

Marie He wasn't on his front, was he?

Andrew No.

Marie No wheezing or anything?

Andrew No.

Marie I think the heat's giving him that rash.

Andrew Yeah.

Marie Did you have a look?

Andrew No.

Marie I don't think he's used to the water.
    Andrew?

Andrew Yeah.

Marie And did you touch his hand?

Andrew I did.

Marie Did he grasp your finger in his sleep?

Andrew Yeah.

Marie I worry about him.

Andrew You worry about him too much.

Marie I know.

Andrew He'll be fine.

Marie I know.

David Marie doesn't like the desert. She doesn't like it when Andrew's filming. She doesn't like staying in hotels. Marie would prefer to be at home, where she understands the hospitals.

Pilot San Diego approach, Speedbird seven november passing one-five thousand descending to one-four thousand and we have visual contact with Bravo.

David Speedbird seven november San Diego Approach Control expect runway two-six right.

Marie Have you got the baby monitor?

Andrew Yeah.

Marie Switch it on.

> Andrew switches the monitor on. He passes it to Marie.
> The sound of a baby breathing close to a microphone.

David Speedbird seven november, turn to heading two-five-zero, join localiser for runway two-six right. Your traffic is twelve o' clock, five ahead now. Do you have the airport in sight?

Pilot We have the airport, but not the aircraft.

David Speedbird seven november, you're cleared the visual approach two-six right, reduce speed to one-six-zero.

Marie After every breath, I'm scared the next breath isn't coming.

Andrew It always comes.

Marie I know.

The breathing continues.
Laura enters, wearing a hospital gown and carrying a mobile phone. She points the phone around, trying to get a signal.

David This is Laura, the Pilot's daughter. She's in hospital in London.
She's not supposed to use that mobile, because it interferes with the kidney equipment in the urology ward.

Laura gets a signal and dials.
In the cockpit a recorded voice counts down.
The breathing continues.

Female Voice *Radio Altimeter.*

Marie Andrew – I know this is quite strange
But I really want to pray.

Cockpit Alarm *Whoop, whoop, whoop, whoop.*

Andrew OK.
I won't, if you don't mind, love, but you go ahead.

We hear the phone's ringing tone. The number Laura is calling is ringing.

Marie I have a feeling that I ought to.

Andrew On you go.

Marie Who shall I pray to?

Pilot Tower, speedbird seven november, heavy fully established two-six right.

Andrew Whoever's up there.

David Speedbird seven november San Diego tower, good afternoon, you're following a Boeing 767, caution wake turbulence, runway two-six right, you're cleared to land.

Marie Perhaps I ought to kneel.

Andrew It's probably all right if you just close your eyes.

Female Voice *Fifty above.*

Marie I ought to clear my head of any bad thoughts.

Female Voice *Decide.*

Marie And I should clear my heart of any bad feelings.

Pilot Land.

Andrew You'll be fine.

Female Voice 100 –

> *The phone continues to ring.*
> *The baby continues to breathe.*

Marie I should be utterly humble.

Female Voice 50 –

Marie What shall my prayer be?

Female Voice 20 –

Andrew You choose, love.

> *They pray*

Female Voice 10 –

Marie Dear . . . dear . . . whoever's up there –

Laura Please be there – please be in.

Marie Please look after us.

The shudderingly huge sound of a jet plane coming in to land.
Marie looks up. Opens her eyes. She is almost blown to the floor by the wind.
The huge sound of the plane overwhelms her.
A screech of wheels burning tarmac and the sound of jets going into reverse thrust.
Darkness.

Marie Andrew?

Andrew Yeah.

Marie There was definitely someone there.

TWO

Gloom.
Laura, in her hospital gown, searching for a signal.
She finds it.
She dials.
A mobile phone ringing somewhere.
The Pilot enters. He opens a huge venetian blind. Behind the blind it is night. He switches a light on.
The Pilot is wearing a vest, his shirt with epaulettes, his tie, his hat, his Y-fronts and his socks.
He scratches his arse.
He looks around for the phone.
He can't find it.
It stops ringing.
Laura exits.
He looks at his watch.

*He sits down on the sofa and flicks through channels
on the TV.*
   *David is walking along dusty path beside a highway.
It is night, he is near a street lamp.*
   *Under the street lamp Daniel is standing. He has a
blue scar across his face and he is carrying a dead goose.*

David I've been in San Diego for six hours and already
I'm lost
   The girl from the theatre who met me at the airport
was called Amy, she gave me a car and a map. It was an
automatic car, I set off on the freeway and I seemed to
drive for hours just following everybody else. Then I was
halfway to Mexico. I decided to stop and ask somebody.

   *Very, very slowly, David approaches Daniel. David
proffers a scrap of a hand-drawn map.*

Excuse me. I'm looking for La Jolla. I'm looking for the
La Jolla Playhouse. It's a theatre. It's supposed to be near
here
   I wonder if you can help me.

   Daniel takes the map. He looks at it.
   *The Pilot picks up a copy of the San Diego white
pages.*
   He starts to flick through.
   He makes a call.

Pilot Hello, yes, is that The Palms?

Woman This is The Palms
   How can I help you?

Pilot I'd like a girl tonight, do you do – you do home
visits?

Woman We do, sir, may I take you credit card details?

Pilot OK. The number is 7577 3543 1985 3776.

Woman Expiry?

Pilot 03/02.

Woman Thank you
    The girl's name is Amy, she's early twenties, very beautiful, very elegant, and she has a great sense of humour
    What name should Amy ask for, sir?

Pilot Kevin.

Woman And where are you, Kevin?

Pilot It's some kind of an apartment block
    The complex is called Pacific View
    And I'm Apartment 3, Block 2
    OK?

Woman What address is that, Kevin?

Pilot Look, I don't actually know
    I'm not from here. I'm –

Woman You're a visitor, Kevin.

Pilot Yes.

Woman Welcome to San Diego.

Pilot OK. Thank you.

Woman We'll have Amy with you in just about one hour.

Pilot Thank you.

Woman Thank you, Kevin. Goodbye.

David notices Daniel's feet. His shoes are torn, his feet bleeding.

David I recognise him. I know his face
    It's unnerving

When I was in London, I was jostled in Camden
Market by someone with his face, the same torn shoes.
The same bleeding feet. The same blue scar
   Who has a blue scar?

Daniel Is that your car?

David It's not my car, it's a hire car.

   Daniel gives the map back to David.

Daniel What type of car is it?

David I don't know.

   Daniel goes to investigate the car.

His name is Daniel
   It turns out he was a fellow passenger on the plane to
San Diego. He ran from the woods, under the fence, as
the plane taxied slowly towards the runway
   He grabbed the big wheels
   He took one wheel, a friend called Edward took the
other
   He held on tight till the plane was in the air
   Stomach in his mouth. Didn't fall
   Then they were raised into the wings like chicks
   Very cold in there
   Eighteen hours of cold, thin air
   He was strong, he never slept, never let go
   Edward was dead when the plane landed
   Daniel saw his friend's body tossed across the tarmac
when the plane landed
   But Daniel hung on tight. He had an appointment to
keep in San Diego.

   Daniel returns.

Do you mind me asking? Your scar, it's quite unusual
   I've seen one like it before. Where are you from?

Daniel takes out a knife.
Daniel stabs David in the stomach.

You can't stab me
  You can't.

Daniel kneels beside David. He kisses him lightly on
the cheek.

Daniel I'm sorry.

David I know.

Daniel I'm sorry.

David That was the wrong thing to do, Daniel
  That was a big mistake. Believe me
  Daniel
  Don't go
  Don't go.

Daniel picks up the knife and runs.
  David lies in the dust.
  The Pilot is standing by the window, flicking
through the channels, looking out of the window.
He checks his watch.
  The phone rings.
  He picks it up.

Pilot Yes?

Woman The girl's having difficulty finding you, Kevin
  Can you be a little more specific about the address,
please?

Pilot I'm sorry, I don't know the city
  It's called Pacific View.

Woman Can you see the Pacific there?

Pilot No
  At least, I don't know

I can see the Hilton Hotel
The top of the Hilton Hotel
And, when I look out of the window, there's a freeway
And it intersects with another freeway
It's a complex, a complex of apartments.

Woman OK, Kevin. I'll tell the girl. We'll try to get her to you.

Pilot OK.

David Hello? Hello? Is anybody there. Hello?

Laura enters and sits down in front of the Counsellor.

Counsellor Hello, Laura. Sit down
How are you today?
Mmm?

A very, very long silence.

Can you say anything about how you feel today?

The phone rings again.
The Pilot picks it up.

Pilot Yeah.

Woman Hello, Mr Kevin?

Pilot Just Kevin.

Woman Kevin, Amy called me just now and she says she's been along the freeway up and down two times now, past the Hilton, and she says she can't find any apartment called Pacific View.

Pilot OK. OK. Right.

Woman We need some more detail of the address here? Can you find out the actual address?

Pilot OK. Wait

I'll go outside and I'll see if I can see any street names,
or any numbers or anything
Can you hold
For two minutes?

Woman I can hold.

The Pilot puts his trousers on quickly and leaves.
The Counsellor pours some water from a jug into
a paper cup and offers it to Laura. She takes it. She
drinks it.

Counsellor You seem very low today, Laura.

A very long silence.
Laura is not hostile.
She looks at the Counsellor.

What can we do to help you, Laura?
What can we do to help you today?

A long pause.
The Counsellor pushes a box of tissues towards
Laura.
Laura pushes the tissues back.
The Pilot re-enters the apartment.
The phone is still off the hook.

Pilot Hello? Are you still there?

Woman Is that you, Kevin?

Pilot Yeah. Look, I went out and had a scout around
and the street seems to be called Coronado Boulevard.
That's the name of the road which is running in front of
the apartment here.

Woman Coronado Boulevard.

Pilot OK, and there's an intersection and I don't know
what the other street is called but I suppose if you look

at the map and you see Coronado Boulevard and you go along it until you're in the vicinity of the Hilton, then you should be able to see if there's a complex of apartments or something marked on the map.

Woman OK, Kevin. Don't worry.

Pilot Do you have a map in front of you?

Woman I don't have a map, Kevin, but don't worry, Amy has a map. I'll relay this information to her.

Pilot Where is Amy just now?

Woman She says she's just by the Hilton.

Pilot Well, look, you know I can see the Hilton from here so she must be very nearby.

Woman Don't worry, Kevin. We'll find you. OK, I'll call you once I've talked with Amy. OK.

Pilot OK. Bye.

The Pilot puts the phone down.

Counsellor It's better if you can talk, Laura. If you can say something. Anything. It just . . . it can help us to start trying to . . . help you get better.

Laura opens her mouth.

. . .

Laura I.

Counsellor . . .
  Yes.

Laura Don't.

Counsellor You don't.

Laura . . .

Counsellor Yes?

Laura . . .

Laura looks at the Counsellor, pleading.

Counsellor It's OK.

Laura leaves the consulting room.
The phone rings again.

Pilot Hello.

Woman Kevin?

Pilot Yes. Hello.

Woman Kevin, I have got to tell you that Amy is looking at her map and she says there is no such place as Pacific View.

Pilot But I'm here. I'm staying here.

Woman But Kevin, you can't see the Pacific.

Pilot No. Not from this apartment.

Woman So why is it called Pacific View, Kevin?

Pilot I don't know. How should I know?

Woman Kevin, my concern here is, that you are some kind of crank
　　Some kind of English crank caller
　　Can you allay my fears on that?

Pilot As a matter of fact I'm Scottish and I gave you my credit card. I'll pay Amy for the time she's been looking.

Woman Well, Kevin. I'm not sure . . .

Pilot Look, I'll walk to the Hilton. Tell Amy to wait in the Hilton car park. I'll walk to the Hilton and I'll find her there.

Woman OK, Kevin, that sounds like a good idea. I'll relay that to Amy.

Pilot Thank you
Tell her I'll be . . . what, ten minutes.

Woman Bye, Kevin.

The Pilot leaves the apartment.
    Marie enters, she sits on the sofa, she switches on the television.

Marie Love . . .
Love? Come through . . .

Andrew enters.

Andrew What is it?

Marie *America's Missing Children's* on TV.

Marie sits down. They watch.
    The Pilot walks down the dusty path beside the freeway.

David Excuse me . . . excuse me . . .

The Pilot sees David.
    He goes towards him. Kneels.

Pilot Oh my God
Jesus
Are you OK? You're hurt? You're bleeding? Can you hear me?

David I can hear you.

Darkness.

THREE

Laura is sitting on the sofa, watching television, wearing a hospital nightgown. She is clipping her nails.
Under the freeway, beside a small muddy gutter.
Daniel is hunkered down a distance away beside a small cooking stove.
Pious and Innocent are sitting on cardboard sheets. In front of them is a melon, the bloody knife, a guide to San Diego, some string, and a zippo lighter.
Pious is holding a small notebook and a stub of a pencil.

Pious One melon
  One penknife
  One book
  One quantity of twine
  One cigarette lighter.

Innocent OK.

Pious OK.

Innocent So – in the event of my death . . . in the unhappy event of my death . . .

Pious Really it's just a matter of who gets what.

Innocent OK
  In the event of my death . . .
  And the funeral arrangements.

Pious And the funeral arrangements.

Innocent OK
  In the event of my death
  I don't like to think about it.

Pious You have to think about it.

Innocent I don't like to think about it
  I may have to – but I don't have to like it.

Pious The sooner you decide who you're going to leave
it all to the sooner you can stop thinking about it.

Innocent You just want the melon.

Pious I want nothing.

Innocent You've had your eye on it all week.

Pious I don't want it.

Innocent You want to have sexual intercourse with my
melon.

Pious I don't want the melon.

Innocent Then you won't get the melon.

Pious It's entirely your decision.

Innocent OK.

Pious In the event of my death, I, Innocent – which is
you – hereby will that my estate be passed over to . . .

Innocent Oh . . . It's a bit much, all this.

Pious Usually, what we do, is we say that we will leave
everything to our wives. In your case, you have no wife.

Innocent I don't need a wife. I have a perfectly good
melon.

Pious You never know, you may find a wife – so can I
put that your estate passes to your wife, and then – if
you have no wife – that it passes to any children you
may have.

Innocent Wives, children. I slave away all my life. For
what? For what? I tell you, Pious, it certainly puts things
in perspective.

25

Pious However, in the event of the deceased having neither wife nor surviving issue – to whom does the estate pass?

Innocent You're so transparent
  You just want it to be you.

Pious As a matter of fact I don't.

Innocent 'As a matter of fact.' Do you have a will?

Pious Yes.

Innocent Who do you leave everything to?

Pious I have left it to you.

Innocent Really?

Pious Really.

Innocent Really?

Pious In trust.

Innocent What does that mean?

Pious It means you have to look after it, until the boy is twenty-one
  Then you have to give it to him.

Innocent That's what I'll do then. That sounds just fine.

Pious OK.

Innocent Except the knife.

Pious You don't want the boy to get the knife?

Innocent No
  The knife will only get him into trouble
  I want the knife to go to . . .

Pious I'll look after it, if you like, until he's twenty-one.

Innocent Don't ever give him the knife.

Pious Never?

Innocent The poor creature's terrified
  He's barely out of the forest. You can't go handing
him knives.

  A *pause.*

Pious Innocent . . .

Innocent Yes.

Pious I lent the boy the knife
  I sent him off to kill a dog.

Innocent You didn't ask me.

Pious You weren't here.

Innocent You're a sly one.

Pious I'm sorry. I didn't know you had such strong
opinions about it.

Innocent You're a cunning jackal.

Pious It was a genuine mistake.

Innocent First the melon, now the knife – what's next –
the string?

Pious I'm sorry.

Innocent Did he kill a dog?

Pious He killed a bird
  A lovely fat goose.

Innocent Well, don't do it again
  The boy's got a head full of electricity.

Pious He doesn't know the ropes, that's all.

Innocent We have to look after him
Is that in the will – custody of the boy?

Pious If you die, I will look after him
If I die, you will look after him
Promise?

Innocent Promise.

Pious Poor lad.

Innocent We'll just have to hope you die first.

Pious What about the knife?

Innocent In the event of my death
Use it to carve my name in a piece of wood
Then I want everyone to sing my favourite song.

Pious What's that?

Innocent 'Band on the Run.'

Pious For goodness' sake.

Innocent That's what I want
And then put the knife in a parcel and post it to
whoever is the President of Nigeria with a note telling
him to use it to kill himself.

Pious OK.

*Laura stands, she takes off her hospital nightgown,
she stands in her pants. She feels the fatter parts of
her body with the calm of a butcher. She chooses her
buttock. She uses the nail clippers to snip a chunk out
of her buttock. She winces in pain. She holds the small
chunk of flesh up to the light. She walks over to the
cooking pot, she puts the chunk of flesh in the pot.*
A pause.
*She dips her hand in the boiling water and removes
the tiny chunk of flesh.*
She eats it.

She chews carefully, then swallows.
She faints.
Darkness.

FOUR

An apartment in San Diego.
The apartment phone is ringing.
The Pilot enters, carrying David.

Pilot We'll get you to hospital, son, don't worry
You're going to be OK.

David I'm not worried
I'm fine.

The Pilot puts David on the sofa and answers the phone.

Pilot Yes? Oh
Yes, this is Kevin
Look, I'm really sorry – something came up
Yeah
No, please . . . I am terribly sorry
There was an emergency here
I know
Look. Please, will you convey to the girl, yes, to Amy,
will you convey to Amy my sincerest apologies
. . .
Well – I really don't know what else to say
. . .
Yes. Yes I realise. Next time I will try to be more
specific about the address. I really am sorry
. . .
I apologise for the inconvenience
. . .
Goodbye.

David You've missed an appointment.

Pilot Yeah.

David I'm sorry.

Pilot It wasn't important.

The Pilot is dialling 911.

David We'll have to get that sorted out.

Pilot Yes
Hello, could I have an ambulance, please?
Yes, it's for . . .
Oh Christ, look I don't know
It's called Pacific View Apartments
No. I can't be more specific
Do you know where we are?

David We're in San Diego.

Pilot Look never mind
I'll . . . we'll get a taxi.

He puts the phone down.

Let's get you bandaged up or something.

The Pilot leaves. He comes back with a T-shirt, he tears the T-shirt into strips.

What's your name?

David David.

Pilot I'm Kevin.

David You're a pilot.

Pilot I am – that's right.

The Pilot starts to bandage David with the strips of T-shirt.

David You fly the new Boeing 777.

Pilot I do. How did you know that?

David I worked it out
Today was British Airways inaugural flight to San Diego in the new extended-range 777s. You're English.

Pilot I'm actually Scottish.

David I didn't know you were Scottish. You don't have the accent.

Pilot You're interested in planes, are you?

David I certainly am.

Pilot I used to be as well.

David You're not any more?

Pilot Well, no, of course I am.

David You still believe in them though.

Pilot Yes.

David Oh, that's good
 . . .
You know the tail-fin designs for British Airways – the mad paintings?

Pilot Yeah?

David Do you like those?

Pilot I hate them.

David Me too.

Pilot Things change. It's a new world
I don't understand it
Now, don't you worry, David
We'll go out on the street and we'll find a taxi and we'll get you to hospital.

David I'm not worried. It's going to be fine
You seem to know what you're doing.

They leave.
    *Laura, in her hospital gown, is standing by a
payphone.*
    *She dials a number which she has written on a
scrap of paper.*
    Somewhere in the apartment a mobile phone rings.
    Eventually the phone stops ringing.

Pilot (*voice on the phone*) *Please leave a message after
the beep.*

Laura . . .
Where are you?

She puts the phone down.
    She limps off.
    *The Pilot holding David on the dusty path beside
the highway.*
    David is visibly ill now.
    The Pilot is frantically trying to flag down a car.
    None are stopping.

Pilot Stop. Stop. Please stop . . .

David What time is it?

Pilot It's five o clock in the morning, David.

David I feel very tired
I've been awake all night.

Pilot You just stay awake
We'll soon have you all kitted out
Don't you worry.

David I'm not worried
I'm just tired.

Pilot Why don't they stop? STOP STOP PLEASE.

David They're on their way to LA
They work in LA, which is an hour's drive from here
They can't stop or they'd be late for work.

Pilot You just . . . that's the ticket. Stay standing
Just stay standing.

David I think I'll just have a sleep
Just for ten minutes
I can't keep my eyes open.

Pilot You just stay awake there
You just stay awake
C'mon
Talk to me
Talk to me.

David I won't die
I'm just tired.

Pilot Stay awake. Tell me about – tell me about San Diego
C'mon
I'm new here
WAIT STOP STOP FUCK
FUCK YOU FUCKING JESUS.

David Don't swear
Please don't start swearing.

Pilot I'm sorry, I'm sorry. Jesus
Look – c'mon.

Holding David up, the Pilot finds the Blue Guide *in his pocket. He thrusts it into David's hands.*

Tell me about San Diego
Where's good places to go?

David Well, San Diego, you may be interested to know that San Diego has the highest quality of life in the whole of the United States.

Pilot Really?

David Yes
San Diego is also unique in having its airport so close to the city centre.

Pilot I noticed that.

David is reading the guide.

David The approach to San Diego at night is one of the most beautiful approaches of any airport. Because you see the ocean on one side, the vastness of the Pacific Ocean, and then on the other side you see the elegant glass towers of the downtown area. And the lights of the Coronado Bridge. Which stretches across the bay.

Pilot Tell me more.

David I'm really quite tired.

Pilot Tell me more. Tell me more.

David Well, San Diego was built mostly in this last century, and mostly since 1950. It has an exact reproduction of Shakespeare's Globe theatre in Balboa Park and it also boasts a zoo with a worldwide reputation.

Pilot Perhaps I'll take a trip down there.

David It's certainly worth an afternoon.

Pilot STOP. STOP. STOP.

David In 1986 San Diego was the setting for the film *Top Gun* starring Tom Cruise and Kelly McGillis. San Diego, while not having many films actually set here, is

often used as a substitute for other American cities
because it is a very convenient place in which to film . . .

David falls.

Pilot Get up. C'mon, son. Get up.

David I can't do that.

Pilot Talk to me.

David I'm not dying, I just feel a little nauseous.

Laura enters with a kitchen knife.
She takes off her hospital gown.
She examines her body.
Innocent is plucking the goose, talking to Daniel.
Pious is sharpening the knife.

Pious Where do you come from, boy?

Daniel I come from Jos.

Pious Jos. Named after Jesus our Saviour. City of Tin
I know Jos. It's lovely place. Very temperate
Is there still a swimming pool at the Plateau Hotel?

Daniel There's a pool. But there's no water.

Innocent Who is your father, boy?

Daniel My father's dead.

Innocent I will be your father
Pious will be your mother
. . .
What is your name, boy?

Daniel My family call me 'little shit'.

Innocent Hmm.

Pious He needs a better name than 'little shit'.

Innocent Son, you killed a fat goose today
　For us to eat at this, the feast of your naming
　A meaty white goose to eat
　Since you brought us the gift of a goose, we'll call you
Grey Lag
　After the goose.

Grey Lag Grey Lag.

Innocent Are you a Christian, a Muslim, or a pagan?

Grey Lag I don't know.

Innocent Do you believe in God?

Grey Lag Yes.

Innocent Then let us pray – Holy Father, help us push
the desert back tomorrow morning
　Help us shape the meat into patties tomorrow
afternoon
　Help us to answer the telephone tomorrow evening
　Dear Lord, thank you for the goose
　Thank you for bringing young Grey Lag here to us
　Roger
　Over and out
　Please cut into the flesh

Laura cuts a thin slice from her body.
　She has to hold herself back from screaming in
pain.

The sound of a car screeching to a halt a little way up
the road.
　The Pilot runs towards the car.

Pilot Please. Please. Wait.

Amy walks along the dusty path by the side of the
road to where David is lying.

36

Amy Oh my God.

Pilot We have to get him to hospital.

Amy Oh my God, oh honey.

She kneels by David and holds him.
Laura starts to bandage herself up.

Pilot Will you drive us?

Amy Who did this to you, honey? Can you hear me?

David Hello.

Amy Who did this to you?

David I don't really know.

Amy Here, call 911. Get them to send paramedics. It'll
be quicker
   Tell them we're on Coronado Boulevard
   Just by the Pacific Heights.

She gives a mobile phone to the Pilot.

Oh honey . . . you hang in there for me, honey.

David Miss.

Amy Yes, honey.

David Are you a hooker?

Amy What kind of question is that?

David I've never met a hooker before
   Outside of a work context
   Not to talk to.

Amy Well . . . good.

Pilot Yes – hello, this is an emergency, a young boy, he's
been stabbed. Coronado Boulevard just by Pacific
Heights, please hurry. It's absolutely vital . . . please. OK.

David What's it really like? Being a hooker?

Pilot They say ten minutes.

Amy Shit, gimme that phone, mister.

She takes the phone.

Get down here now, for Christsakes, the kid's delirious.

The Pilot kneels by David.

Pilot How're you doing, son?

David She's a hooker.

Pilot Yes, son.

David Wow.

Pilot You were telling me about San Diego
    Tell me more.

David I think I like San Diego. I feel very drawn to it
    San Diego is surprisingly familiar
    I recognised it as soon as I stepped off the plane.

Pilot It seems like a fairly anonymous sort of place to me.

David Yes
    Not special at all
    The sort of place one moves to, for a job
    And you know what, no trip to San Diego is complete without a swim in the Pacific. The temperature of the ocean at this time of year is 72 degrees.

Pilot It sounds wonderful.

David When you bathe in the ocean at San Diego – the water is exactly the same temperature as blood
    We could go later today if you like?

Pilot That's a good idea.

David I could take you and the hooker to the beach.

Pilot Yeah.

David Miss? Would you like to come to the beach with the Pilot and me?

Amy Sure, honey.

David We'll go in the afternoon.

Pilot Yes.

David I'm actually slightly frightened.

Pilot Yes.

David I think I'm dying.

Pilot Yes.

David I think that's what's happening.

> *Laura puts the meat into a frying pan on the fire.*
> *Laura faints again.*
> *The flashing red lights of the paramedics.*
> *The Pilot lifts David, cradled in his arms.*
> *He walks towards the lights.*
> *Amy is still kneeling.*
> *David is dead.*
> *Marie is weeping.*

Marie That was very sad.

Andrew Yeah.

Marie That's what it's like out there.

Andrew You shouldn't watch these things, love.

Marie Andrew.

Andrew Yes, love.

Marie I want to pray again

Will you pray with me?

Andrew No, love
But you pray. You go ahead.

Darkness.

End of Act One.

Act Two

ONE

The Nevada Desert.
  Andrew, dressed as a pilot, is talking to the Pilot, who is also dressed as a pilot.
  They sit at a small table and are drinking bottled beer.

Andrew I'm on a routine flight – to the Gulf – when suddenly the cockpit door bursts open and this guy comes in – balaclava over his face – gun – tells me not to panic. Tell's me, 'Stay very, very calm.' I say, 'OK.' He says, 'Right. Are you calm?' I say, 'I'm calm.' He says, 'Right.' I say, 'Wait a minute. Is anybody hurt out there?' He says, 'Not yet. Not yet, but we'll shoot the fucking stewardess if you try any funny business with the fucking plane. Anything the slightest fucking bit funny we'll shoot her. In fact,' says the man, 'if you do anything, if this plane does anything that we don't understand – and we don't understand much about aeroplanes – so if this plane starts doing something and we don't know exactly why it's doing that thing, we'll panic and we'll kill the stewardess. Is that clear?' I say, 'It's clear.' Now, we know each other already from the time in the airport where I find out who's on my flight and my eyes go a bit misty when I hear her name. She's called Amy. Well – what with that moment and the moment when I'm walking on to the plane and I pass her in the aisle and I say, 'Hello Amy,' and she says, 'Ray . . . it's been a long time,' and I say, 'Yeah,' and she says – I don't know, some other shit – so we know that there's a bit of a thing between me and Amy. So anyway, the hijacker says, 'Take the fucking plane to fucking Baghdad.' I start

41

plotting the course. Suddenly, the plane starts emitting this . . . rhythmical sound. 'Thump, thump, thump.' Like great wings beating . . . The hijackers say, 'What's that?' And I say, 'I don't know,' and then the hijacker says, 'Shoot the stewardess.' The co-pilot tries to overpower them and he gets shot, and I cradle him in my arms, the poor fucker – but the shot's damaged the fucking something or other and we're going down and the there's people being sucked out of the plane and then kaboom – we're crashed in the middle of the fucking sand. After that, it's a kind of Moses thing, as I shepherd the survivors through the desert to Abu Dhabi. Amy survives – and in the desert we fall in love.

Pilot Sounds good.

Andrew But is it true?

Pilot I don't know.

Andrew Is it plausible
Take it apart
You're a pilot, Dad, you know.

Pilot Most pilots would attempt to co-operate with the hijackers.

Andrew OK.

Pilot Try to get to know them.

Andrew Sure –

Pilot Try to stay calm.

Andrew Yeah and . . . so is it – the story – does it ring true?

Pilot I don't watch films, really. I don't know
It's a highly unlikely combination of events
How's Marie?

Andrew Fine.

Pilot And the boy?

Andrew Terrible allergy thing, but he's great, he's really great.

Pilot I hope you're looking after Marie?

Andrew That's not what we do nowadays.

Pilot What do you do nowadays?

Andrew I don't know exactly. We're a sort of team.

Pilot Just make sure you look after her.

Andrew . . .

Pilot Have you spoken to your mother?

Andrew She's OK.

Pilot Good.

Andrew You spoken to her?

Pilot I – it's – no.

Andrew What about you?

Pilot Me?

Andrew You all right?

Pilot Yes. Bit tired. Hard night. That's all.

Woman Andrew, you're needed on set
It's the desert decision scene.

Andrew OK.

Pilot They need you.

Andrew C'mon, you can watch the scene
I make a decision in this scene
It's a good scene.

Pilot I'd better go, really.

Andrew No, c'mon, stay – we'll have a drink after.

Pilot I'm a bit tired.

Andrew Stay in my trailer. I've got a great trailer
Have a sleep. Relax. Chill out
Then we'll have a drink.

Pilot OK.

Andrew You sure you don't want to watch?

Pilot Yeah. Thanks. But . . . I'm a bit tired.

Andrew Sure. OK. We'll – we'll have a drink after, then.

Pilot After.

Andrew exits, the Pilot sits.
Pious, Innocent and Grey Lag enter. Pious is
holding three shovels.

Pious Take a shovel.

Innocent Give him the black shovel.

Pious I was already going to.

Innocent The black shovel is the one I started with.

Pious It's just a shovel.

Innocent It was my shovel. Now it's yours.

Pious OK. What we do is, we dig sand from this side
and we move it over to this side.

Innocent Like so.

Pious That's it. Only don't go so fast. If you go too fast
you'll be tired out.

Innocent Don't listen to him. He's a lawyer. He's not
used to manual labour.

Pious We move the sand back across to the other side of the highway.

Grey Lag The sand will blow back in the night.

Innocent Of course.

Pious The sand blows back in the night. And then in the morning we shovel it to the other side again.

Grey Lag I didn't come to San Diego to shovel sand.

Innocent Son – you don't mind me calling you son?

Grey Lag I don't mind.

Innocent Son, if we didn't shovel the sand it would very quickly take over the city.

Pious Three days, they've calculated.

Innocent In three days the city would be covered in sand.

Pious The desert is hungry for this city.

Innocent If you want to make money from the meat and the telephone calls then you'd better start shovelling sand. Because the sand gets in the meat, and it gets in the wires.

Grey Lag . . . I didn't come to San Diego to shovel sand.

> *Grey Lag throws down the spade and walks off.*
> *Andrew enters, crawling. He crawls for some moments. He stops.*
> *He slumps.*
> *Innocent and Pious start shovelling sand.*

Innocent It's just a phase.

Pious You're putting too much pressure on him.

Innocent He has to learn.

Pious He's very sensitive.

A Stewardess enters crawling.
She crawls up to Andrew.

Stewardess We have to rest. The old lady can't go any further.

Andrew If we don't make the city we're all gonna die.

Stewardess She's gotta rest.

Andrew Shit. Shit. Shit. Goddam. Goddam.

Stewardess What are we going to do, Ray? If we go on, the old lady's gonna die. But if we stay here, we're all gonna die.

Andrew Where is the old lady now?

Stewardess She's over there. She's sleeping.

Andrew takes out a knife.

Oh Ray, no.

Andrew Amy, it's the kindest way.

Andrew crawls back towards the old woman. The
Stewardess falls weeping to the earth.

Stewardess You bastard God! God you goddam son of a bitch!

Laura enters.
She is limping and bandaged, and wearing her
hospital gown.
The Counsellor sits, beckons her to sit down.

Counsellor Good morning, Laura.

Laura Morning.

Counsellor How are you feeling?

Laura OK.

Counsellor Good.

Laura . . .

Counsellor . . .

Laura . . .

Counsellor You've been cutting yourself, Laura.

Laura Yes.

The Stewardess gets up, brushes herself down. She looks out into the lights, squinting.

Stewardess How was that?

Voice Fine
Thank you.

The Stewardess brushes herself down.
    Andrew walks on.

Andrew D'you fancy a drink?

Stewardess Sure.

Andrew My dad's here. He's a real pilot. Come and have a drink.

They walk off.
    Pious and Innocent are shovelling sand.
    Grey Lag enters.
    They carry on shovelling sand.
    Pretending not to notice.
    Grey Lag sits, watches.

Counsellor Why are you cutting yourself, Laura?

Laura I'm not cutting myself exactly.

Counsellor What then?

Laura I'm butchering myself.

Counsellor You're certainly doing yourself harm.

Laura At least I'm eating.

Counsellor . . .

Laura I do cook the meat first. In fact I want to be cured.

Counsellor Well, that's good, Laura, that's a start.

Laura In salt. Or maybe smoked.

Darkness.

TWO

*The Pilot sits at a table in the desert under an umbrella.
The Stewardess and Andrew are looking at him.
They are drinking from a bottle of whisky.
The Pilot is sitting in silent abjection.*

Stewardess Andy, listen. I think your dad needs you to hold him right now.

Andrew You do?

Stewardess Yes I do
I really think he needs you to hold him.

Andrew Right

. . .

Stewardess You go, Andy. You go hold your father.

Andrew goes over. He kneels beside the Pilot. He can't quite find a position which means he can hold him. The Pilot continues to cry. The Stewardess watches from a distance. Andrew slowly reaches out his hand.

*He touches the Pilot's hand. The Pilot squeezes
Andrew's hand.*
   The Stewardess watches.
   *Pious and Innocent enter dressed in a uniform of
red dungarees and red baseball caps. They start to
clean the surface of the metal table.*
   *Grey Lag enters dragging a large, heavy see-
through polythene bag full of mince.*

Pious Are you watching?

Grey Lag Yes.

Pious You scoop the meat up with your hand like so.

   He scoops out a handful of mince.

You slap it down on the table.

   He slaps it down on the table.

Then you form it into a pattie . . .
   Like this.

   He forms it into a pattie.

Then you place it here, to form a pile of patties.

   He places it a little in front of him.

When you have a tall pile of patties, you take them to
the freezer
   You understand?

Innocent He has that look again.

Pious You can do it.

Grey Lag What is the meat?

Innocent Pig meat.

Grey Lag Which parts of the pig?

Innocent All of it.

Grey Lag Even the eyes?

Innocent Yes, eyes, nose, lips, all of it.

Grey Lag I didn't come to San Diego to shape pig lips into patties.

Innocent I knew it.

Pious Don't get angry.

Innocent He didn't come to San Diego to . . . Bloody hell.

Pious Innocent. He's only a boy.

Grey Lag I didn't come to San Diego to handle pig noses.

Innocent Listen to me, you little shit
   You're not in Jos now
   If we don't shape the meat into patties the Americans will not eat the meat. And the meat will fill up the storehouse
   And it will rot. And it will liquefy. And this liquid meat will run in the gutters of San Diego, it will soak into the sand and turn it into sludge, it will penetrate the telephone exchanges and cause them to explode in a shower of blood. Do I make myself clear?

   Grey Lag picks up a handful of meat.

Good.

   Grey Lag throws the meat onto the floor.
   Grey Lag walks away.

Pious We have to be patient with him.

Innocent I know.

Pious You called him a little shit.

Innocent Did I? Oh, I did. Oh damn.

Pious You should apologise to him.

Innocent Oh, I feel terrible.

Innocent goes to leave.

Pious Wait. Wait till he comes back. He'll come back when he's calmed down.

They go back to forming patties. Sadly. Serious.
The Pilot stands up. He walks away.

Pilot I've got to go. I've got to get back to the airport.

Andrew It was nice to see you, Dad.

Pilot Good to see you too, son.

Andrew Yeah.

Pilot Look after yourself.

Andrew Will do.

Pilot Nice to meet you, Amy.

Stewardess You too, Kevin.

The Pilot exits.

Andrew Shit.

Stewardess What's wrong?

Andrew All my life he's a fucking cunt
All my life he's a fucking stone
All my life he's a fucking stone carved into a cunt shape
And now he's weeping
Wet
What the fuck am I supposed to say?

Andrew exits.
  The Stewardess follows him.
  Laura enters, limping, wearing a hospital gown.
She sits on the sofa and switches the television on. It
is a cookery programme.
  David enters. Also wearing a hospital gown. He sits
down beside her. She moves up a little.
  Grey Lag comes back.
  He stands watching Pious and Innocent.

Innocent Listen, son, I'm sorry
  I called you a little shit earlier on
  I really shouldn't have done that
  I had no right
  I just want you to know that I'm sorry.

Pious We don't think you're a little shit all.

Innocent Not at all.

Pious But sometimes you behave in a way which makes
us feel like saying the words 'little shit'. D'you see?

Innocent No, Pious, it's more specific than that
  When you say that you didn't come to San Diego to
form pig lips into patties
  I can't stop myself from calling you a little shit
  It's the tone of voice you have
  That's what it is.

Pious But the important thing is, we don't think you are
one
  That thing.

Innocent No.

Pious You're a wonderful young man.

Innocent And we love you.

Pious So, you just hunker down. We'll do these patties.
And afterwards we'll go to the call centre together.

Innocent Here . . . wait.

*He reaches into his pocket and brings out the length
of twine.*

You can play with this if you like.

He gives him the twine.
    Grey Lag hunkers down.
    He plays with the twine.

Laura You're new.

David New. Yeah. Only just come.

Laura What you in for?

David Chronic attention deficit disorder.

Laura What?

David What?

Laura What's chronic attention deficit disorder?

David I don't know
I can't concentrate long enough to find out
. . .
No, that's a joke. That's a joke
Really I'm in for Tourette's.

Laura Right.

David Fuck!

Laura What?

David No, it's a joke. It's a joke.

Laura You're an irritating little runt, aren't you?

David I know. I really am. I'm really sorry. Really.

Laura What you in for then?

David Sex addiction. No, it's a joke. It's a joke.

Laura I'll fucking stab you.

David No, really. It's attention deficit disorder. Really it is.

Laura What's that then when it's at home?

David I'm not interested in anything. It really pisses people off.

Laura Fair enough.

David What about you?

Laura Suicidal. Manic. Self-harmer.

David What's that all about, then?

Laura Very low self-esteem mostly.

David Why's that?

Laura Well, they think it's for some other reason
But as far as I can tell
It's because I'm a useless piece of shit.

David You're very pretty.

Laura You interested?

David I am.

Laura Really.

David Too late. I'm bored again
It's a joke. It's a joke.

Laura I can see why you piss people off.

David Yeah.

Laura You got any fags?

David Yeah.

Laura Gi's one.

David Here.

He gives her a fag. She lights it.

Laura You hungry?

Darkness.

THREE

The ringing of many phones.
    Andrew is sitting on the sofa watching television.
Marie is curled up on the sofa with her head on his knee.

Marie Andrew.

Andrew Yeah.

Marie You know I love you.

Andrew Yeah.

Marie And you know I'd never do anything to hurt you.

Andrew Yeah.

Marie You or the boy.

Andrew Yeah.

Marie Well the thing is . . .
    The thing is . . .
    No I can't say it.

Andrew OK.

*There is a metal bed. With paper across it. Beside the
bed is a bedside table. On the bedside table is a box
of Kleenex. And some pornographic magazines.*

55

The Pilot enters.

Pilot I'm here to see Amy. I called?

Woman Certainly, sir. You're Kevin, aren't you?

Pilot Yeah.

Woman That's right. Eight o'clock. Kevin
    My name is Amy, nice to meet you. I'm Amy's
assistant. If you'd just like to wait here for a moment, sir,
make yourself comfortable, she'll be with you in just a
moment.

> *The woman leaves.*
>   *Kevin sits on the bed.*
>   *He looks at the pornographic magazines.*
>   *Pious, Innocent and Grey Lag enter. They sit down
>   on three swivel chairs and they put telephone headsets
>   on.*

Innocent OK. When you answer the call you say –
'Good morning, Pacific Heights, Amy speaking, how can
I help you?'

Pious OK. In San Diego everybody is called Amy.

Innocent And then let them speak, until they seem to
have stopped whatever it is that they want to say. And
then you say: 'May I have your account number, please?'

Pious Whatever they say after that, you repeat it back to
them, until they stop.

Innocent And then you say, 'May I have your date of
birth, please?'

Pious And then you do the same thing. Just repeat what
they say.

Innocent And your mother's maiden name.

Pious And then you say it back to them, and then you pause, and then you say – 'I have a cousin called –' whatever it is they said.

Innocent Then you let them say another thing.

Pious And then you say, 'Isn't that amazing?'

Innocent And then you say, 'Thank you for calling Pacific Heights'
And when they have emptied themselves of all that they want to say
The call is ended and you begin again.

Pious Do you want to try? You try.

Pious reaches over and clicks a remote so that Grey Lag's headset is connected. The phone stops ringing. They cast encouraging glances at the boy. As if to say – 'Go on . . . go on.'

Grey Lag . . .
   . . .
   . . .
   . . .
   . . .
   . . .
   . . .
I didn't come to San Diego to answer telephones.

Pious reaches out quickly and grabs the headset off him.

Pious For goodness' sake, you little shit.

Innocent Pious.

Pious I've had it up to here with you
   I've had it.

Innocent Calm down.

Pious attempts to hit the boy. Innocent holds him back.

Pious I could show you the back of my hand, son.

Innocent Calm down. Calm down.

Pious You have no idea. No idea
    If we don't answer these phone calls then the Americans will just store up their thoughts until their heads are full and then one day it'll all come pouring out in a great torrent of gibberish and they'll talk and talk and talk until they deflate like balloons
    And then they'll lie exhausted on the streets with the meat piling up in warehouses and the desert lapping at their ankles
    You have no idea
    You arrogant – self-centred –

Grey Lag walks away.

The cheek of the boy.

Innocent We just have to be patient.

Pious I know. I know.

Innocent He's new to all this.

Pious I know.

Innocent The thing is, when he's at his most unpleasant
    That's when he most needs our love.

Pious You're right. You're right as always.

Innocent C'mon
    Let's get to work.

Pious Good morning, Pacific Heights, Amy speaking, how can I help you?

Pious and Innocent answer phones.

Amy enters.
The Pilot looks at her.
She walks towards him and sits on the bed next to him.
They look at each other.

Pilot I – sorry – just thought I'd . . .

Amy I know.

Pilot I don't want to.

Amy Of course not.

Pilot I would like to have saved him.

Amy Me too.

They hold each other's hand.

Marie It's just the thing is . . .
I think I've started to believe in God.

A pause.

Andrew God?

Marie Yes, love.

Andrew Right.

Marie God, love, really believe.

Andrew OK.

Marie Andrew.

Andrew Yes, love?

Marie It's quite a big thing.

Andrew I can imagine.

Marie I really feel it.

Andrew Good.

Marie Really feel it. It's wonderful.

Andrew That's great, babes.

Marie I think
    I think I found something.

Andrew What?

Marie We've brought a boy into a terrible world
    So terrible even his skin reacts to it
    And I've never known what to do about it. How to
cope.

Andrew Yeah.

Marie I just wander round being scared all the time.

Andrew Sure.

Marie But I think I've found the answer.

Andrew Yeah?

Marie I'm going to become a nun.

Andrew What?

Marie A nun, love. A nun
    I think I need to pray more.

Andrew Oh, for Christ's sake.

Marie Don't be like that.

Andrew Don't be like that! Don't be like that! A nun?
Don't be like that! A nun? A nun?

Marie You'll wake the boy.

Andrew A nun?

Marie Andrew
    I – I – just . . . I just . . . I'm sorry
    God

I thought
Jesus
Andrew. I thought you would . . .
God
OK. Forget it. Forget it
I won't be a nun
Forget I said anything
Just forget the nun thing
I should never have mentioned it.

She leaves.

Andrew Where are you going?

Marie I'm going to bed.

Andrew Wait. Wait . . . love . . .

He follows her.
    David and Laura enter. They go up to the fridge.
Laura takes a polythene bag out of the fridge. She
puts it on a plate. She opens up the bag and takes out
about four slivers of meat, different cuts.

David What you gonna do with it?

Laura Roll them in flour and egg
Make rissoles.

She takes a bag of flour and an egg and she gives them
to David. She takes the plate of meat.
    They exit.
    The Pilot and Amy on the bed.

Pilot I'd better go
I've got to fly a plane to London.

Amy Yeah.

Pilot Listen. Thank you.

Amy I know. Me too.

Pilot If you're ever in London or . . .

Amy If you come back – gimme a call.

Pilot Yeah.

Amy You know what?

Pilot What?

Amy If you come back –

Pilot Yeah.

Amy I wanna take you to the beach
Like the kid said
Let's say go to the beach and say goodnight to the kid.
The Pilot leaves.
Darkness.

FOUR

*Under the bridge, Pious, Innocent by the light of a
cooking fire.*
*Grey Lag is kicking the melon about in the dark,
playing football with it.*
*David is lying on the bed, looking at the pornographic
magazines, using a small torch to help him see.*
He looks at them really fast.
Flicking through them.

Pious I'm tired.

Innocent Me too.

Pious Long day.

Innocent Long day.

Pious It's always harder when you've got kids, isn't it?

Innocent Yes
  Good though.

Pious Yes
  Good.

Innocent Look at him with that melon
  He loves that melon.

Pious He's good
  He's a good player.

Innocent You think so?

Pious Potential future international
  He could play for the Super Eagles, that boy.

Innocent You might be right.

Pious I'm telling you.

Innocent He's got the temperament.

Pious And he's strong.

Innocent Perhaps we should write to the manager
  See if we can get a trial for him.

Pious Good idea.

Innocent We'll do it tomorrow.

Pious Yeah
  There's something I want to ask him
  Hey, hey, Grey Lag!

Grey Lag What?

Pious Come here. Come here.

  Grey Lag picks up the melon and approaches them.

Grey Lag What is it?

Pious There's something I wanted to ask you.

Grey Lag What?

Pious Well, you don't have to answer if you don't want
to
  But . . .
  Why did you come to San Diego?

  *Grey Lag reaches into his pocket. He takes out a
  postcard. He gives it to Pious.*

Innocent A postcard of San Diego.

Pious I've never seen one of these before
  It looks beautiful
  Who gave it to you?

Grey Lag My mother sent it
  To me
  It is adressed to me
  See
  The name at the top
  That's my name.

Innocent I can't read the writing.

Pious Give it to me.

  *Pious peers at the writing and tries to decipher it.
    Laura enters carrying a plate.*

Laura You wanking?

David No. Bored. Can't concentrate.

  *Laura takes the magazines and puts them in the
  bedside cabinet.
    She sits beside him on the bed, holding the plate.*

Laura I made these for you.

David They smell great
  What's in them?

Laura Got some herbs from the garden
Apart from that it's just me.

David Can I have one?

Laura If you want.

David looks at the rissoles.
    He eats one.
    She watches him eat.

Pious Dear Daniel, As you may know, I am singing
backing vocals in a band called Wings on a world tour
of America. Tonight I am in San Diego. The tour is going
very well and I love singing. I think of you all the time
and I know I'll see you soon. I'm so proud of you
    You must know so many things that I can only dream
of
    All my love
    Mum.

Innocent Wings – your mother sang backing vocals in
Wings?

Pious Daniel.

Innocent My God.

Pious Daniel.

Daniel When I was a very tiny baby. My mother was
cradling me in her arms as she attended to a chewing
gum stall. In Lagos
    She used to sing to me. And she had a very beautiful
singing voice. One day, she was singing to me when a
man came up to buy chewing gum from her. And he
listened to her singing
    And he said he was making a record right there in
Lagos
    And he asked her to sing on his record. So, right there

and then she put me on her back and went to sing. But I was a bad child. And I cried in the recording studio. And so my mother had to give me to her sister to look after. And when she got married to a man who lived in Ibadan she gave me to her sister, who became ill with fever and gave me to her sister who lived in Jos and that is where I lived until one day I took a mammy wagon up to Kano. And when I got to Kano I found the airport and a man showed me how to catch the wheels of planes as they take off. So I did that until I found a plane to take me to San Diego.

Pious It must have been very cold.

Daniel Very cold
   Very cold.

Laura How does it taste?

David Crap
   No, it's a joke, it's a joke.

Laura Don't.

David It tastes fucking beautiful, Laura
   Tastes fucking great.

Laura Eat another.

   David does.

Innocent How old are you, boy?

Daniel I'm twenty-six.

Innocent No way.

Daniel I am.

Pious We'll help you find her.

   Daniel picks up the melon and takes it off to kick the ball about again.

Laura You can eat them all if you want.

David Can I?

Laura I really want you to.

He eats the other two rissoles.

Innocent McCartney came to Lagos in 1974
The boy is too young
This card is from someone else, to someone else
He just found it.

Pious He says he's twenty-seven.

Innocent No way.

Pious Maybe there is another band called Wings.

Innocent Most likely whatever mother he had was stuffed full of heroin and flown to Amsterdam.

Pious You think so?

Innocent Don't you?

Pious I think we should try to find her.

Innocent Tomorrow.

Pious Tomorrow.

They take out their blankets.

Laura You're smiling.

David Sorry.

Laura Don't be sorry.

David I'm all full up.

Laura I want to kiss you.

David Do you?

Laura Yeah, I do.

David Well, you bloody can't
No, joke. Joke
Do you really?

Laura Really.

David God. I dunno.

Laura Lie on the bed.

David lies on the bed.
  She climbs up.
  Kneels astride him.
  He tries to sit up.
  She pushes him down.

Laura You're skinny. You need feeding up.

Two San Diego policemen with guns come in.
  They pull the guns on Pious and Innocent. Grey
Lag hides in the darkness.

Cop 1 Police. Don't move.

Cop 2 Hands in the air.

Pious and Innocent put their hands in the air.

Cop 1 Get down.

Cop 2 Hands on your heads.

Cop 1 Stay down.

Pious and Innocent lie down with their hands on their
heads.
  The two cops search them.
  Laura leans down to David and kisses his lips.
  She leans back.

Laura Bored yet?

David No.

The cops find the knife on Innocent.

Cop 1 Who's the knife?

Innocent It's my knife.

Pious It's my knife, I lent it to him.

Innocent It's my knife.

Cop 1 shows the knife to the other Cop.

Cop 1 Is that the knife?

Cop 2 Sure looks like the knife.

Cop 1 Who's knife is this?

Innocent It's my knife.

Cop 1 OK. Get up.

Innocent gets up.
The Cop leans down and picks up a stone.
He throws the stone.

Go get the stone.

Innocent looks at them.

Get the fucking stone.

Innocent turns.
He walks slowly towards the distant stone.

Laura leans down to kiss David again. Lingering.
The Cop shoots Innocent in the back.
He falls.

Laura Bite my lip.

David bites her lip.

Oww.

David Sorry.

Laura It's all right
Full of iron
Builds your bones.

Darkness.

End of Act Two.

Act Three

Darkness.

In the darkness, music: 'Band on The Run', Wings, at the instrumental break.

A sudden burst of flame.

Innocent's body lies on a pyre in flames.

Daniel and Pious stand before it. On the ground in the dust, the melon, cigarette lighter, the string and the knife.

The music is coming from a tinny flatbed tape recorder playing an old cassette.

Laura is lying in a hospital bed.

David is sitting on the bed, wearing his hospital gown.

They are holding hands.

Darkness.

ONE

The Pilot, in uniform, his hat on his knee, sitting on the hospital bed.

Grey daylight through a large window.

Laura standing in front of the window in her hospital gown, bandaged, looking out.

An area with coloured bean-bags, a low table and a laptop.

Laura turns to the Pilot. Silence.

Laura Can I wear your hat, Dad?

Pilot If you like.

She approaches him and takes the hat.
  She puts it on.

Laura It's warm. From your head
  Do I look like I know where I'm going?

Pilot Of course.

Laura That's what a hat does for you.

She turns and looks out of the window.
  *David A, David B, David C, and Sarah enter. They
are dressed casually, with an impeccable grasp of the
contemporary. David A approaches a laptop, which
he sits beside and casually types into.*
  *David A, David B and Sarah sit around on the
bean-bags.*
  *The words capitalised in brackets are typed by
David A on the laptop screen.*

David A C'mon
  C'mon
  We're onto something
  OK
  Let's push this
  Let's talk about the village. (VILLAGE) What does a
village have? David?

David B Villagers.

David A Villagers – people – people who live in the
village
  David, yeah?

Sarah The villagers are possessed of a sense of
belonging.

David A A sense of belonging. Belonging. (BELONGING)

Sarah Is there something about birth – place of birth –
Do you have to be born in the village?

David C Born 'into' the village.

David B Brought up in it.

Sarah Because isn't there a symbolic entry moment?
   A ritual of . . .

David B A ritual of initiation of circumcision.

David A Surely not.

Sarah No – yes – A symbol of entitlement. A visible
symbol
   Which is like –
   Yes. Sorry but yes
   Tribal markings.

David B Sorry can I –

Sarah Go ahead.

David B It isn't tribal markings.

Sarah OK.

David B It's your name.

Sarah It's your name.

David A Your name. (NAME) That's good
   Oh that's good.

Sarah There's a dream I have.

David A Dreams. Give me dreams. Dreams work.

Sarah A picture that appears in my dreams
   . . . No, it's gone.

David C Sorry, just while I've got this – fire.

David B Yes. Fire. Fuck. How could we forget fire?

David C A place of fire.

David B Yeah, but also a place of intoxication. A place of drinking or . . . smoking . . .
A transformative place.

Sarah A pub
Whoop-de-do, boys
The village has a pub.

David A (PLACE OF FIRE) Great. Great.

David C Wait. Wait. It's not a pub it's a – public space
Sorry.

David B Go on.

David C I'm thinking of the village square
I'm thinking of the long afternoons
The sun's high so the men sit in the shade . . .

David B Under the banyan tree.

Sarah Like it. Tree. So . . . tree symbol.

David A A banyan is a tree?

David C This was in Nigeria, I saw this in Nigeria.

David A (BANYAN)

Sarah A tree, but it's also a symbolic centre.

David A More
Dave?

David B I don't know. Pass.

David C Men chew betel nut
They spit juice on the ground
In a lazy arc
It's slow. It's a rhythm.

Sarah Wait – the picture. I've got the picture.

David A OK.

Sarah OK, so it comes from a dream.

David A OK.

Sarah But it's very clear.

David A OK. Describe it, Sarah, let's see the picture.

Sarah OK. There's a well.
  And women. Women are . . . They must be going to the well to fetch water. It's hot, so the air is shimmering
  I can hear a sound, there's a low sound. A rhythmic sound.

David This is good. Push it.

Sarah A sound
  It's not even words
  It's . . . um a um a um a . . . you know . . . It's not even in a language maybe
  And
  This is the sound that's coming from the women
  In this picture from this dream
  In the dream I have a sister
  Which is weird
  And she's teaching me . . . the movements . . . um a um a . . .

David B Can I just –

Sarah No, I'm going to finish this –

David B Sorry.

Sarah I have a sister and – the thing is I feel an over-whelming sense of . . . It's as though this sound is a prayer
  Of thanksgiving
  For the going on of things.

David A Hmm.

David B It isn't a place. It's a sound.

Sarah OK. But . . . what I'm saying is . . . in this picture maybe there is a place . . .

David B A crèche?

Sarah It's not a crèche.

David C Is it a well?

Sarah I don't think –

David B Praying.

David C Is it about water, the gathering in of water?

David B A place of praying – to – to who?

David A Yes. Yes. Take it on. This is good.

David B Um.

David A Dave?

David B A place at the centre of it all
A hut
Sarah's sound
A hut in the doorway of the hut . . .
The shaman
The magician.

Sarah The chief.

David A Bingo. (CHIEF)

Sarah Smoke. Darkness. A place you're not allowed into.

David B Not so much a hut.

David C Not so much a hut as a chamber?

Sarah A secret chamber?

David B The people witness their chief turn to enter the chamber.

Sarah It's dark. It's behind a door. And it contains . . . everything.

David A And it is the cockpit.

David B *and* **David C** God, yeah.

David A (THE PILOT IS THE CHIEF)
The Pilot is the chief.

Sarah Yes. Yes. He wears the crown.

David B He wears the crown.

David A OK. Good. Good. Let's look at the plane now
Let's look at the plane.

David brings out a large model of an aeroplane and he takes off the roof of it to reveal the seating. They start to take the model apart.

Laura I tried calling you.

Pilot I know.

Laura Why didn't you call back?

Pilot I didn't get the message until – I was already flying here anyway
I knew I was going to see you.

Laura Sorry.

Pilot I'm sorry. I should've let you know.

Laura No I'm sorry.

Pilot How . . .
How are you?

Laura . . .

Pilot The nurses said you were . . .

Laura Cutting myself. Yeah.

Pilot Laura . . .

He tries to touch her gently.

Laura Get off.

Pilot I'm sorry.

Laura No. I'm sorry.

Pilot I wish I could –

Laura Yeah. So do I.

Pilot Understand, even.

Laura Me too.

Pilot You know I . . .

Laura Yeah.

Pilot And your mother . . .

Laura I know. It's fucking hideous
Last night, I saw the geese fly over
Means it's summer, doesn't it?
Must be going north I suppose
Great big beautiful V
Mad. Fucking insane. How do they know? I don't
know.

Pilot It's in the brain.

Laura In the brain
Goose-brain radar or something
D'you know?

Pilot Nobody knows
Some people think they can read the stars

Some people think they can read geography
Nobody knows.

Laura Geese do
Know where they're going
Don't even know that they know
But they do.

Pilot Yeah.

Laura Remember we saw them
A mad flock by the sea
And they all took off
Fucking all took off in a mad explosion.

Pilot When was this?

Laura Don't you remember?

Pilot Oh. Yeah. I think so.

Laura And you pointed at boss goose
The goose in front
And you said: 'That's what I do Laura
I fly. That's Daddy's job.'

Pilot God. Yeah.

Laura I wanted to go with them
Wherever it is they're going
I want to run and jump through that window and
follow the fuckers all the way to wherever.

Pilot Greenland, probably.

Laura Fucking Greenland
Must be fucking . . .

   . . .
   . . .
   . . .
   . . .
Have your hat back.

Pilot takes back his hat.

Pilot Don't, Laura.

Laura What?

Pilot Don't . . . please don't . . . the window . . .

Laura What? Oh . . .
Oh God
Sorry
Yeah
Scrape me up off the car park and all that
Sorry.

Pilot Please don't
Promise.

Laura Yeah. Yeah.

Pilot They'll help you here
They'll help you out of it.

Laura Dad
I wish.

Pilot They can, Laura. Drugs nowadays.

Laura Yeah, drugs.

Pilot It will. Trust me. It will go away
You weren't always like this
You were cheerful. You were a cheerful kid.

Laura Yeah. Before I fucked up.

Pilot Before . . . before . . . what?

Laura I dunno
I fell down a big well.

Pilot . . .

Laura . . .

Pilot If I ever did anything wrong, Laura
  If I ever – your mother and I . . . if I we ever . . .
  Was it the divorce? D'you think? Was it that? That
sent you like this?

Laura No. I don't think so.

Pilot Then what? Tell me, please.

Laura I honestly don't know
  I . . . It . . .
  It feels like I'm hungry all the time.

Pilot Are you eating?

Laura Not hungry. Like I'm hungry.

  She slumps.

I want to go home.

Pilot I'll take you home.

  *She hugs him, desperately. He tries to respond. Unsure
  of what's required.*

I'll take you home
  I'll take you home
  You can stay in the flat, in Surrey . . . with me.

Laura No.

Pilot In Hong Kong then, with your mother.

Laura No.

Pilot Anstruther, the cottage in Fife, the seaside.

Laura No.

Pilot The *gite*. The *gite* in Provence.

Laura No.

Pilot Tell me, Laura. Anywhere. I'll buy you a house.

Anywhere
Anywhere you'll be happy.

She breaks away from him.

Laura I'm fine, Dad
I'm sorry
I'll stay here
They'll help me get over it.

Laura sits on the bed.
David puts a moving image of a flying aeroplane on the computer.
He stands before it.

David A person needs to know where they are, where they're going and what time it is
But when people fly they feel like they've lost these moorings. They feel anxious
And this anxiety acts as a disincentive to air travel
Nobody wants to feel anxious. We want to feel safe, on earth
But in reality – time and place no longer exist in the world
There is no time in the city
There is no place on the high street
The safety of the ground is an illusion
Co-ordinated universal time – aeroplane time – is the only time we experience which never changes
The cabin of the aircraft is the only space where we can be certain that we belong – we have a ticket with our name on it
On the seat in front of us there is a map which shows us clearly where we are going
And we are going forwards
Did you know, the average child born in this century will spend more of their lifetime on an aircraft than they will with their grandparents? That is fact.

Laura lies down on the bed.

The human mind evolved to cope with a community of two hundred and fifty-six people – which happens to be the number of passengers carried by the Boeing 777, two hundred series.

Laura curls up on the bed.

We don't know how planes work
   We don't want to know how planes work
   We want to believe
   We want to be part of the rhythm
   We want to belong
   We want to see familiar things
   Ladies and gentlemen
   . . .
   The aircraft is your village
   'Welcome home.'

Laura starts sucking her thumb.
   The Pilot kisses Laura, he covers her up as though putting her to bed. He exits.

TWO

Marie, in a nun's habit, is kneeling and praying silently.
   Pious and Daniel on a patch of dusty ground with Innocent's possessions.
   There is also a pile of ashes in front of them: Innocent.
   Daniel is using the knife to carve 'Innocent' into a wooden block.
   Laura curled up on the hospital bed.
   David enters. He sits on the bed.
   She doesn't move.

David I'm hungry.

Andrew enters.

Andrew Love? You've been praying all night, love
Come to bed
. . .
Love, you have to eat
You have to sleep
You have to . . .
. . .
Come on, love.

Laura How do you want me?

David In me.

Laura Tell.

David I want to feel full up again
Like before.

Laura Do you want me tender?

David Yeah.

Laura Do you want me wrapped in foil and butter
And baked
Slowly, slowly, so all my juices keep their flavour.

David Sounds good, yeah.

Andrew D'you mind if I put the telly on?

Laura Or do you want me flash-fried over a hot flame
Hissing and spitting
Herbs rubbed into my skin, rare and red on the inside.

David God yeah.

Andrew I'll put the telly on.

Andrew puts the telly on. Sits on a bean-bag. Watches.

Laura Or d'you want me marinaded in wine
  Paper-thin strips of me
  Soaked in delicious booze.

David Bloody hell.

Laura Or stewed with chilli
  So I burn your mouth off.

David Fuck
  I just want what you want.

Laura I want you to eat me raw.

David God. You sure?

Laura You scared to?

David No.

Laura Go on then.

David Just take a bite?

Laura Taste first
  Lick first.

David . . .

Laura Go on.

  *David gets into bed with Laura. He crawls between
  her legs.*

Andrew The whole nun thing
  The whole – you being one – does it utterly preclude
sex? I mean
  There's the praying
  And so on
  But – does it utterly utterly demand that you don't
have sex at all? Is that a stipulation? I only ask
  I only ask because. Love
  We haven't . . .

85

And . . .

Babes, I know there's a hell of a lot of sadness in the world

Jesus, you don't need to tell me about it. I'm carrying a ton of it on my shoulders. But babes. Seriously. I don't think God would mind . . .

Would he

Could he mind? If we . . . expressed our . . .

He made us sexual beings after all

We have to conjoin, in union, blessed union, isn't it? And we conjoin . . . in a holy way, and . . .

That's a form of worship isn't it?

It's a form of prayer in a way

Isn't it?

When two people lose themselves in each other's bodies it's sacred

Isn't it?

I think, in fact, I know that God, if and when he makes himself available to you in revelation, I know that he, if you asked him would make it very plain to you by sign or symbol that he wanted you to make love

With me

Now

. . .

Besides, love

You do look fantastic in that habit.

Laura screams.
    Marie falls sideways. In a faint.
    Andrew approaches her.
    David emerges from the bed.
    He swallows something.
    Laura kisses him.
    They hold each other.

Pious We should scatter his ashes.

Daniel Two times now.

Pious He wanted me to look after you.

Daniel Two times.

Pious I'm going to look after you now.

Daniel Twice. I've scattered my fathers' ashes.

Pious We'll have to be a team.

Daniel Two fathers.

Pious We'll have to look after each other
We'll have to help each other
He's watching us
He's in heaven watching us and . . .
Daniel.

Pious is overtaken by grief.
He holds on to Daniel.
He shakes.
He breaks off and regains his dignity.

Daniel Tell me, Mother, in San Diego: do they suppose that we are ants? That there are so many of us? Do they suppose that we are dogs? That we love them? Do they suppose that we are cattle? That they can eat our bodies?

Pious You mustn't be angry, son.

Daniel Do they suppose that I came here to shovel their sand?

Pious God will see to it.

Daniel When I was a boy in Jos
I lived nearby a white family
I walked into their garden one day
A boy, about my age
He was playing with a chemistry set

I went to see what he was doing
He threw blue acid in my face
I ran home
And my mother's sister's sister's sister held me
And I asked her
Did the white boy maybe suppose that I was a thief?
And she said, 'No, you little shit. The white boy
supposed that you had come to kill him.'

Pious Everything is written in a map in God's head.

Daniel I know. I know what's written.

Pious We can't know.

Daniel I know. I know exactly where I'm going. I know
exactly
   It's in a map in my head.

Pious Son. You're grieving.

Daniel I didn't come to San Diego to bury my father.

Pious Son
   You came to San Diego to find your mother.

   Marie is on the couch.
      Andrew is caressing her face.
      She wakes up.

Andrew Did you see God?

Marie No.

Andrew Maybe it was just a passing thing and now he's
gone.

Marie No
   He'll come back.

Pious Everyone needs a mother and a father
   You lost you father, son, and you need a real mother

Not some bloody old man
Not some stupid old lawyer
Not me. A proper mother
We'll find your mother, son
Your mother is in San Diego
And we'll find her
We're a bloody team.

Darkness.

THREE

Desert.
  *Andrew, in the costume of a pilot, is crawling across
the desert, near the point of death.*
  Some distance behind him crawls the Stewardess.
  *Pious and Daniel sit, beside them a handwritten sign
that says: 'Are you my mother?'*
  The Counsellor is sitting.
  *Laura comes in, limping badly, wearing her hospital
gown.*
  She sits.

Counsellor How are you today, Laura?

Laura Great.

Counsellor That's good.

Laura Feel fucking fabulous.

Counsellor . . .

Laura No, really
  Really I do.

Counsellor I believe you.

Laura No you don't.

Counsellor I believe you.

Laura It's written all over your face
  I'm happy.

Counsellor I believe that some of your symptoms are in remission.

Laura Yeah.

Counsellor Why do you think that is?

Laura It's because I'm in love.

Counsellor Love?

Laura Love? Don't you fucking add a question mark to that word, you cunt.

Counsellor There's a hostility in what you're saying, Laura
  You are aware of that?

Laura I'm happy. I'm in love. I feel like I'm fucking walking on air.

Counsellor That's great.

Laura You don't seem to think so.

Counsellor Laura
  Love can be . . .
  It can be . . . it can take . . .
  Innappropriate forms.

Laura What?

Counsellor It can be – a – love is – itself – it can be – a disturbance – a . . .

Laura I don't believe this.

Counsellor There is appropriate love
  And there is . . . for example . . . masochistic love

And whilst there is a mild masochism in almost all
relationships
   It is not appropriate, Laura, for your lover to eat your
flesh
   . . .
   . . .
   We found the rissoles.

Laura Love
   It's bloody love.

Counsellor How do you know if it's not . . . an
infatuation . . . a . . . dependency . . .

Laura It is
   It's a crush. I fancy him. It's lust. It's dependency.
It's masochistic. It's pathetic. It's delusional. It's all-
encompassing
   It's obviously just a chemical reaction in my brain
   He looks like my father. He talks like my brother.
He's the part of myself I have still to come to terms with.
I want him to eat me. I want to eat him. I want him in a
way that I can't possibly begin to describe to you except
possibly by performing 'Love Me Tender' at an Elvis
karaoke night
   I feel like I've suddenly fallen into the arms of an old,
old city. Rome. He's Rome and I'm a Roman
   Love
   No question mark.

Counsellor Your dad came to see you yesterday?

Laura I don't want to talk about my dad
   I want to talk about David.

Counsellor How did you feel? Talking with your dad?

Laura Like a useless piece of shit.

Daniel This isn't going to work.

Pious Patience
Patience.

Laura has exited.
David is now sitting opposite the Counsellor.
David is bored and distracted.

Counsellor How are you today, David?

David Mm?

Counsellor David.

David Sorry.

Counsellor How are you today?

David There's a smell
There's a smell. Did you fart?
Oh no. It's my fingers.

Counsellor How are you finding things?

David Looking. Usually looking
In drawers
Try and remember where I put them.

Counsellor I mean how are you . . .

David Joke. Joke. Seriously? Seriously? Being absolutely
serious? To answer the question
Just taking it seriously
To give you – speaking honestly – being frank. Full
and frank. The bottom line? The truth, the whole truth
and nothing but?

Counsellor Yes.

David I suppose . . .
What was the question?
No, joke. Joke
I ate a bit of Laura

Can you believe that? I can't believe that? I ate a bit
of a girl.

Counsellor I know.

David Fuck me.

Counsellor Which bit, David?

David Can't tell you
Secret
Tasted nice, I can tell you that
I love her
I'm finally living. Know what I mean
There's a point
Can you believe it
Jesus
Love – mad – fucking bananas – Jesus – love – me –
girl – There's a point
What time is it?

Counsellor It's midday.

David There's something on telly
It's been nice
Cheers
Honestly. I feel much better after that. I really do
Thanks. Sincerely. Honestly
Load off my mind.

Counsellor We're going to move you to a different ward,
David.

David Are you?

Counsellor We thought a change of scene . . .
It might . . . help you.

David I refuse.

Counsellor David . . .

David No. Seriously. Joke. Joke
Good idea
Like your talk
Change is as good as a rest
Can I go now?

Counsellor David – you can choose what you want to do
Nobody's keeping you here
But you have to start thinking about your choices
You have to start thinking ahead
You have to reflect on what your choices force us to do to you.

David is very unsure about whether to go or whether to stay.

Daniel My mother is not in San Diego
She lied.

Pious We'll talk to Mr McCartney
We'll speak to his people
We'll find your mother.

Pious and Daniel leave.
A Bedouin tribeseman in a white dishdash is holding a water carrier in the middle of the desert. Andrew stops at his feet. He looks up. His mouth open.
The Bedouin kneels and pours water into Andrew's mouth. Andrew drinks thirstily. Then he slumps.
The Bedouin walks towards the Stewardess. He pours water into her mouth. She too drinks thirstily. She too slumps.
The Bedouin tribesman starts calling orders to other tribesmen.

Bedouin Hamdi. Bring the camels
Put the woman on my camel and the man on yours

We can walk beside them
We'll take them to the village
We'll give them clean water from the well
The woman can stay in the women's compound –
with the aunts and the grandmothers
They'll tend her
The man can come to my tent
We'll give him water and dates and wash his feet
Then we will hold a feast for these guests
Then, when they are fully recovered
We'll take them to Abu Dhabi.

Voice (*from off*) Cut. Thank you. Thank you.

David leaves.

FOUR

In a bar. The Pilot is drinking a pint of Guinness, Sarah is drinking gin.
In a bar. The Bedouin is sitting with an empty bottle of beer.
Marie praying.
Laura, in her hospital gown, with a knife, in front of the window.
A woman sitting at a desk with a telephone.

Sarah As you know, the airline's looking at a complete redesign concept to bring us into the twenty-first century. As part of that process we're looking at a few quite small changes to the pilot's role in the whole airline experience. I just want you to look at some ideas.

Pilot OK.

Sarah You've got to criticise – OK? Really lay into them. Any flaws – expose them
That's the idea of the excercise.

Pilot Well, I'll . . . certainly try.

Sarah Good. Don't hold back.

Pilot I won't. Look, before we start
   Would you like another drink?

Sarah Yeah. I'll take another gin. Gin and bottled tonic, please. Double.

> *The Pilot goes to get the drinks.*
>   *Sarah gets out her Palm Pilot.*
>   *Pious and Daniel enter. They look out of the window.*

Pious Look, son. This window is so high that we are in the jetstream
   Look at the city. The desert. The sea
   Paradise. San Diego is most beautiful place on the whole of the earth.

Daniel It doesn't belong to us.

> *Pious walks up to the woman at the desk.*

Pious Miss. We want to make an appointment to see Mr Paul McCartney.

Woman No.

Pious It's very important.

Woman I don't care.

Pious We have to find out about the recording of 'Band on the Run'.

Woman Go away.

Pious We'll wait.

Woman You can wait as long as you like
   Paul McCartney's never going to see you.

Pious We will wait.

David enters.

David We've got to run.

Laura They're going to take you away from me.

David No way. I won't let them. We're going to run.

Laura It's pointless.

David No. No, there's a point.

Laura What is it?

David You. And Me. Now. It's . . .

Laura Where?

David Scotland. The goose place. By the sea.

Laura How?

David I've made a plan.

Laura What?

David We wait till it's dark
Then . . . then . . . we sneak downstairs. OK?

Laura OK.

David Then we wait till the guy at reception's looking the other way.

Laura OK
Then what?

David I dunno. I got bored after that.

Laura I love you.

David No, seriously. We run like fuck.

They kiss.

C'mon. Get proper clothes on.

The both start to get dressed, intermittently kissing and caressing each other as though they are each the other's oxygen and they must get regular draughts to live.

Andrew enters with two bottles of beer. He sits down with the Bedouin.

Andrew There you go. They didn't have any Guinness, I'm afraid.

Bedouin What is it?

Andrew Singha. Thai. Great stuff.

Bedouin I'm very fond of Guinness. When I was a student, I used to go down Kilburn High Road and drink Guinness with the Irish
    Brilliant. Lovely people. Always happy to see a Palestinian
    The Palestinians are the Irish of the Middle East: this guy – Flynn, great guy – big big drinker – he used to say that
    Happy days
    Cheers
    Hows the wife?

Andrew Christ. Don't start me.

Bedouin It's like that, is it?

Andrew There's a whole nun thing happening with her at the moment
    It's driving me mental.

The Pilot comes back.

Pilot Gin.

Sarah Thanks
    OK . . . right
    There you go: it's all on there.

98

The Pilot squints to read the Palm Pilot.

Andrew Since we had the kid, she's had this thing about the suffering in the world. You know? And . . . well, one night she decided to pray and she had a vision of God as an aeroplane. And she said that she was imbued with a feeling that we're all part of something. Something that makes sense. Something meaningful . . . And now she prays all the time to see if she can get the feeling back.

Bedouin Where is she now?

Andrew She's currently in a nunnery.

Bedouin Aisha had a similar thing. Couple of years ago. With her it was Zen meditation. Lasted a few months. Just give her space. She'll find what she's looking for.

The Pilot laughs.

Sarah What? What? . . . Say.

Pilot Nothing.

Andrew God. I'm . . . you've had it too. Jesus. I thought I was the only one.

Bedouin No. It's really common.

Andrew It's shit though, isn't it? When it's happening to you. I mean . . . I love her. I don't want her to be a nun.

Bedouin Just . . . stay cool.

Andrew Yeah.

Bedouin Good scene today, I thought.

Andrew I thought so.

Bedouin I love playing a Bedouin. Bedouins are cool as fuck. They've got it sorted. You just need to put this stuff on and you're . . .

There's a totally natural authority, you know. You just – know.

Andrew I get the same thing in the whole pilot outfit.

The Pilot laughs again.
  Sarah squirms.

Pilot Doesn't matter.

Bedouin Even just then, talking about your wife, you find yourself . . .
  Speaking with authority
  There's a connection to a culture that's a thousand years old, you know. A culture that – it puts things in perspective
  It's – the desert, the desert which is the most hostile environment humans can possibly encounter – and that's where Bedouins live. And it's a spiritual thing
  Why? Because it's empty. Empty. Silent. And all the time you're on the edge of death. So – all you are – your entire being – becomes alive. Truly alive. What's more spiritual than that – that's a five-star place of contemplation. What I'm saying is – it can't be a coincidence that the world's three great religions – Judaism, Christianity and Islam – they all came from the desert. From the Bedouin.

Andrew I didn't know that.

Bedouin Yeah. 'S true. My theory is that it's to do with simplicity
  The community were nomads but – wherever you go in the desert – it's the same – so 'home' becomes the community plus sand. Two hundred and fifty-six people. A well
  The chief's tent. The women's compound. Order. Sense
  Meaning. Belonging.

Andrew Yeah. You might be right.

Bedouin You know I'm right. And I'll tell you what.
I think that's what Marie's expressing. She's expressing
a very deep sense of yearning for the desert. You know.
It's a very . . . that's a symptom of our disease. We need
more desert.

Andrew Yeah.

Bedouin Let me get you another drink
. . .
Listen, Andy – the clapper-loader told me she'd sold
you some coke. You don't have any on you, do you?

Andrew Yeah. Sure
You go on. I'll follow you.

The Bedouin leaves.
The Pilot has stopped reading.

Sarah So . . . what d'you think?

Pilot Are you serious?

Sarah Tell me.

Pilot OK
I think it's the most ludicrous thing I've ever heard
Firstly – 'The Pilot should enter the plane last. After
all the passengers have boarded.' Who does the pre-flight
checks?

Sarah The co-pilot.

Pilot It's the pilot's responsibility. That's the point. It's
his plane
He's got to check it
'The pilot processes through the cabin at the head of
the stewards and stewardesses in order to be witnessed
by the passengers.' No way

The passengers don't want to see the pilot
The pilot's going to keep them in the air
They want to imagine the pilot. They hear the pilot's voice on the tannoy, they imagine a man in control. They see a human and they think – he's just one of us. It's utter drivel.

Sarah What about the new uniform design?

Pilot Stupid. Pointless.

Sarah The idea is . . . that the naval metaphor doesn't resonate as strongly as the monarchic metaphor.

Pilot You're in a plane. You want a man who knows. A man with the hat that says, 'I know.' That's all you want. Nothing else.

Sarah You didn't like the crown idea?

Pilot The crown idea has no merit in it whatsoever
It's beneath contempt
How did you think it up
What jelly is there inside your head that you think up this stuff? How pointless can an excercise possibly be? Jesus
You're like my daughter
Useless. All over the fucking shop mooning about from half-arsed crisis to half-arsed solution without a single fucking sensible idea in her head. Look at the world. It's a practical place. Jesus. Get a fucking job. Get your hands dirty. This . . . God . . . this . . . world of mental masturbation you live in – learn to fly a fucking plane. Do something. Who gives a shit what the world's like? Live in it. Do the work. Have kids. Pay the mortgage. And get on with it
Don't dwell
Pull yourself together
You make me sick.

Sarah is crying.

Pilot . . .
I'm sorry
I'm sorry . . . you – oh . . .
You said to . . .

Sarah Doesn't matter.

Pilot You said to criticise you.

Sarah Forget it. I'm being silly. I'm being weak. I'm . . .

Pilot You asked . . .

Sarah I'm just . . . God. I'm just . . .
It's the gin. It's the gin
. . .
. . .

The Pilot awkwardly kneels beside her chair.
He holds her.
A little self-consciously.

I'm useless.

Pilot No.

Sarah I am. I'm a waste of space.

Pilot No. You're . . . you're . . .

Sarah I'm a useless piece of shit.

Pilot No
No
You're . . . beautiful. You're beautiful.

Sarah Stay with me.

Pilot I can't. I have to fly to San Diego tonight.

Sarah Stay with me.

Pilot I can't.

Sarah exits.

David Let's go.

David and Laura exit. Laura limping.
The Mother Superior enters.

Mother Superior Have you found him, Marie?

Marie No.

Mother Superior Don't worry.

Marie I need him.

Mother Superior I know.

Marie Otherwise what's the point?

Mother Superior Can I let you into a secret?

Marie If you want.

Mother Superior He doesn't exist.

Marie No.

Mother Superior Yeah. I'm afraid so.

Marie But . . .

Mother Superior I know
That's why we have nuns
We pretend
As long as we pretend convincingly, everyone else
doesn't have to worry. We mainly do it to humour the
priests
But basically. No.

Marie I don't believe you.

Marie exits.

Daniel I didn't come to San Diego to wait for Paul
McCartney.

Daniel walks off.

Woman You can't go in through that door.

Daniel Who's behind it?

Woman I can't tell you.

Daniel takes out the knife.

You can't
  You can't go in.

Daniel goes in.
  Pious follows him.
  Darkness.

FIVE

David Greig is sitting at a desk.
  Pious and Daniel enter.
  David looks up.

Pious Are you Paul McCartney?

David No.

Daniel We should go.

Pious We're looking for Paul McCartney.

David I'm afraid he lives in the the Mull of Kintyre
  Which is well over three thousand miles away from
here
  I tried to bring him over but I wasn't able to.

Pious Do you have his phone number?

David I'm sorry, I don't.

Daniel We should go. Come on, Mum. Let's go.

Pious We're looking for Daniel's mother. All we have is this postcard. It says she sang backing vocals for Wings.

Pious gives David Greig the postcard.

David I don't know. McCartney definitely went to Lagos. They recorded in the EMI studios there. It's possible he heard a woman singing in the marketplace. But she's certainly not listed on the album. In fact the only Nigerian who contributed to the album was the recording engineer. I heard the marketplace story myself when I was living in Nigeria but I think it's – one of those stories that get told whenever a global superstar turns up in a third-world country.

Pious So the postcard is a lie.

David No. It's true. She's not on the album, but she was on the US tour. McCartney invited her to sing backing vocals
    She still lives in San Diego. This is the address
    Her name's Patience but she calls herself Amy.

Pious Thank you.

David Don't thank me.

Pious C'mon, Daniel. Now we can find your mother.

Daniel Wait outside, Mum. I want to talk to him.

Pious leaves.

David I've been wanting to talk to you.

Daniel Why did you bring me here?

David I wanted to get to know you, I suppose.

Daniel It's not possible for you to know me.

David Was it you I saw in London?

Daniel Yes.

David And it was me who threw the acid in your face?

Daniel I don't know. Was it?

David Why did you come to San Diego, Daniel?

Daniel I came to San Diego to kill you.

David I want to –

Daniel I am utterly uninterested in what you want.

David There must be a –

Daniel You are no longer in control
San Diego, from now on
It belongs to me.

Daniel leaves.
   Darkness.

Act Four

ONE

Pious and Daniel are sitting on the balcony of an expensive beachfront house in San Diego.
  Marie and Andrew in the desert.
  Andrew dressed as a pilot, Marie dressed as a nun.
  Laura and David on a beach beside a pile of wood arranged for a bonfire.
  A can of petrol.
  Also a huge pile of meat products.

Andrew I've arranged for you to stay in a Bedouin encampment
  It's the one we used for filming the last scene
  I thought you'd need some time alone
  But if you need me, the mobile's switched on, and it's great reception here. They have total coverage
  . . .
  Boy's with the nanny, so happy with the nanny.
Brought you a photo.

  Andrew gives Marie a photo of the boy.

My dad's flying in tonight. I'll probably have a drink with him. But call – any time – anything.

Marie It's perfect.

Andrew I love you.

Marie It's perfect.

  She kneels and begins to pray.

Andrew So
  You'll be – all right then
  . . .

I love you
OK
I'm thinking of you
OK
Whenever you're ready
I hope you get through to him.

Andrew leaves.

Laura Didn't think we'd get away.

David Plan was bound to work. Plan was genius.

Laura It's cold.

David Yeah. We'll light the fire.

Laura Geese and everything.

David Sodding geese. Would you believe it? You want
them to be there
    And there they are
    Hundreds of the fuckers.

Laura On their way to Greenland.

David Mad geese cunts.

Laura Don't say that.

David Sorry.

Laura Don't be sorry.

David Sorry.

Laura This is the place, David
    We found it
    You – and sodding geese – and grey sky and grey sea
    And it's a bit cold
    It's definitely the place.

David I knew it was.

Laura How did you know?

David I can concentrate when I'm with you
My whole brain – on the one subject
You. And what you want
And I just know
I just completely know what you want
Totally bonkers but it's the truth.

Laura Cocky.

David I am right, Laura. I'm serious.

Laura No joke?

David No joke.

Laura Go on then
What do I want? Right now.

David Oh God
. . .

Laura Go on. What is it.

David I'm embarrassed now.

Laura Tell me.

He suddenly starts to open the packets of meat products.

I want you to cut me.

David You don't.

Laura I do.

David You don't
You want me to need you
And I do. Laura
Without you – I can't concentrate.

Laura I want you to eat me.

David Pretend
  From now on. We can pretend.

He gives her a packet of meat product and a knife.
She cuts the packet open. She takes out some ham.
She gives it to him.

This is you
  I'm eating you
  All I'm ever going to eat
  From now on
  Is you.

Patience/Amy enters carrying bottles of beer. She sits.
  She looks at the postcard.

Patience Jesus. I remember writing this. I was so strung
out
  During the tour I got badly into drugs and I remember
one day this roadie just told me I was fired and I went
out, scored, and wrote this to you
  Jesus
  Different woman. Thank God. Different woman.

Pious You've done very well for yourself in San Diego,
Patience.

Patience Actually, do you mind, calling me Amy? It's just
– that's who I am now.

Pious Amy.

Amy Amy.

Pious Patience is a good name too.

Amy But Amy's the name I use in San Diego.

Daniel Why did you never come to get me?

Amy Well, son, the thing is at first I had no money
  Then, when I set up the massage parlour I started to
make some money, I was embarrassed. I didn't want you

to see me doing a job like that. So I sent the money for you to go to school. You know. I thought you were going to school in England. My sister's sister's sister kept sending me letters telling me that you were in England doing your A levels

And then, when I diversified into real estate and I wanted to see you – I wrote and they told me you'd become a lawyer and you didn't really want to get in touch with me because you thought it would upset you in your new life. So I respected that.

Daniel I was in Jos.

Amy I know that now, son
But I didn't know before.

Daniel I looked for you.

Amy I know, son. But look – you can stay with me now. I'll get you enrolled in some adult education classes and you can come work for me. You can stay here, in this house. We'll get to know each other. We'll walk the dogs together. We'll go swimming in the ocean together. We'll talk about old times together

I'll cook Nigerian food for you and it'll be just like we're back on the streets of Lagos

And before you know it, you'll feel at home

When I take people round to buy real estate now –
I always say – you'll see many houses – but you'll only ever see one home

When you see it, buy it

This is your home now, son.

Daniel I don't belong here.

Amy Nobody does
Nobody's from here
San Diego is a place people come to.

Daniel I belong under the freeway
  I didn't come to San Diego to do adult education
courses
  It's too late. I don't know you
  Come on, Mum. Let's go. We need to scatter Dad's
ashes.

Pious Son.

Daniel I belong with you.

  Daniel leaves.

Pious I'm sorry, Amy.

Amy It's OK.

Pious At least – he knows you exist.

Amy I know.

Pious He's very temperamental. Very – he's got a head
full of electricity. But – you'll see. He'll come round.

Amy I feel so responsible.

Pious Don't worry. I'll look after him. He's a good boy.

Amy Thank you.

  Pious shakes Amy's hand and leaves.
    *David and Laura, lying on the beach, entangled
  and enraptured.*

David You see
  I knew
  I knew, didn't I?

Laura You did.

David And you don't need to cut yourself any more.

Laura No.

David And I can concentrate
  As long as you're with me. I can concentrate.

Laura I know.

David And we can pretend. Eat ham with mustard, and
Cumberland sausages, and pork chops, and rissoles and
mince and . . .
  Anything you want.

Laura When I'm with you, I don't feel like like shit.

David That's right.

Laura I know where I'm going
  It's in my brain
  I know – I can see a direction.

David Yeah.

Laura Like – Greenland – I can see sort of Greenland.

David That's it. That's it.

Laura Dave –

David Yeah.

Laura Dave I've fucked up
  I've really fucked up badly.

David No you haven't.

Laura I have
  I've done a fucking stupid thing
  Really really fucking stupid.

David What?

Laura Before – when you were getting the meat
  And – I sat here – and – I saw the geese and
everything
  And I knew it was the place.

David I told you. Yeah.

Laura I knew it was the place. But I got it wrong about what the place was for
  I thought – I did a really stupid thing.

David What?

She shows him an empty bottle of pills.
  Darkness.
  In the darkness.
  A sudden noise in the darkness.

Marie Hello? Is there anybody there? Hello
  Who is it?. . . Andrew?
  . . .
  Hello
  HELLO
  . . .
  I don't have anything
  I have nothing to steal
  . . .
  Go away
  GO AWAY
  Shoo
  Shoo animal shoo
  . . .
  God? . . .

Marie laughs in embarrassment.

  . . .

Marie sings.

'Stuck inside these four walls
Oooh
Sent inside together
Ooooh
Never seeing no one nice again like you ooooh

Mama
Yooooh.'

Bright sunshine.
    The Pilot is sitting on the beach, with his trouser legs rolled up.
    Marie is praying. Tired. Very tired.
    Laura is almost unconscious on the beach.
    David is holding her.
    He slaps her. He sticks fingers down her throat. He pushes her stomach. All in an attempt to make her vomit.

David Concentrate, David. Fucking concentrate
    Jesus. Don't sleep, Laura. Wake up. Concentrate
    TELL ME WHAT TO DO.

Laura Sea.

David What? See what? What? Concentrate.
Concentrate.

He thinks, panicking.

Pious and Daniel at the end of the runway. The objects in front of them.
    Pious puts the objects into a plastic bag.

David Concentrate. Think. Think. Concentrate
    Geese
    Sky
    Meat
    C'mon
    What is it?
    Geese
    Sky
    Meat.

Pious You might as well eat the melon
    It'll fill you up

The string. Could be useful. Perhaps you could use it to tie the bag to your wrist. So you don't drop it when you run for the plane wheels
The cigarette lighter
Do you smoke?

Daniel No.

Pious Maybe you could use it to keep warm. When you're high up in the atmosphere and it's cold. You could make a small flame
And the notebook
I've written your name in it, and my name and an address where you can get hold of me. And –

The Pilot takes out his mobile phone.

You will write?

Daniel Of course, Mum.

Pious I didn't think I would feel so . . .

Daniel Don't cry. Please don't cry, Mum.

Pious My little goose is leaving the nest.

Daniel I'll be fine.

They embrace.
    The phone beeps to indicate a message is waiting for him.
    The Pilot listens to the message.

Voice First new message
Received today at 7.21 p.m.
To listen to the message, press one
. . .

Laura's Voice Dad
I'm in Scotland
I'm at the goose place

I'm with a boy. And I'm dead happy
I'm really really happy
The goose place is where I'm supposed to be
OK
So I want you to know
That I'm sorry
I'm sorry I can't explain better
But – it's OK
Thanks for everything
All right so – bye then
Bye-bye.

Voice To listen to the message again, press one
To delete the message, press two
To call the person who left this message, press three.

The Pilot looks at his watch.
He decides it is too late to call.

David See what? I can't think. I can't? See what? See
what? Wake up. Wake up.

Voice Message deleted
Next new message
Received today at 11.25 p.m.

Amy's Voice Kevin? It's Amy – remember?
I got your message
I'm at the beach
Why don't you come down to the beach?
Gimme a call when you get there
I'll tell you how to find me
Please come
OK
Bye now.

Pious and Daniel break their embrace.
The Pilot starts to take his clothes off, down to his
shorts.

Pious Take your father. (*He gives Daniel the bag of ashes.*) When the plane is in the air, high up in the jetstream, say a prayer for him and scatter his ashes.

Daniel I will.

Pious And take the knife.

Daniel He didn't want me to have the knife.

Pious I want you to have the knife
   When you get to Nigeria
   Put it in a box and send it to whoever is president
with a note telling him to kill himself with it.

Daniel I will.

   Pious gives Daniel the knife.
      The Pilot combs his hair and puts his hat on.

David See? Sea. Sea. The sea
   Sea.

   He runs to the sea.
      He runs back with a cupped hand full of water.
      She opens her mouth.
      Drinks.
      He runs back.
      Cupped hands.
      Water, mouth drinks.
      Again and again.

Sea.

Laura Sea.

Pious Here is ten dollars
   This is all the money I have
   When you get to Nigeria, write to me with an address
   And I'll send you more money.

Daniel I will.

The Pilot walks towards the sea.
Amy enters. She is in a bathing suit, with a towel.

Daniel The plane is waiting.

Pious I know.

Daniel I should run.

Pious I know.

David Wake up. Wake up.

Laura Sea
I feel sick.

David Sick
Seasick. Concentrate
Wake up. Wake up.

Laura's eyes open.
She looks at him.

Laura It's all right.

Daniel Good bye, Mum.

Pious Be safe.

Amy and the Pilot walk into the sea holding hands.
Daniel suddenly runs.
The noise of a plane about to land.
Laura pukes. At first dry, then vomits. David holds
her as she vomits and vomits until eventually, a small
posset of pills is vomited up.
The huge sound of the plane as it is right overhead.
Pious kneels to pray.
Pious looks up at the aeroplane.
Marie opens her eyes.
The wind blows.

David Thank God
Thank you God

Thank God.

The bump and screech of a plane landing.
  The reverse thrust of the engines.
  The noise quiets.
  Darkness.
  In the darkness.
  The Pilot's voice.

Pilot Ladies and gentlemen, welcome to San Diego, we hope you've enjoyed flying with us today. The temperature outside is a rather warm 82 degrees and the local time is 3.37 p.m.

Thanks once again for flying with us and we hope you'll fly with us again soon.

. . .

Cabin crew, door to manual.

The End.

OUTLYING ISLANDS

For Rory

Acknowledgements

With grateful thanks to Catherine Bailey Ltd,
without whose support this play could not
have been written.

I would also like to thank the following people for
their help, support and advice during the writing
of *Outlying Islands*:

Marilyn Imrie, Louise Ludgate, William Houston,
Oliver Milburn, Sean Scanlan, Stuart McQuarrie,
David Harrower, Katherine Mendelsohn and,
as always, Mel Kenyon.

Heartfelt thanks for this and so many other plays
go to Davey, Nathan, Katherine, Vanessa and
all the staff of the Traverse Bar for putting up
with me so kindly, feeding me espressos
while I sat in the corner.

*Although the depiction of the characters and the
story of the play are entirely the playwright's fiction,
David Greig and the Traverse Theatre gratefully
acknowledge* Island Going *by Robert Atkinson
(Birlinn, 1995) as the inspiration and starting point
for the play.*

Outlying Islands was first produced by the Traverse Theatre Company at the Traverse Theatre, Edinburgh, on 12 July 2002. The cast, in order of appearance, was as follows:

Robert Laurence Mitchell
John Sam Heughan
Kirk Robert Carr
Ellen Lesley Hart
Captain Robert Carr

Director Philip Howard
Designer Fiona Watt
Lighting Designer Chahine Yavroyan
Composer Gavin Marwick

Characters

Kirk
tacksman of the island

Ellen
Kirk's neice

John
a naturalist

Robert
a naturalist

The Captain

Setting

A small island in the North Atlantic
in the summer months before the Second World War

The sound of water on a shore.

Robert I have noticed that something draws us towards outlying islands. Some force pulls. A quiet bay, an island in its middle – we take a small boat and we row out from the land. We circle the island, looking for a beach. We pull up the boat and light cigarettes. We walk the island's boundaries. We make a fire.

We sit on the beach and drink beer.

We cast our eyes back to the far shore from which we've come.

Night falls and the mainland slips into darkness.

We listen to the waves.

The island claims us.

The crash of the sea on rocks.
A cliff.
A thousand seabirds.

I have noticed from the study of maps.

The more outlying the island –

The further out it is in the remote ocean –

The stronger the force that pulls us towards it.

TWO

On an outlying island.
In the chapel.
The chapel is a roughly built stone building, half underground, with a roof of turf. Once it was a primitive church for the small community that occupied

the island. For a hundred years now it has only been
occupied once a summer by mainland shepherds.
Late afternoon.
John outside, struggling to open the door.

John Mr Kirk – I can't seem to –
The door won't budge. The stones must have shifted
during the winter. It's stuck fast.

Kirk Force it.

John tries to open the door.

Give it a kick, boy.

John What – just . . . ?

Kirk Kick it.

A kick.

Harder boy.

A harder kick.

Take a run at it.

Pause.

John hurls his full weight at the door.
He grunts with effort.
The door-frame cracks and splinters. The door falls.
John crashes to the floor.

John We're in.
Oww.
I think I might have done something to my shoulder.
I can't see a bloody thing, excuse my French.

John lights a match.

Good God.
What a mess.
Some of your sheep must have got in over winter.

Kirk It's a roof.

John It's – it's perfect. Ideal. Table. Fireplace. We can lay out the sleeping bags over there.
  A lamp.
  Does it work?

Kirk Try it.

John lights the paraffin lamp.
  The chapel is illuminated.

John Light.

Kirk That door's broke.
  Took me best part of two days last annual to fix up that door.
  Now it's broke.
  I'll need compensated for that.

John It doesn't look too bad.

Kirk According to my letter the ministry are liable for any losses incurred during the course of your survey. Would that be right, now?

John Of course.

Kirk There is an inventory of goods, sir.
  It is all to be accounted for.
  I'll need to claim now for the work and the materials.
  To the cost of one door.

John It was stuck. I don't want to pick nits, Mr Kirk, but there was no other way of entering the property.

Kirk It was stuck.
  But if you ministry boys weren't come to my island – to make your studies of the birds –
  No one would be wishing to open it.
  So, sir, you could say –

It was a door serving its purpose.
Until your arrival.

John Perhaps I did take a bit too much of a run at it.
Still.
We'll need to repair it as soon as we can, anyway.
Against the weather.

Kirk You'll be using peats for the fire, I take it.
From the peat store.

John We're only staying for a month.

Kirk And there will be disruption to the sheep.

John What?

Kirk They're easily disturbed.

John By what?

Kirk Human presence. They see no people most of the year.

John They see you – once a summer.

Kirk They know me.
I am a friendly face.

John Mr Kirk, I don't have any power in these matters.
If you talk to the right official –
I'm sure he'll see you're fully compensated.
Right.
I'll go and see where Robert's got to with the rest of the kit.
We'll get ourselves set up in here.

Kirk My niece and myself will be sleeping in the shepherd's bothy.

John Right.

Kirk I'll take the table now if you want.

John Table? Oh – but we'll need the table to work.

Kirk There was no mention of your needing a table.

John We need to write up our notes and develop photographs and so on.

Kirk The island has no other table.

John I see.

Kirk At what are we to eat?

John You could eat with us. We'll all eat together. At the table.

Kirk I wouldn't want to disturb your work.

John Of course.
   You must.
   I mean – I wouldn't have it any other way.

Kirk If I'd been informed about the need of a table.
   I could have brought one on the boat.

John No. No.
   It's quite all right. We'll eat together.
   Simple fare. But –
   We didn't come here expecting a grand hotel, Mr Kirk.
   Robert and I –
   This is perfect.
   Ideal.

Kirk This was their chapel – if you can call it a chapel.
   The last people.
   It gives me no pleasure to eat amongst their stoor,
even for a month only.
   But it has the table and the hearth.
   It will suffice for the purpose.

John Amazing, isn't it, to think that a hundred years ago there were people who actually lived here.

Kirk They were pagans. It is a pagan place.
Make yourself at home.

Kirk exits.

John Right.
Jesus, it stinks in here.
Right.

Wind.
John tries to shut the door.
He succeeds, partially.
Quiet.

Fire.
Right ho.
Fire . . .
Peats.
. . .
Jesus, dark as the buggering grave.

Lights a match again.

No tinder.

Tries to strike a match.
Fails.

John Damp. Right. Damp. So.

From outside, the arrival of Robert, out of breath and shivering.

Robert Johnny. Johnny. Have you seen the cliffs yet?

John The door's stuck.

Robert tries to open the door.
Fails.

Hold on, I'll –

Robert kicks the door.

Robert Let us in, Johnny, I'm freezing.

John I'll just give it a tug here –

Robert runs at and shoulder-barges the door.
He knocks John down under the door and falls
himself into a heap on the floor.

John Oww.

Robert Stinks in here. Smell of bird. Fulmar oil.
Can't see a thing.

John God.
Can you just –
You're on top of me, old bean.

Robert gets up. His eyes adjust.

Robert This is perfect. Perfect. The village chapel. The
stink. Hasn't been occupied for years. The shepherds use
the bothy, you see. Kirk told me on the boat – they won't
sleep in the chapel. Stones must have shifted in the
winter. What are you doing on the floor?

John Nothing. Just – well – I was pushed over. You
pushed me over.
Where's the kit?

Robert On the beach.

John What?

Robert I went exploring.

John You're wet.
It's not raining is it?

Robert I went for a swim.
At the the cliff bottom, there's a rock stack, about
twenty yards offshore.
It looked inviting.

John Wasn't it cold?

Robert Burning cold.
  At first your nerves don't feel it. You're numb.
  Until you climb out.
  And it hits you like a whip.
  Took the breath right out of me.
  You should come.

John You'll catch your death.

Robert I've never felt more alive. I promise you.

John There's weather coming, Robert, we need the kit in.
  And we'll need to fix up the door.
  The old man wants to write to the ministry for
compensation.

Robert We're a long way from the ministry now.

John Let's just fix the door before you freeze to death.

Robert You could have got the fire on.

John No tinder.

Robert What's this? Paraffin. Drop of that'll soon get us
started.

  He unscrews the lid from the paraffin bottle.
    He pours the liquid on the peats.

John The matches are damp.
  The sea must have got in on the crossing.
  There's dry matches with the kit.

Robert The cliffs, John – you must see them – the noise
of them. Kittiwakes, guillemots, razorbills, puffins,
fulmars, shags . . .

John I know.

Robert No sign of the fork-tails. I was hoping for a glimpse of one.

John They're here. We've a whole month to study them.
   And we're not even unpacked yet.

Robert Here we go.
   Fire.
   I've got a cigarette lighter.

John Wait, Robert – you just poured.

   The cigarette lighter is lit.
      An explosion.
      The two boys knocked backwards.
      Pause.

John Paraffin.

Robert Gosh.

John Half a gallon.

Robert I smell burning hair.

John Yes.

Robert I've never smelt that before.

John You blew us up.

Robert Hair and skin burned.

John Yes.
   Oww.

Robert Sudden light, then a sucking of air, an engulfing roar, the sound of a flame taking but amplified to a factor of what?

John My shoulder hurts.

Robert Would you say thirty? A factor of thirty. Absolute clarity of vision for a second then we go backwards, but we weren't knocked backwards.

John I was knocked backwards.

Robert We jumped backwards. Instinctively. Tremendously fast.

John Tremendously.

Robert To the extent where you could say there was no – decision – no moment where we made a choice but simply an entire nervous system's sudden and violent response to threat. The brain was cut out of the process – straight to the body – jump.

John Robert, we have been on this island which is forty miles away from the nearest inhabited land which itself is some forty miles away from a hospital if we could get there given that the boat will not come for us till the end of summer and we have no radio so we are utterly alone and we have been on this island not more than an hour and you have already smashed the door on top of me, and blown us both up. You don't think, Robert, that it might be wise – from now on – to at least try to think before you act –

Robert You're cross.
 Which comes from fear – shock – fear – anger –
 I'm cross too. Now.
 Bloody hell.
 I nearly killed us.
 Christ.
 Now I'm angry – now – the adrenalin comes rushing – heart beats and so forth – now – I'm sweating –

John I'll go and get the kit.

Robert Shaking – raging – fear comes after – which is what it must be like for a soldier – under fire – because we nearly died. Nearly.

John You bloody bugger, you bloody irresponsible bugger.

Ellen appears in the doorway.

Ellen Hello.

John Excuse my French.

Pause

Ellen Soot-black on your faces.
Your hair, sir.
Like minstrels you look.
Like off of a film.

Robert It seems we were at the centre of a conflagration.

Ellen It would seem so.

John I'm afraid we haven't – tidied up much yet.

Ellen No.

John But we will, of course.

Ellen I came to ask if you'd be ready to eat soon?

John I'm certainly famished – you, Robert?

Robert Appetite – normal – it would appear – neither hungry nor otherwise.

John Right. Right ho.
I think that means yes, Ellen.
I'll go and fetch the rest of the kit.
Clean yourself up, Robert.
And get the fire started – properly – would you?

John exits.

Robert Come in.

Ellen Thank you.
Stinks in here, sir.

Robert Birds – the fork-tailed petrel nests in burrows,

under stones. This place is half underground – it must be riddled with them.

Ellen Uncle's caught a fowl for tea.

Robert Fowl?

Ellen A puffin.

Robert Never eaten a puffin.

Ellen Tastes of fish oil.

Robert Of course. It must. It must.
We taste of what we eat.
Humans, apparently, taste of sour milk and rotting flesh.

Ellen I'll see if I can get this fire going, sir.

She starts to arrange and set the fire.

Peat's dry enough, so it seems you need to put heather under it, sir, it's no use trying to start it without.

Robert Your hands.
They're . . .

Ellen Sorry, sir.

Robert What's wrong with them . . .?

Ellen Eczema, sir.

Robert Do you suffer from eczema?

Ellen Bad, sir. Since I was a bairn.

Robert Really?

Ellen It's nothing.
Makes my hands look like claws.
Put them in my pockets most of the time.

Robert Your hands don't look like claws.

Ellen Feel like claws. When they're looked at.
There's your fire.

Robert Thank you.

Ellen Well, sir.
I'll go and get tea.

Robert Wait.
Shh.

Ellen What?

Robert Listen.

Silence.
Pause.
A petrel calling from somewhere in the room.
An eerie, almost electronic sound.
Robert listens intently.

Robert goes to investigate.
In a corner of the chapel, amongst some debris,
there is a box.
The noise is coming from the box.
Robert looks into the box.

An old candle box.
She's made a nest in it.

He shows Ellen.

A fork-tail.
Hen and chick.
See how the she tries to bite me.
Leach's fork-tailed petrel. *Oceanodroma leucorhoa.*
Somewhere between the size of a sparrow and a thrush,
slim and light, dark-feathered with a white rump and
the eponymous forked tail. It's webbed feet cold to the
touch. The hooked beak of the petrel family, black with

a soft tubular nostril. Dark, passive eyes. Beautiful –
don't you think?

Ellen It's a bird, sir.

Robert First time I've seen one.
  Here she is, in my own billet.
  They must be all over the island.

Ellen Is that what you've come all this way from
London for, sir – that bird?

Robert Not only this one. We'll be surveying and taking
photographs of all the birds. But, this is the real prize –
Leach's petrel – barely known, never studied.

Ellen It must be a very special bird, for you to come all
this way.

Robert There are rarer birds, but not many so hard to
find. She lives at sea and only makes landfall to breed on
outlying islands. The fork-tail's not rare, but where she
nests, people are. Let's take her outside and see how she
flies.

Ellen But that's her nest there, sir. With her baby.

Robert I want to see how she moves through the air.

Ellen Will she find her way back to her nest?

Robert I don't know.
  Let's find out.

  Robert carries the box and bird outside.
    Ellen follows.
    Wind. Sea. Birds.

Off you go.

  The bird flaps away.

Ellen She's going out to sea.

Robert Sickle wings, jerky, bobbing flight blown on the wind.

Ellen She'll tire surely. She doesn't glide like the gulls do.

Robert She'll stay at sea for two days, maybe longer, before she comes back to land.

Ellen Nest'll be cold now, sir. Chick'll die.

Robert Yes. Interesting, isn't it? Not very maternal of her.

Ellen I hope she finds her way home.

Robert When's food, Ellen? I'm hungry now.

Ellen Soon, sir. I'll fetch it shortly.

Robert Ellen, I notice you've taken to calling me 'sir'.

Ellen Uncle says I should, sir. Since you're from the ministry.

Robert Call me what you like.

Ellen Right, sir.

Robert My name is Robert.

Ellen Robert.

> *Ellen exits.*
> *Robert returns to the chapel. He replaces the nest box.*
> *John returns carrying kit, struggling.*

John Give me a hand with this stuff, will you?
That's the last of it.
Any sign of food?

Robert Apparently we dine on puffin tonight.

John For Christ's sake.
I thought we brought rations.

Robert Better to eat fresh.

John Puffin.
Puffin, though.
They're so endearing.

Robert They're also edible –
And . . .
Plentiful.

The kit is all inside the chapel and heaved down onto the earth floor.

John That's all the gear in. Looks in good shape.

Robert Is the camera safe?

John Let's have a look.

He opens up a crate.

Newspaper. I packed them in newspaper, you see.

Robert What about the flashes?

John All intact. Thirty-six.

Robert We'll survey the burrows first, find out where they all are. Take a few days to get the feel of the night-flighting. Then we'll take photographs. No point wasting flash.

John I'm bushed.
Arm hurts.
Up since half-six.
Famished.
Billeted in a mud cave half underground on a sodding rock somewhere in the middle of the sea.
We've only just got here and I want to go home.

Robert No you don't.

John I bloody do.

Robert Why do you say that?
  What's the point in saying that?

John I'm just – moaning.
  Letting off steam.

Robert We're here, Johnny. We made it. We're the first.

John I know.

Robert Nobody else has done this – nobody has come here, lived here and photographed these birds ever – we are the first.
  This is your chance to experience the blinking limit . . .

John All right. At ease, sir. I'm only carping.

Robert Don't.
  And don't 'sir' me.

John Sorry.

Robert You could be dead next year.

John I know.

Robert Sent off to some blinking foxhole and blinking gassed or something.

John Robert . . .

Robert So don't carp.

John I won't.
  I'm just hungry.
  . . .
  Looking forward to a tasty puffin.
  You got a smoke?

Robert Here.

John Ta.

  Robert throws John a packet of fags.

John lights up.

Fag makes everything seem all right.

Robert I found a nest over there in the corner.
    In an old candle box.
    Fork-tail must have crawled in through a gap in the stonework.

John Let's have a look.

John looks at the box.

There's a chick.
    D'you think the mother will come back tonight?
    Maybe we've frightened her off?

Robert Humans don't scare her. She's a flyer. We lumber about so slowly. As far as she's concerned –
    We're just a larger variety of sheep.

A blast of wind from outside.

John Christ, we'll need to fix that door.
    The wind'll blow the fire out.

Robert The chapel, the bothy, the rest of the old village, it's all underground. Did you notice that?

John Give me a chance. I was humping kit.

Robert Burrows. We're living in a burrow.
    The fork-tails burrow.
    Nothing to stop the wind from one side of the Atlantic to the other and this rock in between – so the humans and the birds go underground.

John Very sensible.
    If we don't fix that door we'll freeze our balls off, excuse my French.

Robert The gannet takes a gamble, lays her egg on the cliff, spends nothing on the nest, there's eggs rolling

148

about everywhere. Mess and madness. But the petrels
invest – they dig – they come back. It takes a lot of effort
to dig a pit.
   Gamblers and savers.

John What?

Robert Nature divides us into the gambler and the saver.
   I'm a gambler. You're a saver.

John Am I?

Robert You wrap things in newspaper.
   Do you ever do the gee-gees?

John Do them?

Robert Bet.

John No.

Robert You'd hate it.
   My family lost half of Hampshire because a paternal
uncle of mine got into the gee-gees.
   It's not an activity you ought to go in for.

John You do, though?

Robert I have done.
   My point is this –
   The cliffs and the burrows are related to each other.
   Like men and women.

John Hold that, would you?

   Robert holds the door closed.
      John hammers the nails in.

Robert What d'you make of the girl?

John Ellen?
   She's . . . nice.

Robert Sexually. What do you make of her?

John For Christ's sake, Robert.

Robert It's an important observation.

John It's damn prurient and none of your business as it happens.

Robert You exist in a stupor. Are you aware of that?

John I'm fixing a door. It's actually quite an energetic task.

Robert You are mentally stupefied.
The chloroform of the bourgeoisie.
Watch yourself.
Notice.
Rise out of the mess of the present and observe.
You are a sexually active male.

John I wish I were.

Robert You are – in terms of natural history.

John A hand on a pair of silk knickers at May Ball, that's all the natural history I've ever experienced.

Robert Because you remain in a stupor.

John Just don't say that will you, Robert?
You do this – you perpetually insult.

Robert Why is it insulting?

John I'm trying to make this place watertight with no help from you and all you seem capable of is a succession of these somewhat stinging barbs about my sexual success.

Robert The comments sting because you are a sexually active male who cloaks his natural urges in the stupefaction of civilised morality.

. . .
She's got lovely jugs.

John What?

Robert Ellen.
Her jugs, good God, they're fabulous.

John I wouldn't know.

Robert On the ship, on the way over, she's leaning over the side.
I caught a glimpse.

John That's it fixed.

Robert She's a young female of the species. It's fascinating to watch her so close up. She moves with an acute awareness of being watched and judged. Even the way she set the fire – before – when you were fetching the kit – every step she took was considered as to the eyes watching. And when she finished she stood back to be sure she'd be taken in – as a picture. Every movement of hers is arranged into a small performance for the spectator. When the performance is over she drops her eyes to the floor and awaits applause. She's concerned that her hands, which are riven with eczema, look like claws.
They do, rather.

John I'll be frank with you, Robert. I don't think a chap ought to talk about girls like this.

Robert It's absolutely as it should be. She is sexually ready and on the look out for potential mates. We are both sexually ready. We observe her and she observes us.

John It's a damn fine line between that kind of talk and perversion.

Robert It will be interesting to see what happens.
According to Darwin –
We should both fight for her.

John I don't think that's wise.

Robert Don't worry. According to Darwin, she'll sleep with the loser as well. She's claimed by the winner but she'll mate with the loser when the winner isn't looking. That's her strategy.

John Look, old bean, I think I've made myself clear.
   If we're going to spend a month on this island with the girl and her clearly grim-faced uncle I don't want you talking about this type of stuff. It's asking for trouble.

Robert It'll be interesting to see.

John No it won't.
   We're here to survey the island. To take our notes.
   Write up our conclusions and send them in to the ministry. Girls – observation of – appreciation and general perverted staring at of their as you call them 'jugs' is not what we're here for.

Robert You're a prig.

John Perhaps.

Robert You can't be a prig and a scientist, you know.

John I can attempt to remain civilised in the face of –

Robert In the face of the truth. Turn your face to the truth, Johnny.
   The darkest thoughts, observe.
   Know thyself.

John That door is solid.
   Thank you, John, for fixing the door.
   Now I won't die of cold.

Robert Of course the interesting thing would be to observe the girl when she is not aware that she is being observed. That's the real meat of the work. To see that which is normally not seen.

John Will you stop this right now?

Robert How many girls have you had?

John Had?
None – not that I care for your language on the matter.

Robert Your reticence interests me, that's all.

John I'm well aware of your conquests.

Robert There is no conquest.
Only a surrendering to natural behaviours.

John Yes, Robert, so you've told me, but do you enjoy it?

Robert What?

John Do you enjoy it? Fluffing some weeping lab assistant in her rooms on a Friday night?

Robert I can't say I do or I don't.
It's interesting.
Are you referring to any specific incident?

John Linda Jameson.

Robert Oh her.

John Did you enjoy it?
Did she have lovely jugs?

Robert Not as lovely as Ellen's.

John That's an opinion, not an observable fact.

Robert On the contrary, old bean.
Ellen's breasts are perfect.
Two island hills.
Low and rounded.

John Pale and soft.

Robert You've noticed.

John Of course I bloody have.
Excuse my French.

Robert laughs.
Kirk enters.

Mr Kirk.

Kirk I see you've fixed the door.

John Yes.

Kirk I could have done that.

John I just thought –

Kirk It'll do.

John finds a bottle of whisky amongst the gear.

John Would you like some whisky, Mr Kirk, for our first night?
A welcome celebration.

Kirk I don't drink.
Doctor says it'll kill me.
I take pills –

John That's a shame.

Kirk Bloody doctor. He's on the mainland.
Go on, boy –
I'll take some.
It's never killed me yet.

John Sit down. It's only crates I'm afraid.

John starts to pour whiskies.

Kirk Ellen's bringing food across shortly.
You eaten fowl before?

John No.

Kirk I like my food in tins.
A tinned sausage.
You didn't bring any tins, did you?

Robert Just dry rations.
And whisky.

The drams are poured in tin mugs.

John Slainte.

They drink.

Kirk You don't look like ministry men.

John Surveying's just leg-work. They send out the juniors.

Kirk Counting birds.

Robert The first comprehensive survey of the island's wildlife. We'll be taking observations. Studying the habits of the birds. The petrels in particular. This is an almost pristine habitat, Mr Kirk, it's barely been touched by humans. It's unspoiled.

Kirk Preparations, is it? Hush-hush.

John Preparations?

Kirk For war.

John There's nothing hush-hush about what we're doing.

Kirk This island – all the way out here on the sea.
This is a diamond for you ministry boys.
Am I right?
You can do what you like here and nobody need ever know.

John It's more of a . . . an inventory – of the natural contents of the island.

Kirk It'll soon be boats back and forth – and buildings for accommodation, and tins.

I expect to be considerably inconvenienced.

Robert The army may station a few troops. A gun maybe. But I don't think there'll be any interference with the annual.

Kirk Don't mistake me, this island's sat here a hundred years waiting for its time. Sheep and fowl hardly make the trip worth taking every summer. If the island sheep can be put to use for military purposes let the military come. As long as I receive due compensation. I'm a patriot, but I'm not a fool.

John We're here to observe. That's all. We won't be in your way.

Kirk It's not yourselves – although you broke the door and who's to tell what else you'll break – but it's what you'll leave behind that I'll need compensated for.

Robert Our purpose is the close observation of nature, Mr Kirk.

Kirk God put the birds here for man to eat.

And God, in all his graciousness, has afforded me the fowling rights.

That's all I need to know about nature, boy.

Ellen from outside.

Ellen Bird's hot – can somebody open the door?

John Just a moment.

John opens the door.
Ellen enters carrying a metal pan.
In the pan is a fried puffin and boiled kale.

John It looks . . .

Robert It looks intriguing.

Kirk It'll do.
  Sit.

John It's only crates to sit on, Ellen. I do apologise.

Ellen Eat – while it's hot.
  There's boiled kale with it.

John Right-ho –

  Plates and forks are found in the kit.
    The food is set out.
    They begin eating.
    Wind from outside.
    Silence.

John Mmm.

Ellen Is it all right for you?

Robert It tastes like chicken cooked in axle-grease.

Ellen I'm sorry, I –

Robert Fascinating.

John It's . . . nice.

Kirk If you'd brought a tin.
  You could have had a tin.

Robert They should introduce it in restaurants.
  As a delicacy – don't you think, John?
  They'd lap it up in London.

Kirk I've been to London.

John Really?

Kirk In the last war.

John It must have been . . .

Kirk It reminded me of nothing so much as a gannetry.

John Right.

Kirk A place of howling and squawking.

John Yes.

Kirk A place of random defecation.
Of eggs dropped and birds whirling.

John I know exactly what you mean.

Robert John's from Edinburgh, Mr Kirk.
Nobody defecates in Edinburgh. Do they, John?
Randomly or otherwise.

Kirk Not yet. But it's coming.
Chaos and filth.
Women have begun to uncover their heads.
Cinemas have arisen.
We are becoming a pagan people.
Ellen and I are Christian still, thank God.

John I see.

Kirk pours another whisky.

Kirk Slainte.
A month's a long time for a study of birds.
They leave eggs.
What more do we need to know?

Robert Much much more, Mr Kirk.
There's always something waiting to be uncovered.
For example, did you know that in a gannetry about
a third of the eggs laid, don't belong to the male bird of
the pair guarding them?
They are bastards.

Kirk Is that a fact?

Robert Established fact.

Kirk The creatures know no better.
We are their husbandmen.
God made them for our food.

Robert A study I would like to undertake – using blood
type – would be to see how many children in London
belong to the male who guards them.
Or how many children in your village, for example?

Kirk The child I guard does not belong to me.
Not in the way you mean, boy.

Ellen Uncle – he was talking of birds.

John He didn't mean . . .

Kirk I guard her for a brother who lies at the bottom
of the sea.

John I'm sorry.

Kirk Drowned coming home from the war.

John How awful.

Kirk How does your natural history help you with that,
boy?

Robert It's one of the most interesting questions of all.
War.
Is it natural?
Two men fight, two birds fight, that's natural enough.
But do you ever see a thousand or a million birds
flock together to attack a million others?
Birds kill, but you never see them massacre.
War and God.
Perhaps they are peculiarly human inventions.

Kirk Godless are you?

Robert I only ask.

Kirk Shame.

Robert What do you think, Ellen?

Ellen I think it's a shame to serve you this poor fowl and make you eat it for your first time with us.

Kirk No shame in fowl, Ellen.

Ellen It is, uncle.
We could have given them better food.

Robert We'll eat what you eat.

Ellen We may be remote from London, but we're not remote from the sensibilities of people such as yourself. We're not strangers to your world.

Kirk You're too familiar with certain sensibilities.

Robert Are you?

Kirk She is familiar with cinemas, and the darkness you find in them.

Robert Are you, Ellen?

Ellen You shouldn't be drinking, uncle.

Kirk I'm on the island.
Away from the doctor.
I'll do as I like.

Ellen You'll regret your speaking.

John Gosh – quite filling – puffin – isn't it?

Kirk The pagan is always desirous of something new.
Desire being sown amongst us by the devil.
It is his strongest weed.
It chokes our soul.
We should take what we're given and be thankful.

But Ellen has given ground to desire.
Ellen has visited the cinema.

John Do you like films?

Ellen I like some films.

Robert I like films.
What films do you like?

Ellen I like a film – do you know a film called *Way Out West*?

Robert I do – I love that film –

Ellen I've watched that film thirty-seven times.
How many times have you watched it?

Robert Once.

Kirk A hundred years ago there were people living on this island.
Godless they had become through isolation.
Fallen to blasphemous practices.
Till God sent a famine that drove them to the mainland.
Now their descendants live amongst us and build cinemas where there were churches before.

Ellen It is a bad thing, uncle.
We all agree.
Bad.
Wicked.
But we are on the island.
There is no cinema for me to visit here.
No need to speak of it.
If you're all finished.
I'll take the dishes to be washed.

John Let me help you.

Ellen It's all right – I can manage.

John Let me. Please.

Kirk Leave her.

John It's quicker with two hands.

Kirk I don't want to know what you do with your hands, boy, in the presence of my niece.

Robert I think you can trust John, sir. John thinks girls break if you touch them. He'll keep his hands to himself.

Kirk I'll carry the plates to the stream.

Ellen I can do the dishes fine myself.

Kirk This is my island, boy.
Decency will be observed upon it.

Ellen and Kirk leave.

John Bugger me, he's hard work.
Excuse my French.

Robert Ask yourself this question, Johnny.
To what military purpose can you put a sheep?

John What?

Robert When he was grilling us about the survey, he said that the ministry wanted the island for military purposes.

John There's a war coming, everything's got a military purpose. He's just grubbing about for compensation.

Robert He said the flock. He said the flock had a military purpose.

John He's an old man.

Robert Military purposes.

John Perhaps he thinks the sheep are to feed the army.

Robert He didn't say that.
He implied there was a plan.

John A top-secret sheep-related war plan?

Robert I'm asking myself, why are we here?

John To survey. Look, they'll be planning an artillery battery or something and . . . I don't know. The ministry probably don't know. There's a war coming and they want to seem like they're doing something.

Robert I'm sitting in Cambridge. I get a call. Come and see the ministry, am I interested in going to the island? – of course I'm bloody interested – it's the chance of a bloody lifetime and I don't question it. I don't ask myself, why is the ministry interested in an an outlying island?

John I suppose you could stuff explosives up a sheep's arse.
A crack team of collies.
Trained not to panic under shellfire.
Herding a flock of living sheep bombs behind enemy lines.
Come by, come by.

He whistles for a sheepdog.
He makes the sound of an explosion.

Achtung! Gottinhimmel!

He makes the sound of an explosion.

I don't think the ministry are interested in Mr Kirk's ewes, Robert.

Robert They're interested in something.

Kirk re-enters.

Kirk I washed the glasses.
Where's that whisky?

Robert Here.

Kirk Very civil of you.
Sit.

Kirk pours the measures.

Drink.

Robert To the ministry.

Kirk To the ministry.

Robert To a rewarding trip.

Kirk Rewarding. Aye.
Now tell me, birdman –
How many of my fowl are to die?

Robert This year?

Kirk Aye – how much am I looking at for the birds?

John I don't understand you, Mr Kirk?

Kirk The birds, boy, I've been told about the sheep but the birds – nobody's talked to me about the birds.

John That's what we're here for. To find out about the birds.

Kirk I need to calculate my losses.
In the letter they asked me to calculate my losses.

Robert What exactly did the letter say?

Kirk I cannot divulge its contents.
It was marked as a confidential communication.

Robert Of course.

Kirk I know the value of what's here now.
The question is, what am I to lose?

Robert Well, we would need to know what value the island holds for you.

Kirk It's grazing land. I hold the rights to the grazing. Eighty sheep. If I'm to lose my flock to this . . . thing, that's eighty sheep. And then, after. Will I be able to graze next year or will the land be poisoned? That's eighty times two which is one hundred and sixty sheep. But I'm not asking about the sheep . . . I'm aware of the destruction of the sheep. I'm asking about the birds.
    And the birds – nobody has considered the birds.

Robert What have the ministry said to you?

John Robert . . .

Kirk They told me their plans.

Robert Of course.

Kirk But the ministry don't know about the fowling rights. They don't know that I take some two hundred fowl from this island every year. Does the germ kill birds? That's what I want to know.

John What germ? What are you talking about?

Robert They told you about the germ?
    I didn't realise the ministry had told Mr Kirk about the germ.

Kirk It was a slip of the tongue. Not my place to have mentioned it.

John What germ?

Robert John, it's that project.

John What project?

Robert The one they told us about.

Kirk Mum's the word.

Robert Exactly, Mr Kirk.
Top secret.

Kirk That's the story.

Robert The letter must have been from Porton Down,
was it?

Kirk That's right, aye.

John Porton Down?

Robert That's the project.
Porton Down.

Kirk But what I want to know is – the birds – how
many of the birds will I lose . . . how long? Because
I need to make the calculation of my losses, d'you see?
I need to make the calculation.

Robert Well, that all depends. It's difficult to say.

Kirk But you can guess.

Robert Well, which germ is it?

Kirk The man said it was the germ that causes
Woolsorters.
There was a Harris man got it years ago.
Black sores all over his arms, they said.

Robert Anthrax.

Kirk Is that its name?

Robert That's its name, Mr Kirk.

Kirk It's well named.
It has the sound of the devil about it.

John Anthrax.
Bugger me.
Excuse my French.

Kirk I'll lose the flock to it. That's clear enough. But
they have asked me to calculate the losses per annum.
Now, the birds, the birds, you see – will they be lost, will
they be lost for a summer only? Because that is part of
the calculation.

John What on earth do the ministry want with anthrax?

Robert The ministry's intention, Mr Kirk, is to bomb
this island with anthrax in order to see how many living
things will be wiped out. And for how long.

Kirk Bombs. That'll not be good for the grazing.
    I'll want something for that.

Robert Mr Kirk, this island is a sanctuary.
    It's pristine. This cannot happen here. It must not be
spoiled.
    You'll simply have to recommend another.

Kirk I don't want to recommend another.
    I want to recommend this one.
    This one is mine.

Robert You don't seem to grasp – Mr Kirk.
    If the ministry – if they infect it – the island will be
dead – for years . . .

Kirk How many years?

Robert Nobody knows. Five, ten, twenty, fifty . . . It will
not support life.

Kirk It is a useless lump of rock.
    A pagan place.
    I'd have sold it years ago if there was ever a buyer.
    Let them have it for as many years as they need.
    For seven hundred pounds my niece can be married
and her husband given a share of a herring-drifter.
    That is supporting life.

Robert No. No. No grazing here, no fowl taken –
nothing.

Kirk It's a hard place to take a living from.
    Let me be the last.
    Let them compensate me.

Robert The island will die.

Kirk It has no soul.
    And let that be the end of it.
    Make your survey. Conduct your studies. Undertake
your preparations.
    We shall be the last people here.
    To the ministry.
    I must piss.
    Tempted though I am to piss in the corner.
    I will have a care for your comfort and take myself
outside.

    Kirk exits.

Bloody door's jammed.

    He laughs.
        He kicks it.

It's broken again.

    He laughs again.

I'll want compensation for that door.

    He exits.

Robert I should have realised.
    Damn them.
    Of course they were up to something.
    The old man's face in Whitehall.
    Over the desk when he asked me, in his eyes –
    Deceit.

They don't want us to observe, Johnny,
They want us to take a census of the living dead.

John We don't know that. We can't be certain.

Robert The last wild scrap of rock and soil.
And they want to make a laboratory of it.
To enculturate it with their germ.

John If there's going to be a war, we'll need weapons.

Robert Let them use bayonets.

John That's hardly sensible.

Robert How dare they interfere!
What's the bloody point of coming here if it's to be
wiped out?

John Maybe we can persuade the ministry.
If we make the scientific case –

Robert The ministry doesn't care.
They have cities to destroy.
What does anyone care about an outlying island?

John Weapons have to be tested.
Maybe we just have to accept . . . there are other islands
we can study.

Robert Let them infect themselves.
This is a landfall.

John You have to admit Kirk has a point.
It's a good choice. Remote and . . .

Robert He's nothing but a parasite.
Did you see him?
Sitting there gloating over the loot he's going to rake in.

John It's unpleasant but – perhaps . . .

Robert Perhaps nothing.
Let them test their fucking bombs on London.

John Excuse your French.

Robert Why don't they infect the salons and gas the slums?
Spread botulism in the suburbs?

John Steady on.

Robert People are the problem, Johnny, not the birds.
Wherever they gather they spread contagion.
Let them take the mainland, and leave me the island.
It's not his island.
I've been here a day barely but it's more mine than his.

John He does have a claim to the place. His family hold the lease.

Robert He's no more claim to this place than a tapeworm has claim on the stomach it feeds off.

John We'll talk to him tomorrow.
Maybe we can persuade him.
He's drunk now – we'll wait till he's sober.

Kirk re-enters.

Kirk That's better.
One more drink.
Then bed.

Robert We were just talking, Mr Kirk, about how you are a parasite.

John Robert . . .

Robert I'm just making an observation.
A parasite – or even a germ – who lives off a host body and then kills it.

Kirk You watch your tongue, boy.

Robert In the face of the annihilation of this . . . sanctuary, you're looking forward to fattening yourself up on the profit.

John Robert –
    You could be a little more temperate.
    We all have to live together.

Robert What right have you –?

Kirk It is the ministry that is making the proposal.

Robert Parasite.

Kirk I take what I'm given and I'm thankful.

Robert I won't allow it.

Kirk It's not your place to allow or disallow, boy.

Robert I have no 'place'.
    Don't 'place' me.

Kirk You're a young Englishman who knows nothing.
    I thank God he gives me the forbearance to forgive you your tongue.
    Goodnight.

    Kirk gets up to leave.

Robert Mr Kirk.
    What's to stop me from hitting you?

John What?

Kirk Hold on, boy.

Robert I should hit him.
    It's obvious.

John Hit? Don't be ridiculous.

Robert Not hit, beat – beat.

Kirk Don't you lay a finger on me.
  This is my island.

Robert We're here. Forty miles from anywhere and
a month before we see another human.
  He's a weak old man.
  Let's knock some sense into him.
  Let's force him to write a letter to the ministry.
  Force him to sign.

John Don't be ridiculous.

Kirk I'm going to my bed.
  You boys have taken too much drink.

Robert Stay there.

  *Robert holds the old man in front of him, his arms
  pinned against his side.*

Hit him – you've done basic army training, haven't you?

John I will not hit him.

Robert Before the girl gets back.

Kirk I think it would be better if you take your hand off
my shoulder, boy.

John For God's sake, Robert.
  I'm terribly sorry about this, Mr Kirk –

Robert Beat him – if he doesn't change his mind, we'll
beat him again.

John Apart from anything else it's against the law.

Kirk I will be informing the ministry about this.

Robert Be quiet, old man.
  What's he going to do – call the police?
  The man's drunk – he's an easy target.

John He'd call the police when we get back.
  And if he didn't, I would.

Robert Would you?

John You hit him if you're so keen on hitting.

Robert What if we killed him?

Kirk You're deranged. Tell him to take his hand from me.

Robert Look, I'm just interested.
  We're in a position to kill this man –
  And no one would know.

John Ellen would know.

Robert He fell – he's drunk – he fell and hit his head –
on the stone hearth.

Kirk ELLEN! ELLEN!

Robert Calm down.

Robert puts his hand over Kirk's mouth.

Robert There are some verifiable facts we have to
consider here, John. If we don't stop him, this old man
will sell the lease to the ministry and the island will die.
Worse than that it will propagate death. It will become
a killer itself.
  The birds, John.

John He's struggling.

Robert Of course he's struggling. I've got my hand over
his mouth.

John Let him go.

Robert Not until you have a better idea.

John Persuade him – let's – Mr Kirk – we can be
reasonable . . .

Robert He can't answer you – my hands are over his mouth.

John If it's money you're worried about, Mr Kirk, there is a possible income for you from tourism, Mr Kirk – have you considered that?

Kirk struggles, he's suffering.

Robert John – the man's point is valid. The ministry will give him the best price. If he wants to sell, he has every right. Tourism's a side issue – with a war coming there'll be no tourists anyway.

John But there's a moral point. Mr Kirk – the island is a haven, it's unique, it's a wilderness – you surely don't want –

Robert He's got to make a living, John.
As long as he's alive.
No. It really does come down to what he wants and what we want.

John He's – Jesus, Robert – his eyes are rolling back he's –
LET HIM GO.

Robert lets him go.
Kirk breathes in heavily.

Kirk Monstrous . . .
Monstrous . . .

John Sit down, Mr Kirk . . . please . . .

John sits Kirk on a crate.

Kirk Evil . . .

John You're all right now.

Kirk groans.

Kirk Ellen . . .

John I don't think he's well.
I think he's . . .

Kirk . . . bring Ellen . . .

Robert He looks like he's having a heart attack.

John Christ. Christ.

Robert He said he had pills.
He must have a weak heart.

John Where are your pills, Mr Kirk?

Kirk . . . Ellen . . .

Robert He's old. He's just old.

John Mr Kirk?
Do something.

Robert What?

John I don't know – water or – oh God.

> *Kirk falls unconscious.*
> *A moment.*
> *His body fallen to the floor. Still.*

Robert He said himself he shouldn't have been drinking.

John Mr Kirk – Mr Kirk – wake up . . . wake up.
There's a first-aid kit. Get it from the bag will you . . .?

Robert I think he's beyond that.

John Mr Kirk –
Oh. Oh dear. Robert, he's . . .

Robert He's dead.

. . .

He's actually – he – expired.

Literally.
Taken his last breath.

John Mr Kirk.
Mr Kirk.

John slaps Kirk.

Robert I've never seen that before.

John What'll we tell Ellen? What'll we say to her?

Robert Nothing.
Not yet.
He looks like he's asleep.
Leave him there.
Let her make the discovery herself.

Sudden sounds of thumping and bird calls from outside.

John What the hell is that?

Robert Listen.
Listen . . .
The night-flighting.
The fork-tails.
They're coming in from the sea.

Robert pulls open the door.

Good God, it's chaos.
There are hundreds of them.
John, come and see.
They're throwing themselves at the ground.

Ellen's voice in the distance.

Ellen Birds have come, sir.

Robert The birds have come.

Ellen What a sight, sir.
Never seen it.

Robert Me neither.

Ellen Tumbling and falling.
  Fighting.
  Hundreds of them.
  Falling out of the sky.
  What a sight.
  What a sight.

THREE

The sea crashing against rock.
  The sound of thousands of seabirds.

Ellen I sat with the body for three days and three nights
and on the morning of the third day I rose from a half-
dream and came out from the ground and into the
daylight. I walked to the good well looking for water
to wash and I saw the boy –
  I see him at the cliff top standin' like he's got a
thought in his head a thought like a midge botherin' him
and he's looking away away out over the blackness of
the sea towards the mainland where we've come from
and I'm thinking why's he come here this boy this boy
to stand on this cliff and why's he come all the way here
from London from there where all waits for him why's
he come and as I'm thinking he vanishes over the cliff
edge like he's jumped and I so I howk up my skirts and
go over to see where he's gone and I find the cliffs not
sheer as it looks but sheep-pathed and he's running or
more like falling down through the gannetry with the
birds raising hell about him and stabbing for his head
and the fulmars spitting oil at him and the noise and
eggs falling and he's waving his hands about him and
laughing and shrieking like he's found his own family
and at last he reaches the water's edge where the sea

177

swell's rising and falling and sucking and blowing at the
rocks and I'm thinking he'll have trouble climbing back
up here and I'm half away to fetch my uncle with his
long rope for the fowling when I remember that uncle's
dead and cold in the pagan chapel lying way way out
of reach of me and so I stand and I remain watching and
the boy starts to stripping his shirt and trousers from
him his body white and skinny and he strips it all, he
strips off all his clothes and they lie in the puddle of hot
sun about him and I watch him and he doesn't know
and he closes his eyes and his hands fall to touching
himself to the giving of himself pleasure and there in the
hot sun on the rock like a young gull preening I watch
him and I'm thinking this is the thing of the most beauty
I have ever seen this badness this fallen thought and I
want to drink it this moment like a draught of whisky
when the boy rises from the rock and all of a sudden
dives into the sea and the boy swims the twenty yards
it takes him to the stack of rock where he comes out and
shakes himself down and he shivers the water from him
and I think I think I think what is this feeling I'm having
here this feeling of affection that's rising in me what is
this feeling and I'm thinking this when all of a sudden he
touches his hair and pulls it from his black gull eyes and
he looks right at me and I realise –

This affection is an affection I have felt before.

This affection has come to me in my dreams before.

This is the same feeling, the way two sorrows can be
the same the same affection as I have felt thirty-seven
times in the darkness.

It is the affection I have felt for Stan Laurel.

Beautiful and tender, Stan Laurel.

And that is what I saw.

FOUR

Afternoon.
 Inside the chapel.
 Ellen with the corpse of Kirk.
 She is shaving the corpse.

John Ellen?

John enters. He is carrying a mug of tea.

I brought you some tea.

Ellen Thank you.
 Sit.

She returns to her work.

John You're shaving him.

Ellen He looked untidy.
 I washed his clothes.

John He looks a treat – tidy.

Ellen He looks old.
 He was old.
 With him these three nights.
 Watching him.
 Nothing makes you seem so old as to be dead.

John You haven't slept.

Ellen Nor have you.

John We've been working.

Ellen Every night you've been out amongst the birds.
 And still bringing me tea.

John We've slept in the day.

Ellen You've been very kind to me.

John Really it's – nothing.

Ellen You see it in people. Goodness.
A spirit.
You can see it in them.

John Maybe you should sleep.

Ellen Maybe.

John Ellen – I –
Your uncle and you –
Were you very close?

Ellen My uncle was not a close man.

John No.

Ellen But he was not cold.

John No.

Ellen Most of the time I hated him.

John I'm sure you didn't really.

Ellen No – I did. For being an old man.

John Yes well, all of us –

Ellen I hated him.
But it was a warm hate I felt for him –
The hatred of a familiar thing –
Your home, your village, the winter.
It's gone.
He was not cold.

John The thing is, Ellen, the boat won't be coming for another three weeks.

Ellen No.

John And unless some ship happens to pass there's no way of us leaving the island.

Ellen I've sat with him three days and three nights.

John So – he will – his body will . . . unless we –

Ellen I've done my duty.
It's enough.

John We really ought to bury him.

Ellen Yes.

John Is that all right?

Ellen We have to bury him.

John You don't mind?

Ellen He has to be buried.
It's all right.

John Good.
Well – not good, but . . .
Good.

Ellen Where's Robert?

John He's at the burrows. The fork-tails have all flown for the day. Every dawn we check the burrows to see which eggs have hatched and weigh the chicks to see how much they've eaten.

Ellen Have you weighed yourselves?
You've not eaten – I've cooked nothing for you.
You must be hungry.

John We've had our rations.

Ellen Nothing cooked.
I've neglected you.

John No. I won't hear of it.

Ellen You've slept in the bothy.
While I've been here with the table and the fire.

John Really, you mustn't think of it.

Ellen He was old.
   We must bury him today.
   Before he begins to stink.

John Robert and I have dug – in the cemetery – by the others . . . well . . . a grave, I suppose.

Ellen Is there weather?

John It's a beautiful morning.
   Warm.
   And not even a wind.

Ellen I'll sleep.
   And then we'll bury him.

John Yes.
   We'll – I'll – I just – warmed up now . . .
   I only thought I'd bring you tea.

Ellen Don't go yet.
   Would you sit with me?

John Sit. Of course.
   Right-ho.

Ellen I've been in and out of dreams.
   Don't know what I saw and what I dreamed.
   I seen you two boys out with your torches in the half-dark.
   The flash lighting up your faces.
   And the birds flying all around you like a crowd of women at fishmarket.
   I seen that – was that dream?

John We've been watching the fork-tails flighting these past two nights. We're going to take photographs tonight.

Ellen The noise they make.
  Thumping.
  Like the roof's come falling in.

John They're strange creaures. They live for two days at sea, and they make the most elegant flight, but when they come back to land, to their nests and chicks, they crash and thump on to the ground – they fly into each other – they attack each other. It's an amazing sight.

Ellen And you and Robert –
  Laughing and shouting.

John Did we disturb you?

Ellen When the torchbeams hit your faces you were smiling like children.

John He's always wanted to come to this island and study these birds. When we met at Cambridge Robert said, let's be the first to study them. I never thought we'd get the chance to come here.
  We don't mean to be disrespectful to your uncle.

Ellen Not a dream then – but it seemed like a dream.

John Not a dream.

Ellen I dreamed a bird.
  A gull sat in the hearth.
  Amongst the embers.
  Watching me.
  Black eyes on me.
  Seeing into me.

John That was probably a dream.

Ellen And I dreamed a boy swimming.

John Swimming.

Ellen Naked. In the sea.

John Could have been – a seal you saw.

Ellen He reminded me of Stan Laurel.

John Who?

Ellen Off of the films.

John Oh. I don't watch films I'm afraid.
Robert does. I read mostly.

Ellen I watched him lying on a rock in the sun.

John I haven't swum. Too cold. It must have been
Robert.
Robert swims. Didn't mention he'd seen you.

Ellen More likely a seal.
Or – maybe I dreamed it.
Does Robert have a girl?

John A –
Well, no. No.

Ellen Does he have his eye on someone in London?

John No. But –

Ellen Do you think he would notice me?
A girl of my type?
Does he –

John He has noticed you – he – said to me – the first
day, he said –

Ellen Did he? What did he say?

John He said you had – lovely eyes.

Ellen Did he?

John You do.

Ellen My uncle wanted me kept for a village man – a
man at the fishing. Married and three-bairned, with my

claws in a bucket of nets for the rest of my life. But uncle's dead now.
  Isn't he?
  So – I will cast my eye about whomsoever I like.

John Perhaps it's best if you – if we – eyes casting and so forth – if we don't – at least until the boat has come to take us back.

Ellen Yes.

John This is a very distressing time for you.

Ellen It's a strange time.

John When we're on the mainland.
  You'll see things more clearly then.

Ellen You're kind.

John No.

Ellen A good friend to me for a stranger.

John You need to sleep.
  Rest.

Ellen Thank you.

John That's it, lie there, that's it.
  And I'll cover you with this blanket.
  There.
  And . . .
  I'll stoke up the fire.
  And . . .
    . . .
  Sweet dreams.

John stokes up the fire.
  Ellen is asleep.
  Robert knocks on the door.

Robert Blinking door's stuck again.

John Shh.
  She's sleeping.
  Hold on –

  Robert opens the door.
    They speak in whispers.

Robert Only half the chicks got fed last night.

John Keep your voice down.

Robert Only half – I weighed every one – only half had
an increase. Some nights some get fed, some nights some
don't – no discernible pattern. They all came back, but
some of them don't bring food.

John Why would they – what, deliberately? – starve
their chicks?

Robert It could be to do with the absorption of oil.
It takes time to metabolise oils, so perhaps if they're fed
too often they'd gain too much weight and be unable
to fly. But there is another possibility.

John What?

Robert That they're being tested.
  How far can they go?
  And if they fail –
  The death of a weakling chick is a good thing.
  A saving of resources.

John It seems unlikely.

Robert Does it?
  Still – it's a promising start. Only here three days and
already we're breaking new ground.

John I can't help feeling that the survey, the island – it's
all been put into a little perspective by events.

Robert You're just tired.

John I don't know.
I'm in a daze.
Lost, a bit.

Robert We're a long way away from London.

John A long way from Edinburgh.
Three days here and I feel all I know's this patch of land in the middle of the sea and all the rest has faded away.

Robert It's a natural reaction.
We've witnessed one of the most – powerful moments it's given humans to observe.
We watched a man die.
Your response is natural –
Like when the paraffin exploded – in the moment you suddenly react and then – anger.

John It was our fault, Robert.

Robert A period of reflection when the chemicals, the adrenalin that's been swimming around in your system, suddenly dissipates and there's a slump.

John We could have done something.

Robert That's the slump.
Think about it – what could we have done differently?

John We shouldn't have given him whisky.

Robert He shouldn't have been drinking.

John No.

Robert And the strain of a day's sailing and then carrying those loads up the hill from the beach – it was obviously too much for him.

John He seemed at the top of his game –

Robert It's often the way –
Look – he'd just had a full meal.
His digestion was working overtime.
He was drinking as well – which was putting a strain on his heart.

John I suppose.

Robert And we challenged him. Challenged his authority.
He stood up too quickly – the sudden movement must have triggered something.

John He staggered, didn't he?

Robert The attack was probably already coming on.
He seemed to have pain.

John He seemed – distracted.

Robert I held on to him.
He looked like he was about to fall.

John I tried to get him to calm down.

Robert So did I – I had to physically hold him – because he wanted to hit us.

John He – I mean although we argued with him – and it did get quite heated – you didn't actually – I mean you held on to him but you weren't actually exerting force –

Robert Good God, no – I didn't exert force.

John It was the kind of thing that a younger man would easily have shrugged off –

Robert Exactly.

John I still feel as though we could have done something.

Robert Do you think so?
I don't.
It's strange, isn't it?

Look, Johnny, don't upset yourself.
It was my fault.
I challenged him.
I expected him to back down.
He should have backed down.
I've been cursing myself.
It was my fault.

John No. No, it was . . .

Robert If it was anybody's fault it was mine.

John It was an accident.

Robert If you say so.

John It was.

Robert But, you know, it was also a lucky accident.

John Lucky?

Robert Not for Kirk – obviously – but for the island.
For the birds.
The ministry will never get their hands on the island
now.
With Kirk gone –
They're waiting for a letter that will never come.
They'll forget about it.
They've probably forgotten already.
We can do what we like, John.
Complete a full study of the fork-tail.
An absolute first.
Not just the fork-tail but the whole island.
A whole, pristine, unobserved, unsullied, pure
environment.
Only for us.

John They'll want to see our report, though. We have to
do a report.

Robert We lost it.

In the files.

We'll deposit a copy somewhere in some departmental basement under 'P for Petrel, habits of' . . .

It'll never be found.

John It all seems a bit . . . rash . . .

Robert Who's to stop us?

John Nobody, I suppose.

Robert No one will notice. Not for months and by then they'll have contaminated some chunk of Dartmoor with their poison.

John What about Ellen?

Robert What about her?

John She holds the lease on the island now. It's hers.

What if she wants to sell it?

Robert Ellen won't be a problem.

John We can ask her not to. Persuade her.

Robert We can do what we like.

That's the luck of it.

When the old man died – it was like a fog fell away – I realised nobody really knows we're here.

We can do as we please.

We're alone.

Dead to the world and –

Free.

Look at him.

Lain there – he bears the shape of a living thing but every thing about him is still and dead. A stone. And then you see her sleeping, tiny tremors of movement passing across her skin – her eyes, her finger, the breast rising and falling, a shift of bodyweight.

She's at rest, but she's a living thing.

John She's beautiful.

Robert He's beautiful too. His is the beauty of absence. The way an outlying island is more beautiful than the mainland. Things at a distance are always more attractive – a girl, a hill.
Looking at him you see life, at a distance, receding.
Looking at her, and looking at him, you realise that when people say the dead look as if they're asleep – they are either not looking closely enough at death, or they are not looking closely enough at sleep.

John He's beginning to smell.
I noticed.

Robert Maybe we should bury him now.
Before she wakes up.

John Don't you think she might want to say goodbye?

Robert He's dead.

John I know but – the final moment – the last time she sees him.

Robert She doesn't want to see him humped about like a sack of potatoes.

John I suppose not.

Robert The pit's dug.
We'll put him in it.
And then we'll wake her.
Cover him.
A few words in my capacity as senior chap.
And then it's over.

John Come on then, give us a hand, you take his feet.

Robert Got him.

John Right-ho. Lift.

They lift.

Robert He's a heavy beggar.

John To me, to me . . .

Robert Shh. You'll wake her up.
Get the door.

John It's stuck.

Robert Give it a tug.

John I'm about to drop him.

Robert Hold on, swing him round – I'll have a try.
Watch the tea.

*They knock the mug of tea over.
It clatters.*

Watch where you're going.

John I can't hold on to him much longer.

Robert Here we go.

He tugs the door.

Come on . . . come on . . . it's jammed –

It comes free.

John Watch out.

*John falls, knocks Robert, the body falls.
Ellen wakes up.*

Robert Oww.

John Shh.

Ellen What are you doing?

Robert Bloody idiot.

He cuffs John.

John Oww.

Robert Now look what you got us into.

Ellen laughs.
  The boys scramble to retrieve the situation.

John Ellen, I'm most terribly sorry.

Robert We wanted to lay him out before you woke up –

John Please – we'll – I'm so sorry about this.

Ellen That's another fine mess you got me into.

She laughs again.

John What?

Robert I see.
  I suppose it is a bit –
  Comical.

John It's not funny at all.

Robert Laurel and Hardy – she's talking about –

Ellen whistles the tune.
  Ellen laughs again.

John I think it's rather morbid.

Ellen Hit him again.

Robert Why you . . .

He cuffs John again.

John Oww.

Ellen laughs.

John Is this part of the joke?

Ellen You boys.
You're a tonic.

Robert Stanley . . .

Robert cuffs John again.

John Oww.

Ellen and Robert are in hysterics.

John I really can't see the joke.

Robert No.

John We simply fell over.

Robert I know.

Ellen Hit him again.

Robert cuffs John.

John Oww.

John cuffs Robert back.

Robert Owww.

Ellen is practically wetting herself.

John I just don't see where the humour is.
The whole thing's quite unpleasant.

John stands up.

I don't know about anyone else but I need a stiff drink.

Robert Do you, John?

Ellen A stiff drink?

They collapse again.

John What's so funny about that?

Robert (*doing an impression of Kirk*)
You need a stiff drink.
What about me?

John Oh for God's sake.
It's a corpse, Robert – not a ventriloquist's dummy.

Robert I'm sorry.

Ellen He's dead.
He doesn't care.
And I'm . . .
Awake.
Half-dreaming for three days.
And it's enough.
Seeing him dead there.
It's the first time I've known that I'm alive.
I want to drink.
I've never drunk.
I want to drink.

John It's awfully early in the morning for it.

Robert No, she's right.
Why not drink?
Here – we'll all have some.
We work at night, we sleep in the day, we can do as
we please.
Isn't that right, Ellen?

He pours her a drink.
Ellen coughs.
Drinks more.

Ellen That's right.

John I'll have one.

Robert Me too.

They all drink.

Ellen Happy.
Do you think it's normal to be happy at death?
Maybe I'm a monster.

Robert Why shouldn't you be happy?

Ellen I'm supposed to weep.
He's blood of mine.

John I've never been bereaved. I don't know – can't
know –

Robert Nature does not require that you weep for the old.
Birds on the cliff top clear the corpses without pity.
Your feelings are perfectly natural.

Ellen Awake. Is all. After winter, spring.

Robert Here – in a natural environment – death means
exactly what it should. More room for the young.

Ellen Like when the lights go down in the cinema.
And the music starts.
And the film begins.
Only now I'm in it.
With you two.

Robert Laurel and Hardy.

Ellen Laurel and Laurel.
You – your hair sticky-uppy from being under your hat.
Your eyes black and –
And Johnny – always anxious and lost-looking.
Laurel and Laurel you are.

John I wish I knew what you two were talking about.

Ellen I've had three nights in a half-dream.
I've felt alone.
I don't want you to go back to the bothy.
It's cold in the bothy.

This is to be my island now and you my guests upon it.
I want you to stay here.

John I'm not sure that's . . . for the best . . . is it?

Robert It makes sense for us to share the same room.
For heat.

John But there's still weeks till the boat comes.

Ellen Let there be weeks.
We have food.

John You don't mind . . . ?

Ellen They call this the chapel but it is a pagan place.
This was their church, you know, if church they
called it.
Their priest lived here.
They were fallen, the last people, uncle wouldn't have
us talk about them but in the village they spoke of it.
Fallen. They'd come to the mainland from time to time
and take a girl out to be married and the people would
give them a fallen girl – never a girl like me – because the
fallen were damned already and only fit to be brides for
pagans. They'd speak of it as a warning but I used to
dream of the boat coming to take me. Wouldn't you?

John Well I don't know, I –

Robert Of course.

Ellen Do you know how the island came about – truly?

John Volcanos.
There's a fault line under the Atlantic –

Ellen Truly.
At the beginning of time there was a giantess, and she
was in the business of carrying rocks from Ireland over
to Scotland where she was building a home for herself

and her daughter. So every morning as the sun rose she filled her basket with stones and hitched up her skirts and walked out from the beach into the sea – which for her was no more that a burn for the crossing. And so it was that from time to time as she delivered her loads she slipped sometimes on the ocean bottom and spilled her stones – and the stones that fell were made islands and that was how we came to get Lewis and Harris and Skye and Mull and Rum and Muck and Eigg and so it was also that the pebbles she dropped from her basket fell and made islands also and that is how we got the islands outlying – the flannans and the monachs and the shiant and all the islands outlying the outliers, the black islands and the sheep islands and the goat islands and the small islands and all those of that desert type that lie scattered in the sea. And so it was that one day the giantess was hungry and she saw a bird she wanted the eating of flying far out in the distance so she bent reached her hand into her basket she was carrying and she fetched a stone which she threw at the bird with all her strength to bring it down. But the stone missed its target and sailed on and on to the north far out forty miles or so before it hit the cold sea and settled down on the sea bottom and it was a mile broad and a half-mile long and that was this island, the most outlying of all the islands and the one which has on it the chapel of the priest who was fallen and driven out from the mainland with his woman and who came here to hide himself away and there were his people here who lived for three hundred years until they were cleared by a famine from God and they came to the mainland once more and were saved. And the island was kept for sheep only and shepherds and the houses to fall to ruin.

And that is the true history of this island.

This island which is mine.

John What will you do with it . . . after you go back?

Ellen I don't know.
   It has no use.
   Maybe build a house on it and use my claws at the
fowling and grow kale to live.
   Maybe sell it and build a cinema.

Robert You can do exactly as you please.

Ellen Drink.
   Let's bury him.
   But first – we must have a service.

Robert Yes. A funeral. He must have a send-off.

Ellen A few words.

John Robert said he was willing to say a few words . . .

Ellen He must have a eulogy.
   I'll speak it.
   Sit – the congregation must sit.

   The boys sit.

Ellen Now you must look like stones.
   Still and in heavy consideration of God.
   That's right.
   So.
   We are gathered here to pay tribute to Iain Kirk.
   An island man.
   He was a man – look at him – dead there – up in
heaven now –
   He was a man –
   Who knew the evils of womanhood.
   Who fought all his life against the decoration of nails.
   Who kept our house shut against the cinema.
   Who saw Stornoway for what it was – a house of sin.
   Who was never happier than when amongst fish –
   Or at the funeral of an old friend.
   Who knew well the value of pennies.
   And oatmeal.

And darkness.
And work.
And now he is gone.

Robert Amen.

John I don't know if that's appropriate.

Ellen Amen.
A hymn. A hymn now.

John I'm afraid I only know episcopalian hymns.

Ellen This is a pagan place.
We'll sing a pagan hymn.
After me.

'In the Blue Ridge mountains of Virginia,
On the trail of the lonesome pine.
In the pale moonshine, our hearts entwine
Where she carved her name
And I carved mine.
Oh June,
Like the mountains I'm blue.
Like the pine,
I am lonesome for you.
In the Blue Ridge mountains of Virginia,
On the trail of the lonesome pine.'

John and Robert join in.
Eventually lustily.
The song ends.

Ellen Now put him in the ground and cover him.
He's gone from here.

FIVE

A cliff full of sea birds.
The sea swell washing against rocks.

John In the days since the burial of Kirk I have noticed that time has begun to evaporate. The summer day stretches on long into the night and just as the darkness finally falls so the first soft light of dawn appears on the far horizon. I am aware of seconds and minutes but hours and days merge into each other and wash away. We measure our time in the photographs we take of the birds – nesting, with their chicks, flighting, resting on rocks, or mating on the clifftop colonies. Each photograph, each phosphorescent burst of flash, is a solid instant of time, a branch to hold on to in the flood.

I swim. I lie on the rocks like a white seal in the hope that she will see me again. I lie beside her in the manse and listen to her breathing. I have noticed my mental capacities for sound judgement crumbling away under the force of her presence like cliff stone being pounded by the sea. I am no longer confidently aware of whether a memory of her is real, or something I wish were real. I dream persistently of forcing myself on her and in the hours of the early morning when I am at my weakest I feel only a thin wall separates me from rising and going to her bed and –

I feel myself to be falling.

I must remember – there is a boat coming.

I must remember – there is a war coming.

I must remember – there are other people to consider.

SIX

A phosphorescent flash.

The early hours of the morning, towards the end of the night-flighting.

Darkness outside.

Heavy rain and wind.

Robert and John are outside the chapel taking night photographs of the birds arriving at their burrows.

Robert Did you get it?

John I don't know. I can't see a bloody thing.

Robert Me neither. Only three left.

John Jesus! Blinking sod!

Robert What?

John Bloody gannet got me in the leg.

Robert Come on.

> *Inside the chapel, Ellen is sitting by the dying embers of the fire, in lamplight; she has opened Robert's notebook and is reading from it.*
> *From the candle box, the cheep of the fork-tail chick.*

Ellen 'Day Four. New Moon. Thirty-two birds returned to their burrows. Fifteen burrows left unattended. See map below. Two eggs remain unhatched, 21 and 44. Two adults lost in predation by gulls.'

> *A second phosphorescent flash.*

John I can't feel my fingers.
I'm numb.

Robert Did you get her?

John Perfect.

Robert Last one. Wall by the field.
Come on.
Soon be done.

John I'm soaked to the buggering bones.
My actual bones are wet.
I'm going to die.

Robert You can't die yet.
  I haven't given you permission.

Ellen 'Nest Number One, chick remains unattended
since the first day.'
  That's you he means.
  Number One is you.
  Because he found you first.

  Ellen goes over to the candle box.

Poor chick.
  All the mother birds come home but yours.
  Who's to keep you?
  Who's to give you warmth?
  Poor chick.

  A phosphorescent flash.

Robert Beautiful.
  Did you see?

John I saw.

Robert Perfect.

Ellen He's a bad man.
  Isn't he a bad bad man?
  A bad bad man he is.

  Ellen takes a small stone from the floor of the chapel.
    She puts the stone in the hearth.
    She finds a piece of oily rag beside the lamp.
    She lifts the stone from the fire and wraps it up in
  the oily rag.
    She puts the wrapped stone in the candle box.

Keep you warm a while.
  Fires dying.
  Need more peat.

A moment.
  The boys outside the door.

John I can't open it.

They enter.

John (*imitating Kirk*)
  'I'll want compensation for that door.'

Robert and John giggle.
  Slightly hysterical.

John 'If you boys weren't come here to my island.'

Robert 'Making your studies of jugs.'

John 'Interfering with my sheep.'

Robert 'Falling to blasphemous practices.'

John 'It would be a door serving its purpose.'

Ellen pulls her shawl over her head.
  She opens the door.
  Ellen leaves into the darkness and rain.

The boys are soaked, cold, muddy and exhausted.
  They sit. Silent.
  John, scrabbles about in his pack.
  He finds a packet of biscuits.
  He eats one.
  He throws one over to Robert.
  Robert catches it.
  Robert eats the biscuit.
  John takes his boots off.
  Takes his socks off.
  Squeezes the water out of them onto the floor.

Robert You are my madeleine, Johnny, do you know that?

John What?

Robert They say that smell is the key to the door of memory, don't they? Didn't old Proust get transported to the bosom of his mother by a whiff of cake?

John Buggered if I know.

Robert He did, no, he did and I must say . . . catching the aroma of your socks, Johnny, wafting across the chapel like some . . . like some pagan incense . . . a heady mix of regurgitated fish oil and sweaty wool, I am transported . . . I really am.

John Are you, old bean?

Robert I am.

John And where are you transported to?

Robert Somewhere in between Linda Jameson's thighs.
   Of course, that's not a place you would be familiar with.
   Is it?

John Transported, are you?
   You asked for it.

   John takes his sock and rubs it in Robert's face.

Robert Get off.
   Get off.

John Not until you apologise.

Robert Never.

John You know you can't win.

Robert I submit.
   I'm sorry.
   Mercy.

John breaks off.
  Sits back down.
  Sniffs his sock.

Robert laughs. John laughs.

We did it.
  All the burrows photographed.
  We got flying, fighting, feeding, everything.

John We're the first.

Robert The first by a mile.

John We'll die if we don't get dry.

John starts to take off his wet clothes down to his underpants. He hangs his clothes off the table.

Where did Ellen go?

Robert She's probably gone to get breakfast.

John I'm starving.

Robert also strips and hangs his clothes.
  He pulls a blanket over his shoulders.
  He takes a damp notebook from a pocket of his trousers and sits down to write up his notes.

Robert What time is it?

John I don't know.
  Nearly dawn I suppose.
  I don't even know what day it is.

Robert Most of the chicks are hatched. Only a few weeks and they'll be flying. They'll start going south.

John I don't blame them.
  If this is what it's like in midsummer.
  How people ever survived a winter in this place is beyond me.

Robert You adapt. That's all. You stay underground.

John goes to the candle box.

John This one's still not been visited.
Old Number One.
He's still alive.

Robert I know.
I don't understand.
Four whole days without warmth.
He should be dead.

John Why doesn't his mother come back?

Robert I don't know.

John Maybe she died at sea.

John gets a cigarette.

Poor little bugger.
You look out at sea and there's so much of it.
And it all seems so buggering empty.
You got a light.

Robert throws him a lighter.
John lights up.

Robert We have to follow them.

John What?

Robert They live at sea. We're only getting glimpses of
them here.

John I suppose.

Robert They'll all be flying soon. What if we tag them,
before they leave, every one, adult and chick . . . ?
What if we follow the migration? All the way down to
the Azores.

John That would be . . . it would – has anybody ever done that?

Robert No.

John To follow an entire colony.

Robert Observe the pairing patterns. The survival rates. Study the distances travelled at sea. Follow them south and then all the way back here again – next summer.
And this is only one population.
There are colonies in Greenland, Newfoundland . . . in the Pacific even.
Imagine it. Imagine really understanding them, John.

John The ministry won't send us to Greenland.

Robert We don't need the ministry. We can do it ourselves.

John Hardly.

Robert Why not?

John A chap has to earn a living.
Not much money in birds.

Robert Sod money.
Money's never a problem.
We don't need much anyway.
Some grub, we've got kit.
It's not as if there's anything to spend it on.

John What if there's a war?

Robert There won't be.

John D'you think?

Robert Look, fuck their war.

John Steady on.

Robert Let them. Let them tear each other to pieces. Good.

The more of them that die the better.

We'll get out of it. Anybody with half a brain can get out of a war. It's only the boneheaded, the cattle, the boys who like sport who walk out in front of guns.

They bloody love it. Let them. We'll be far away.

John I was thinking of applying for the air force.

Robert Why in Christ's name would you want to do a stupid thing like that, Johnny?

John I don't know.

I suppose I fancied being a flyer.

Robert Then follow the birds.

You want to come back, don't you?

You do want to?

You want to come back for Ellen.

John Of course I do.

Robert I don't know why you flinch.

John No, I don't imagine you do.

Robert You draw back.

John I don't know what you're talking about.

Robert Your hand hovers, Johnny, it's quite transparent . . .

A half an inch from her skin when she stands by you.

And then you draw back.

John I do not.

Robert You must sicken,

With every dawn that passes and yet still she remains untouched.

John Don't, Robert.

Robert Don't what?

John You know perfectly well what I'm talking about.

Robert You'll tire.
Hovering is tiring.
Eventually you'll lose strength.
Your hand will move.
You'll fall.
It's perfectly natural.

John How do you do it, Robert?
You always – you . . . get what you want.

Robert Do I?

John That's what it seems like.
To us ordinary mortals.

Robert How could you possibly know what I want?
You don't even know what you want, John.

John I want to remember what it feels like to be warm.
I want to sleep.

*John gets up. Goes through his kit. Finds a pair of
shorts and a vest. He takes off his underpants and
puts the shorts and vest on.*

John We may be far away.
But there is a boat coming.
At the end of the summer.

Ellen returns.
  She stands in the open doorway.
  She sees John changing.

Robert How do they fly?
You saw them in the storm.
How do they do it?

John I could hardly open my eyes.

Robert There was a moment, in the dark, crossing the
bog near the cliff top, when the mist was everywhere and

the rain was whipping in off the sea and I thought . . .
My clothes are wet. My skin is wet.

John I was too numb to think.
Except bacon and eggs.
I kept seeing bacon and eggs and a hot fire.
Hovering in front of me.
Just out of reach.

Robert The whole world's water . . . the world's water . . .
Nine-tenths of our bodies is made of water. The substance
of us is water. I thought . . . so little of us is solid we
might as well be made of mist. Mist clinging to hollow
bones.

Outside the chapel, the call of a petrel.
Ellen still waits.

John They must be dry by now.

Ellen enters.

Ellen Never dry in front of a fire like that.
Fire's about dead.
You'd have let it go out.

John Dry enough. They'll dry on. Once the fire's going.

John puts his clothes on.
Ellen puts peat on the fire.

Ellen There's a bird outside.
The rest have settled but there's one still flying above
the chapel.
She's calling fit to burst.

Robert The light! It's the light!
You blinking idiot.
That's his mother.

John Whose mother?

Robert Number One.

Ellen She's calling and calling.

Robert She won't come because of the light.

John Come in – in here?

Robert They always land at night, why?

John To avoid predation.

Robert To avoid the gannets who'd snap them out of the sky like that.

So they wait for dark to come back to their nests.

Dark – dark – she doesn't know what's sun and what's lamp.

Dark's all she wants.

No wonder she's left the chick five days.

She's been waiting for night to fall and it never has.

Switch the lamp off.

Ellen blows the lamp out.
    The chapel is dark but for the glow of embers from the fire.
    Robert crouches in front of the fire, the blanket round his shoulders.

Robert Get the camera.

John I can't see anything.

Robert Quiet.

She'll come in if we're quiet.

They are all quiet.
    John looks for the camera in the dark.
    John knocks into the table.

John Owww.

Robert Shut up.

John Sorry.

Found it.

Nearly broke my shin.

Robert Will you shut up, you blinking idiot.
Stand by the candle box.

John Will you not call me a blinking idiot.

Ellen giggles.

Robert I hear her.
She's coming.
Ready.

In the darkness.
The flapping of a bird as it enters the chapel.
The bird makes her way swiftly to the nest.
The bird calls.
The chick calls.

A phosphorescent flash.
In the flash, Robert, crouched in the hearth, blanket around his shoulders – a bird.
Ellen looking at him.

Darkness.

SEVEN

Night.
Weather.
A real storm.
Ellen and John in the chapel.
John is processing negatives.

Ellen He's still out there.
It's darkening.
Rain's come heavy.

John He shouldn't be out tonight, he'll freeze, but he insisted on it. He wanted to watch them flying in a storm.

He puts the plate into the processing canister.

Ellen Abracadabra.

John What?

Ellen What magic you got hidden in there?

John It's not magic.

Ellen Magic to me. Pictures coming out of water.

John It's the chemical process. The light reacts with the film to make a plate. The plate reacts with the fluid to make a negative. Once the negative is fixed, you wash it. And then you get the image.

He pours out the first fluid and pours in the second.

Ellen Light. Water. Magic.

She retrieves a processed negative.

John A fork-tail chick.
A week old.
This one hatched on the second night.

Ellen It's a picture of Robert.

John It's a fork-tail chick.

Ellen It's Robert.

John Robert's in the picture.
He's holding the chick.
A human figure helps to visualise the scale.

Ellen The chick fits in the palm of his hand.
His eyes.
Look at them.
Do you see it?
What he does with his eyes. When he looks at a person.
When did you meet him?

John At college. We were both interested in natural history. He – I met him – I don't remember the exact moment. We sort of fell in together.

Ellen He picks you out.

John He's mostly, generally speaking, a trial.
Quite liable to leave halfway through dinner, or to talk about the sexual habits of primates to a roomful of dowagers.

Ellen He's always looking about.

John What I can say for Robert is that he has some gift for observing nature. Better than anyone I've ever met. In so far as one can predict these things I suspect he may be very great in the field and –

Ellen Very great.

John So one holds on to his coat tails given the chance and puts up with the sheer bloody irresponsibility of the man.
Excuse my French.
He shouldn't be out there.
The lightning.
Maybe I should go and get him.

Ellen He watches me.

John I know. I know.
He does the same to me.

Ellen As though I'm worth watching.

John You learn to ignore it.

Ellen I know what he wants.

John He doesn't want anything.

Ellen He does.
Five days he's been watching me.
This morning I woke up.

I opened my eyes.
And he was sitting by the last embers.
His eyes on me like hands.
Touching.

John If you felt uncomfortable – because I can – talk to him if you want.

Ellen I didn't feel uncomfortable.

John Oh.
Well. I . . . I see.
If –
Maybe I should get him.
The lightning.
It's really quite –

Ellen I rose, he watched me rising, the morning was warm.
I went to bathe.
At the stream.
I looked up the hill towards the village.
And he was still watching.

John When you were bathing?
Good God.

Ellen I wondered if he would come to me but he stayed where he was.
I think he's afraid of me.

John Now see – Ellen, if you have feelings for Robert,
And I don't pretend that I can deny he's spoken to me about –
That he has reciprocal –
But only in the sense that –
Any man would.

Ellen Any man?
Claw-handed?

John I – your hands are –
   I didn't notice – I wouldn't say they were –
   What I mean is any man – essentially alone with a
woman of your – is bound to feel –

Ellen What about you?

John Well I – of course – but only in so far as – it's . . .

Ellen As far as what?

John It's natural, that I should feel . . .

Ellen Natural.
   But you will not name it.

John What I want to say is that Robert – he's . . .
   A –
   The way he wants you is –
   Purely . . .
   Not genuine affection.
   So I think you should be careful.

Ellen Abracadabra.

   *John removes the processed negative from the canister
   and places it in the bath for washing.*

John He is not a man who will marry.
   Or at least, if he does, I don't believe he'll make
a woman happy.

   Ellen laughs.

Ellen You're like uncle.
   Marrying me off.
   I said nothing about marriage.

   Ellen looks at the new picture. Ellen laughs.

I don't see what's so funny.
   It's not bloody funny. Excuse my French.

Ellen This picture – this is not a bird.

John What?

Ellen This one here – no bird in this picture.

John No – it's – Robert must've – oh, my God.

Ellen That's a picture of me.

John I had no idea – this is – scandalous . . .

Ellen It's me.
Never seen a picture of me before.

John He had no right.
No right at all.

Ellen At the stream. In the morning.
My body.

John You were bathing.
. . .
He –
I'll –
I'll put it on the fire.
Don't worry. I've not looked at it. I've – nobody will
see it.

Ellen Am I so monstrous you'd rather it burned than
look at it?
. . .
Give it to me.
Hang the picture up.
Let it dry.

John You want to keep it?

Ellen I've never seen myself.
Look at it.

John You look . . .
And it certainly doesn't take away from the sheer
liberty of taking the picture – but you do look –

Very beautiful.
If you don't mind me saying so.

Ellen I don't mind.

John I'll have a word with him.
I'll get him –

Ellen Don't.
Let him be.
Look at the picture he's made of me.
This is how he sees me.

John No –

Ellen Yes –

John It's – I'm warning you – it's instinct.
Animal –

Ellen Natural.

John You can't.

Ellen I can.
This is my island.
Nobody here, except Robert, and me and you.

John Simply because we are somewhat isolated –
There are limits of decency which we must observe.

Ellen I've upset you.

John He has upset me.

Ellen I have broken the limits of decency.

John No – but . . .

Ellen I will break them again.

John Have him then.
You have him.

Ellen Why are you angry?

John I'm going to get him.
I'm going out.

He tries to open the door.
It sticks.

Bloody door.

He pulls hard. Opens it.
Weather.
He goes out.

ROBERT.
ROBERT.

His voice is drowned on the wind.

Ellen He won't hear you.

John ROBERT.

Ellen There's nobody there.

John re-enters.

John Everywhere he goes he does this.
At Cambridge. In London.
He watches and he captures.
I drag along behind him.
You have him.
Rise with him.
Rise above and watch me disappear.
I try – I have been trying – to be decent.
But you go on – he goes on –
And I – And I – And I –
. . .
I can't do it.

Ellen What?

John I follow you around.
I'm like a damn dog at your heels.

Ellen What can't you do?

John I can't.
   I want to –
   I'm sorry.

Ellen Do you want to hit me?

John Good God no.

Ellen You moved – like you were to hit me.

John I don't want to hit you.

Ellen Then what?

John I'm going to the bothy.
   I'll sleep there tonight.
   I think it's better.
   Don't you?

Ellen Why?

John Go with Robert. Go with Robert if you must.
   Just don't make me witness it.

Ellen We're on the island.
   Amongst birds, and rock, and water.
   This is not London.
   You talk about me as though I'm from a twopenny
novel.
   I'm flesh.
   Look at me.
   I like you, John.

John I see.

Ellen I want you.

John You want me?

Ellen Yes.

John And him?

Ellen Yes.

John That's monstrous.

Ellen I am monstrous, then.

John He is. He's monstrous. He's planted this . . .
You want me?

Ellen I said so.
Is that monstrous?

John Well. No.

Ellen I'll go to the bothy.
I'll sleep there.
I should never have spoken.

John Surely you can choose between us.

Ellen I don't want to.

John What – what – it's – what are you suggesting?

Ellen I want you to touch me.
Here's my hand.
Hold it.

John He'll come back.

Ellen Quiet.
Take the water off the table.
Bring the blanket.
Put the blanket on the table.
Now come by the fire.
Stand in the warm, in front of me.
Look.

She undresses.
Her clothes fall to the floor.
She laughs.

John What's funny.

Ellen You look afraid.

John I am.

Ellen Take off your clothes.
Take me to the table.
We'll lie on the blanket.
I'm cold.
Warm me.

They move to the table.

John Look – before – I ought to say –

Ellen Shut up.

John So that you know.
Before we –
That I do – love – my intentions –

Ellen Birds and rock and water and us.
We're on the island.
No need of intentions here.

John Right.

Ellen Right.

A moment of touching.
Kissing.
Suddenly.
A kicking at the door.

John Oh my God, he's come back.

Ellen Stay.
Let him come.

The door kicked open.
Wind and weather.

Robert They still fly, Johnny. I've been watching them.
In the storm. They still fly – it's as if they're part of it.

John Robert, I – it's – I –

Robert takes in the scene.
Robert shuts the door.

Ellen It's fine.
Let him sit by the fire.

John I know it seems a bit rum.

Ellen Look at him.

John Robert, I can explain . . .

Ellen Quiet.
Let it be dark.
Let him be silent.
Let me see him seeing us.

John Robert, I – look, it's a bit awkward.
I do wish you'd say something.
Ellen and I – we – she –

Ellen Put your hand on my breast.
Leave it there.
Feel my breathing.

John Breathing –
I –

Ellen Slowly.

John I can't, I – stop.

Ellen If you're going to make a fuss about it, then stop.

John No. I . . .

Ellen Go to the bothy.
Sleep there.
If you want to bring decency back to me.
Go.
Take yourself away.

John No, I want to. I want –

Ellen Then stay.

John It's just a bit – off-putting – having a spectator.
On a chap's first time.

Ellen Look at him.
Like a gull.
On his haunches.
Watching.

A crash of thunder, lightning from the storm.

John We're going to be struck by bloody lightning.

Ellen We're caught in his gaze, boy.
This bird's look.
Gull Robert-watching.
Drawing us into his gull eyes.
Into his gull mind till.
I'm watching myself.
Watching me and you.
Let me take you in.
Look at your white seal skin.
Like film stars we are, boy.
Made film star by his gull eyes.
Dark.
Light flickering.
The falling away of all things.
Gone from ourselves.
In a pagan place.
Under the eyes of the gull.

A moment.
Their bodies perfect.

John Robert.

Robert Notice it, Johnny. Remember.
Remember the surprise of her body.

Remember very precisely the heat of her breath.
The heat of her.
Which is life, remember, Johnny.
Life.
Life contains heat which you only notice when you
touch.
When you stop hovering.
When you fall.

Perhaps Robert is weeping.

John This can't be, Robert.
It can't be.
You know that.
The boat will come.
It has to end.

Robert Does it?

John pushes Ellen from him.
   Rises from the table.
   Covers himself.

Ellen We'll send the boat away.
We'll stay.
I'll not go back.

Robert I've been watching the petrels, Johnny.
Watching them in the storm.
And I saw something.
They allow themselves to be taken.
They're drawn on currents of air and currents of
water. They throw themselves into the storm and allow
themselves to be taken.
Where d'you think they go, Johnny?
They land on the island, but they don't live on it.
It's a landfall but it's not their home.
They live unweighted by mainland, tethered only to
an outlier.

226

Imagine.
Living without time.
Because time, Johnny, time belongs to the land.
Not to the sea and the air.
Imagine entering their world.
Imagine that.
No beginnings and no endings.
Limitless.
Imagine departing from the land.

John It can't be.

A moment between the two boys.
Calmly, Robert walks out into the storm.

Ellen Bring him back.

John Leave him.

Ellen He was weeping.

Ellen goes to the door.

John He's wet from the storm, it's rainwater, that's all.

Dawn.
The sea crashing against rocks.
Thousands of seabirds.
Wind.
A bird rising.
A bird flying.

EIGHT

Some weeks later.
Inside the chapel.
Ellen is looking at the candle box.
The door is kicked open by the Captain.
Ellen and John enter with him.

Captain Bloody door.
You mean to say, lad, you were on this island for a
month and you never got round to fixing the door?

John Sorry, sir.

Captain No need to be sorry.
It's your lookout.

John The stones seemed to shift.

Captain I daresay they did.

Ellen I've gathered my things, sir, from the bothy.
Shall I take them to the boat?

Captain Leave them there.
I'll have one of the chaps take them down to the beach.
Can't have a lady carrying loads, can we?

John No, sir.

Ellen He's big now, John.
Number One.
He's grown.

John One of the birds, sir.
Ellen's sort of adopted him.

Captain A pet.

Ellen He'll be flying soon.

John They migrate.

Captain Fascinating.
Well, if you're all packed up.

John Ready as we'll ever be.

Captain You can get yourselves down to the launch.
Quick as you can if you don't mind.
I'd like to be sailing soon.

Ellen Is it all right, Captain.
  If I take a moment to say goodbye.
  To my uncle.

Captain Ah, yes . . . yes . . . right-ho. You do that.

Ellen Thank you.

Captain Poor girl.

John She's been a brick, sir.
  A real brick.

Captain They're made of stern stuff.
  Women here.
  Bred in the bone.
  I have a theory that it's the puffin.
  I take it you ate puffin.

John I did, sir.

Captain Rank. Isn't it?

John Chicken cooked in axle-grease.

Captain Food on board. Cook'll sort you out for a
roast-beef dinner.
  You deserve it.
  Still, you seem to have made yourself quite at home.
  'The chapel', you said.

John That's what the shepherds call it.

Captain Poor-looking chapel.
  No doubt he was a poor-looking priest.
  Have you boxed up all your documents?

John Yes, sir.
  All the survey notes.
  Photographs.
  All there.

Captain The ministry chaps are eager to see what you've got.
Whether the island is suitable for the project.
I have to say, it looks ideal to me.

John I think it will be suitable, sir. Pristine. A diamond.

Captain Now listen,
Before we go.
About the other lad.

John Robert, sir.

Captain Robert, yes.

John Fell, sir.

Captain So you said.

At the cliff top, Ellen stands, looking out to sea.

Ellen When it was over.
He walked out into the storm and I followed him because he seemed to have been weeping.

John He was in the habit of swimming.
In the morning.
He would swim.

Ellen Into the dawn he walked. Up the hill he walked.
To the cliff top.

John I thought he can't be going to do that.
Not now.
Not in a storm.

Ellen And he made a short run.

John I feel just awful about the whole thing.

Ellen He ran at the cliff edge
And spread his arms out and flew.

John It was typical of him.
  Not thinking.
  The complete absence of questions.

Ellen He flew.

John By the time we got down to the rocks on the shoreline, the storm had taken his body away.

Ellen Away, away. Far out to sea.

Captain Careless.

John Yes, sir.

Captain Cliffs.
  Always a gamble.

John I should have done something.

Captain Not your fault.
  He was the senior.

John About Robert, sir.

Captain We'll need a report, of course.

John He – I wondered – telling his parents.

Captain Ministry'll see to all that.

John Right.

Captain Come on then. Ship's waiting. Let's get a move on.
  Take the stuff down to the beach.
  Where's the girl?

John I'll fetch her.

Captain Right-ho.

John Captain, would you mind, since the island's going to be – well – out of commission shall we say . . . ?
  Would you mind – is there room for the table?

Captain The table?

John Yes. It's a couple of hundred years old I think.
A souvenir if you like.
And besides.
Just to have it sitting here while the whole island around it is incapable of supporting life.
Seems an awful waste of a table.

Captain Of course.
If you put it like that.
I'll mention it to the chaps.
Have them bring it down with the rest of the gear.
Right-ho.
Back to civilisation.

He tries to shut the door.

Can't shut the bloody door.

John Doesn't bloody matter now does it?
Excuse my French.

*The Captain and John walk away from the chapel.
A fork-tail calling in the corner of the chapel.*

The End.

PYRENEES

In memory of Morag Hood

Pyrenees was first produced by Paines Plough and the Tron Theatre Company, Glasgow, in association with Watford Palace Theatre, at the Tron Theatre, Glasgow, on 9 March 2005.

The Man Hugh Ross
Vivienne Paola Dionisotti
Anna Frances Grey
The Proprietor Jonathan McGuinness

Director Vicky Featherstone
Designer Neil Warmington
Lighting Designer Natasha Chivers
Original Music and Sound Nick Powell

Characters

The Man

Anna

The Proprietor

Vivienne

We should have been galloping on horses, their hoofprints
Splashes of light, divots kicked out of the darkness,
Or hauling up lobster pots in a wake of sparks. Where
Were the otters and seals? Were the dolphins on fire?
Yes, we should have been doing more with our lives.

Michael Longley, 'Water Burn'

Act One

Anna and The Man are seated at a table on the terrace.
   A mini-cassette recorder sits on the table between them.
   Anna is dressed smartly, for work, but with a nod to the unusual location of the interview and the season.
   The Man is wearing a borrowed suit without a tie.

Anna loads the machine with a cassette.
   She spends an awkwardly long period of time trying to get it to work.
   She consults a little folded instruction leaflet.
   She's a little nervous.
   The Man watches her.

Anna It's OK.

The Man Would you –?

Anna No. I've used this machine before.

The Man Sometimes they're temperamental.

Anna Mm.

The Man Would you like –?

Anna I think I've got it.

The Man Good.

   Anna tries the machine.
      It seems to work.

Anna Instructions in five languages, none of it makes any sense.

The smallest of laughs from Anna.
  Something of a pause as she fiddles with it.

The Man There's no rush.

She rewinds.
  She presses play.
  The recorded voice is distant, barely audible.
  The laugh is audible.

*Tape: 'Instructions in five languages, none of it makes
any sense.'*
  The smallest of laughs.

She switches it off.
  The Man is smiling.

Anna Right.
  . . .
  I know.
  I'm terrible with . . . equipment.
  Cars. Things that have a manual.

The Man I'm not laughing at you, honestly.

Anna It's funny.
  I deserve it.

The Man No.

Anna Anything mechanical – I get a bit – (*She makes
a hand-gesture which seems to conjure clumsy indecisive
hands dealing with a small, technical object. Simultaneously she is searching for a word.*) – you know . . .
spazzy.

The Man I'm sorry?

Anna I shouldn't really use that word, but you know
what I mean.

The Man Spazzy?

Anna It's a bad habit. You don't need to tell me.

The Man I've never heard it before.

Anna Oh.
It's just a childish . . . at school they used to . . .
Really?

The Man It sounds American.

Anna No, it's – it's – gosh –
It's from – I don't even like to say it – spastic. It's –

The Man Spazzy.

Anna But actually it's quite offensive.

The Man Spazzy. (*He laughs.*)

Anna It's not really appropriate any more.

The Man It's a funny word.

Anna At school – it was just – but kids do, don't they?
So – because I'm epileptic.
'Spazzy Anna'.
I just picked it up.
So I should know better, actually.

The Man 'Spazzy Anna'.

Anna Actually really I shouldn't have said it.
Would you mind not mentioning it to anybody?

The Man Not at all.

Anna It's a slight breach of guidelines, you know. That's all.
Anyway – we'll get started.
I don't want to keep you too long.

The Man Keep me as long as you like.
It's a glorious morning.
It's nice to have company.

Anna Yes.

The Man Since my experience, Miss Edwards –

Anna Call me Anna.

The Man Anna – the smallest things seem –

Anna Let's be informal.
Sorry.

The Man It's quite all right.

Anna The smallest things.

The Man The smallest things –
You know, a bird or the way a person plays chess.
They seem part of – I do understand that this is
embarrassing for people – a greater one-ness.
I feel awake to the wonder of being alive and amongst
things.
So unfortunately I smile at people more than I should.
In fact,
It was your laugh which made me smile.
Hearing your laugh on the tape.
That's all.

Anna It's all right. Really.

The Man I probably seem a bit 'spazzy'.

Anna Not at all.

The Man Pay no attention.

Anna No I – it's – actually.
I know exactly what you mean.
. . .
OK.
Let's . . . so . . . if you could just say something. For a
level.

She switches the tape on.
  She stands the recorder on the table between them.

The Man . . .

Anna What did you have for breakfast this morning?

The Man I had an English breakfast. Bacon, eggs, sausage, tomato.
  Just the usual.

Anna I had the continental.

The Man I dithered over the continental, but in the end I plumped for the English.

Anna OK, that should do.

She rewinds the tape a little.
  Plays it.
  Both listen.

Tape: '. . . dithered over the continental, but in the end I plumped for the English.'

The Man Do I sound like that?

Anna Yes.

The Man It's strange.

Anna It's always horrible hearing your own voice on tape.

The Man I suppose so.

Anna Does it trigger anything for you? Any memories?

The Man It sounds like –
  It's softly spoken.
  It's quite a softly spoken voice.
  That's all I could say about it.

Anna When I was an actress, I had a voice coach once, and she told me that people carry a landscape in their voice. This was to help us find the right accent. She said that, you know, if a person's from Glasgow their voice would be low, held in the back of their throat, like this: '*Hullo*'. Because in Glasgow it's always raining, you see, so everybody has their heads down.

The Man Play it again.

Anna rewinds and plays the tape again.

I don't know. What do you think?

Anna I suppose it sounds soft. Like you said.
Softly spoken.
Maybe you come from a soft landscape?

The Man Somewhere with rolling hills. Low hills.

Anna Yes.

The Man And farmland. Copses.

Anna Does that landscape ring any bells?

The Man It certainly feels familiar.

Anna Of course it may not mean anything. I'm not really here to investigate that per se. Really I just need to establish that you're British and see if I can set out a process for the investigation. Hopefully just by talking we can establish a few background details. Then we'll send the tape to a forensic specialist in the UK who can analyse the tape.
Come up with something more specific.
And eventually we'll try to match what we've got against the missing-persons records.

The Man I do seem to feel an affinity with nature.
I've been appreciating the arrival of spring.

Seeing the birds come back.
Just these past few days.

Anna It's gorgeous, isn't it?
Not like Britain.

The Man Things coming to life again.

Anna You feel it, don't you? One does.

The Man Very strongly.
You were an actress?

Anna Yes. Well, you know, a long time ago.

The Man Can't have been that long ago.

Anna I gave it up. It wasn't really me.

The Man That's a shame.

Anna Well, it's not so much that I wasn't any good. I was – well – that's for others to judge. I just don't think I was cut out for it.

The Man Learning all those lines.

Anna No. I could learn the lines. I think it was more that I didn't seem to fit a 'type'.

The Man is staring at Anna.

In theatre people often cast by 'type'. And I – didn't seem to have one – well, I don't know – my face didn't fit. Whatever it was. Maybe it was that I'm – you know, my weight.

The Man . . .

Anna Anyway, lah-di-dah.
It doesn't matter.
Is everything all right?

The Man Hm?

Anna It's just you were . . .

The Man I was looking at you. Sorry.

Anna It's all right.
I don't mind you looking.
I was just worried for a moment.
That you were ill.

The Man Sometimes I get a feeling when I'm speaking
to a person.
Like an undertow.

Anna Oh.
Perhaps that's important.
An undertow?

The Man I can't really describe it in more detail than
that, I'm afraid.
But I have that feeling with you.

Anna Is it a feeling of recognition?

The Man I don't know.

Anna Of course, if you felt you recognised me, that
would be odd.
I mean, I know you've never met me before.
Because I would remember.

The Man You're right.

Anna But maybe I remind you of someone?

The Man No. It isn't that.
It's gone.
I'm not sure I could have put a word to it anyway.

Anna OK.
Never mind.

The Man Sorry.

Anna God, there's no need to apologise.
I wasn't –
This must be very difficult for you.

The Man It's embarrassing.

Anna Please don't be embarrassed.

The Man No, I mean, not knowing who I am.
It isn't difficult really except when . . . well, in social situations, it's embarrassing.

Anna Please don't be embarrassed with me.
I'm here to help. You're not under suspicion or in any kind of trouble. Far from it.
A lot of people have an idea about consular staff that we're stuck up, or cold, out to get them. But we're not.
I think we're like doctors.
We just try to sort out people's problems.

The Man Have you ever had anyone like me before?

Anna I believe it's happened, not in France but somewhere.
I once heard about it.
It isn't common, no. But that's the thing about consular work – every day is different.

The Man Today you're a detective.

Anna Not really a detective.

The Man A puzzler.

Anna It's certainly one of the more interesting cases I've had.

The Man If it's any help.
I'm pretty sure I'm British.

Anna We can't be sure of anything.

The Man You're right but, you know, just then – when you were talking about the consular staff. Suddenly I felt proud. It was a feeling of pride in the British Diplomatic Service.

Why would I feel proud of the British Diplomatic Service?

Unless I was British?

Anna I'll just take a note of that. (*Anna takes a note of that.*) Maybe we should begin with – if you're comfortable, if you could just – for the tape, to get an example of your speech down, if you could just – I don't know – describe where we are, what you can see?

The Man Um.
We're on the terrace. A terrace.
Around us there are tables and chairs.
Below us there's a steep slope, a mountain pasture,
Stretching away down.
Over there – there's a sheer rock face.
It's very rugged.
Beautiful.
Very typical of the Pyrenees, I suppose.
Is that enough?

Anna Perhaps a little bit more.
It's not so much what you see as the words you use to describe it that are important.

The Man . . .

Anna Just keep going.
Try to be natural.

The Man The sky is blue. Porcelain-blue.
White cirrus clouds high up.
Evangeline's hanging up laundry.
She's talking to one of the climbers.
She's laughing.

I can see the climbers' tents further up in the pasture.
. . .
A pine forest behind us.
The smell of a thaw.

. . .

Look, as a matter of fact, describing things feels unnatural.

Anna It's good. Keep going.

The Man A . . . through the pines . . . a river, not a river but a . . .
There's a word for it.
Smaller than a river –

Anna Stream?

The Man Stream. Yes. I suppose. Running through the pines.

Anna It wasn't the word you were looking for?

The Man No.
'Buh . . . ' 'Buh . . . '
It's on the tip of my tongue.

Anna Brook?

The Man No.

Anna Beck?

The Man No.

Something of a pause.

It's gone.

Anna If it had been 'beck' then we could have said that you were from Yorkshire, you see, or at least the north of England, or at least that you have some connection with the north.

The Man Right. I get you. The words are a clue.
I'm sorry I can't –
'Buh . . .'
No.

Anna We'll tape some more later.
There's no rush.
I'm just here to get to know you and write down
whatever I think might help the experts.
I think we should try to be relaxed about it.
No point rushing.
Just . . .
Take it as it comes.

The Man I might be from Yorkshire.
York.
No.
Nothing stirring.
York.

Anna While you think about that, I'll just write some of
this down.
Do you mind if I smoke?

The Man Not at all.

Anna takes out a cigarette and lights it.
She writes on her pad.
Something of a pause.

There's something about the smoke.
The smell.

Anna I am sorry. Is it blowing in your face?

The Man It's familiar.
Do you – do you mind? Could I have a cigarette?

Anna I'm sorry. I didn't offer. I just assumed you didn't
smoke.

The Man I haven't. Not since I've been here.
But the smell is definitely familiar.
I'm just wondering if it's familiar because I'm a smoker.
Do you see?

Anna The smell of smoke would be familiar to someone who lived with a smoker. Just because it's familiar doesn't mean that you're a smoker.

The Man I won't know unless I try it, will I?

Anna Yes, but that's something you wouldn't want to find out.
You don't want to discover that you're a smoker.
Not if you've given up.

The Man No. I'm pretty sure I am a smoker.

Anna People go to endless lengths to give up smoking.
I know – believe me – I'm weak myself.
So even if you were a smoker – you've given up so –

The Man Just give me a fag.

Anna . . .

Anna offers him the packet.
He takes a cigarette.
He lights it.

The Man Yes. This feels very familiar. This feels . . . yes . . .
Like coming home.

Anna I'm sorry.
I shouldn't have been smoking myself.
Not when I'm working.

The Man Don't worry about it.

Anna Now I've got you started.

The Man You didn't offer me heroin, Miss Edwards.

Anna I know.

The Man We're making progress.

Anna Anna.

The Man I know.

Anna Sorry.

The Man I'm a smoker.
I'm not from Yorkshire.
It's not much, but it's a start.

Anna This must be terribly difficult for you.

The Man It's fine.
I have money. A place to stay. My health.
I'm happy.
There are people much worse off than me.
It's kind of you to be concerned but –
I don't think I like fuss.
I think I'm the kind of person who doesn't like a fuss
being made of them.

Anna I know what you mean.
I'm like that myself.

The Man Are you?

Anna I like to be left alone.

The Man Not completely alone.

Anna Can't get into trouble on my own.

The Man Not fussed over.

Anna No.

The Man That's it.
That's what I'm like.

Anna I respect that.

The Man Thank you.

Anna Do you mind if I ask, as much for my own curiosity as anything else: what do you remember? – I mean – do you have any memories?

The Man I remember being found in the snow.
  I remember everything since then.

Anna But before? I mean, how do you know where you are?

The Man Well, I'm here.

Anna No – but where is here?

The Man The terrace.

Anna Yes but –

The Man The Pyrenees.
  France.

Anna And France – what is France?

The Man I'm not clear what you mean?

Anna Does France mean anything to you?

The Man France is a country.

Anna Do you know what a country is?

The Man Yes.

Anna I see.
    . . .
  What's the capital of Uruguay?

The Man Montevideo.
  Look, I can see what you're getting at. Clearly I still have whatever bank of general knowledge I built up in

my previous . . . existence. But when I bring that
knowledge to mind, what's missing is my place in it.
I'm absent. I have no idea how I came to know it. Do
you see?

Anna Your accent has a lilt.
 You became quite animated just then and I noticed a
slight lilt to your accent.

The Man A lilt?
 Maybe it does.
 Can you place it?

Anna No . . . Wales? . . . '*know* it', 'no idea how I came
to *know* it'.
 Wales?
 '*Know* it'.
 The experts will get it.
 We should tape you when you're animated.
 Hold on.

 She picks up the tape recorder again.
 Prepares to press record.

You're looking at me again.

The Man I know.
 It's an undertow of warmth.
 I'm getting it again.

Anna Warmth.
 That's interesting.
 Particularly when I just mentioned Wales.

The Man Miss Edwards. Anna.
 This is a little embarrassing.
 . . .
 I seem to want to hold you.

Anna I see.

The Man It's going.
The feeling's fading.

Anna Get it back, try – describe it.

The Man Wanting to hold you.
And a feeling of wanting to tell you about the feeling.

Anna Hold me.

The Man Are you sure?

Anna It's quite all right.

The Man leaves his chair. He goes over to Anna's chair.
Anna stands up.
He holds her. He remains that way for some moments.
He breaks off.

He returns to his chair.
He sits down.

Anna Gosh.

The Man I'm sorry.

Anna sits down again.

Anna No. It's good. It's –

The Man I can't help it. I just had the feeling –

Anna Actually, because I used to be an actress, and also because I've worked so long in a Mediterranean country, I'm actually more comfortable with that sort of spontaneous physical contact than most people. It's really – it's OK.

The Man I feel embarrassed now.

Anna Don't.

The Man I'm sweating.
  God.
  I'm really sorry.
  You're here to do a job, not to have me pawing over you like some Norwegian pig.

Anna It's OK.
  It's OK.
  Norwegian?

The Man What?

Anna You said, 'like some Norwegian pig'.

The Man Yes.

Anna Why Norwegian?

The Man It's just, 'Norwegian pig', a figure of speech.
  Just –
  . . .
  Isn't it?
  'Norwegian pig'. Surely that's a phrase, isn't it?

Anna I've never heard it before.

The Man Disgusting pig. Pig anyway. It doesn't matter.

Anna You held me.
  It wasn't disgusting.

  Something of a pause.

The Man In the snow, the feeling I had when I opened my eyes.
  I had a feeling of extraordinary –
  I can't put a word to it.
  Cleanliness.
  A feeling of whiteness, of cold, but also a feeling of
  The most enormous relief.

As though I'd woken up screaming from a dream I couldn't remember.

Sometimes, when you ask questions, I feel as though I'm going to fall somewhere. In my head.

Anna I understand.

The Man If I've forgotten, maybe I had good reason to forget.

Anna I don't believe, if this is what you're saying, that you're –

I'm no expert, but if it's any comfort, the impression you give me is kindly. You seem kindly.

The Man What does that mean?

Anna A kindly soul. I'm known as being quite a good judge of character. I often wonder if I'm not slightly psychic actually.

I once met Slobodan Milosovic at a reception and I got an intense feeling of evil from him. As physical as if he was radiating heat. From you I get kindliness. Warmth. Strength.

The Man . . .

Anna We'll get to the bottom of it.

Anna holds his hand across the table.

What's your name?

The Man . . .

Anna . . .

Anna withdraws her hand.

The Man Why did you ask me that?
You know I don't know.
Were you trying to trick me?

Anna No.

The Man You don't believe me.

Anna Of course I do, I'm sorry, I –

The Man I don't know what my name is.
I don't know who I am.
How could I know what my name is?

Anna I thought, for a second, that you might answer from instinct.

The Man Don't you think I haven't tried that?

Anna It was silly of me.

The Man It's fine.
I'm sorry.
You didn't mean anything.

Anna No. It was clumsy. I overstepped the mark.

The Man I overreacted.
I think you touched a nerve.

Anna That might be significant, you know.

The Man Maybe.

Anna Sorry.

The Man Look, do you mind if we break for a bit?

Anna No. It's OK. It's a good idea. We'll take a break.

The Man My head's –

He makes a gesture with his hands, suggesting his thoughts are in a jumble.

Anna Of course.

*The Man retreats to the edge of the terrace.
Something of a pause.*

The Man returns.

The Man Do you mind if I borrow a cigarette?
I'll buy some.

Anna Not at all.

The Man Thank you.

She offers a cigarette. He takes it and lights it.

I just need a moment to recover.

Anna Of course.

The Man retreats again.
He smokes.
He looks at the view.
The Proprietor enters.

The Proprietor Good morning, Miss Edwards.

Anna Morning.

The Proprietor Spring-like.

Anna Isn't it just?

The Proprietor And it's quiet. You can enjoy the peace.

Anna Yes.

The Proprietor The season hasn't really begun yet. This
is the first time I've put tables out on the terrace. At the
moment there's just you, the gentleman and the lady in
room one hundred and eight. There are some climbers
about but they camp on the pasture. They don't spend
any money here. They'll be on the mountain soon. You
can watch them. People watch them from the terrace
with binoculars. Every year one or two of them falls.
They want to climb. We want to watch. Some of them
are bound to fall. What can I do?

I prepared a room for you. Room one hundred and nine. Whenever you're ready I'll take your bag up for you.

Anna Thank you. I think I'll be all right.

The Proprietor Whatever you prefer.
How is he?

Anna Oh, you know. It's . . .
It must be terribly difficult for him.

The Proprietor Obviously since he arrived I've been expecting a visit from someone, although you could have called ahead and I'd have prepared things for you. Yesterday, the gendarme, Bernard-Marie, told me to expect someone at some point, he wasn't any clearer than that – but then Bernard-Marie is not noted for his clarity. I hope there isn't a problem. Is the gentleman in trouble? He's been very quiet. He comes down from his room every morning and sits on the terrace. He looks at the mountain. Bernard-Marie comes by in the afternoon to check he's still here. He talks to him. Bernard-Marie is struggling with inner demons, don't tell him I told you that, and I think he likes to talk things through with an Englishman. I don't count. If you ask me the man's a pilgrim. When they found him he was clutching a scallop shell. In all likelihood he's a pilgrim who's had a nervous breakdown, got lost in the snow, and . . . now here he is.
I play chess with him. He's a poor chess player, but no one else here plays at all so . . . He pays for the room by the day. He doesn't complain. I'll be sad to see him go. Do you have an idea who he is? I don't want to know. If he's done something awful, I don't want to know.

Anna What makes you think he's done something awful?

The Proprietor How old do you think he is?

Anna I don't know, late fifties . . .?

The Proprietor Do you know any man, or any person for that matter, but let's be more specific, do you know any man, any man at all who has reached the age of fifty without at any stage in his life having done something awful. Some awful act, or failure to act, which he regrets bitterly. Some act which would come back to him nightly and bring beads of sweat to his forehead. Some act which he would yearn to erase.

Anna Well, I don't know . . .

The Proprietor Take it from me.

Anna But people . . . sometimes people are ashamed of perfectly reasonable things. Maybe he wanted to erase something that happened to him. Something he was a victim of.

The Proprietor Perhaps. I hope you're right.

Anna And people are capable of good.

The Proprietor Sporadically.

Anna So, you know, he's just as likely to have done good things, to be a good person, a person whom someone loves. Someone who someone else needed, needs even.

The Proprietor What are the chances?

Anna Do you speak to him about this?

The Proprietor No. Of course not.
I play chess with him. That's all. Really. He's been the perfect gentleman. Can I bring you a pot of coffee?

Anna Thank you.

The Proprietor Shall I ask him if he wants anything?

Anna Leave him just now.

The Proprietor Do you have inside information?
  You must have an idea.
  The British police must have an idea.
  Has he done something awful?
  No I actually don't want to know.

Anna Really I'm only here to establish if he's our responsibility.
  Once I've done that I'll be out of your hair.

The Proprietor Oh, he's definitely British.
  I'll go further than that. He's English. I'd put my shirt on it.
  I haven't lived in England since I was a tiny boy.
  Who'd want to?
  Really.
  I occasionally go to London on business.
  Dearie me.
  But I can tell an Englishman when I see one.
  We still carry a certain bearing.
  Wouldn't you say?

Anna I don't know. I'm not an expert. I'm just . . . I'm really just a . . . it's quite an unusual job for me, in fact. It's not part of my regular duties.

The Proprietor Suggestion.
  Ask him if he likes to spank or be spanked.
  I've never known an Englishman who doesn't like one or the other.
  For a Spaniard, like me, to have sex is to enter into a zone of ritualised combat between oneself and death.
  The German in me thinks of sex like eating – a gustatory business, all fingers, juices and smells.
  My Italian side requires an audience and applause.
  The Portugese in me simply wants to weep at the sadness of beauty.

Ah well.
Do you like to spank or be spanked?

Anna . . .

The Proprietor You're embarrassed. It's well seen you're English.

Anna Actually I'm not. As it happens I'm Welsh.

The Proprietor Fiery.
  Don't mind me. I flirt with all the clientele.
  It's the Frenchman in me.
  You musn't take me seriously.

Anna Right.

The Proprietor It's been a long winter.
  I've barely talked to anyone since last November.
  . . .
  I'll get your coffee.
  He's looking over here.
  Morning.

The Man Morning.

The Proprietor Well. Good luck.
  I don't want to know.
  I take as I find.

  The Proprietor exits.
    He returns with a tray and a coffee.
    He puts it down in front of her.

Will there be anything else?

Anna No. I'm fine. Thank you. This is fine. Thank you.

  The Proprietor remains for a moment.
    Anna takes out her purse.
    She takes out some money, offers it to him.

Thank you.

The Proprietor It's not necessary to offer me a gratuity.
I am the proprietor, madam.

Anna Oh, I'm so sorry.

The Proprietor If there's nothing else.

Anna No. No. I'm fine. I'm sorry.

The Proprietor It's not necessary to be sorry for offering
me a gratuity, madam.

Anna Right.
Silly.

> *The Proprietor exits.*
> *The Man comes back over to Anna and sits down.*

The Man I've been thinking.
I'm wondering if I might be from Bristol.
Or at least the West Country.
Cheltenham, or Swindon, or Gloucester.

Anna Right.

The Man It's the landscape. It's . . . soft, and I do seem
to have a sense of low hills, woodland and mists . . .
which is –

Anna You don't have a strong accent.

The Man That doesn't necessarily mean anything.
I may have lost the accent.
Or else I may be – you see I have money – maybe I'm
middle-class.
Perhaps I'm a person from the West Country but with
a standard accent.
R.P.
Neutral.

Anna I suppose it's worth following up.

The Man There's something else as well.

As I was standing there, smoking, and by the way I'm convinced now that I am a smoker, I saw a woman walking on the pasture. The woman from room one hundred and eight. She was walking down the path towards the . . . what's that word – stream. And I had a feeling . . .

Anna The undertow.

The Man That's right. And I thought to myself, 'There she is, walking the downs.' The word 'downs' came to me. From nowhere.

But that's a West Country word, isn't it?

Anna You might be right.

The Man It might be nothing.

. . .

I just started to get a picture of myself.
As a boy, amongst a soft landscape.
And growing up, and needing to leave.
A sense of myself as a sailor, of some kind.
Of the pull of the sea.
And a feeling that life held more for me.
Adventure.
Dolphins – a picture of dolphins amongst the foam at the prow of a fast-moving boat.
The company of men.
It's all very vague, but . . .
What do you think.

Anna I'm sorry?

The Man You seem distracted.

Anna Oh. Yes.
I think I just offended the proprietor.

The Man Pedro?

Anna Is that his name?

The Man One of them.

Anna He was hovering.
  I offered him a tip.

The Man Oh no.

Anna I know. I didn't realise.

The Man It's fine.
  Pedro's –
  He'll understand.

Anna Maybe I should go and apologise.

The Man Pedro's fine.

Anna I'm Welsh but I'm so bloody English.
  Ugh.
  I often think. I often think India would never have
been part of the British Empire if, when the first ship
came, the Indians had stood on the shoreline looking as
if they might or might not require a tip. I think the
English would have frozen. I think they would have run
away.

The Man I never tip. On principle. I'm a socialist.
  Born and bred.

Anna Really?

The Man I don't know where that came from.

Anna What?

The Man I wonder if it's true.

Anna About tipping?

The Man About me – being a socialist – what I said.
  I don't know where it came from.
  But the words felt familiar as I said them.

Anna Maybe things are starting to come back to you?

The Man Maybe.

. . .

Why would a socialist be against tipping?

Anna When I was a waitress, I hated non-tippers.

The Man You would.
It seems perverse.

Anna It's downright inconsiderate.

The Man I must have been a git.

Anna Mean.

The Man A Jock.

Anna laughs.

Anna I shouldn't laugh.

The Man laughs.

The Man A mean-spirited, depressed, dour, violent, Jock.
Making everybody miserable.

. . .

No wonder I went mad.

They both laugh.

Anna I was just thinking – about the breakfast – you mentioned you had the full English?

The Man You're worried about my health again.

Anna Well – yes – smoking, cholesterol . . .
No, it's just I wondered – the full English breakfast.
I wondered.
Is that what you've had every morning.

The Man Since I've been here.

Anna I just wonder if that – might mean you're English.
If you see what I mean.

The Man I do.

Anna You're a man who eats a full English breakfast.
That's your preference.

The Man Although I always dither over the continental.

Anna Maybe in your previous – maybe – before – maybe
–

The Man Maybe.
But then – what if I was the sort of man who ate a
continental breakfast out of concern for my health but
deep down had always wanted to eat a full English?
That would explain the dithering.

Anna You're right.
It's probably nothing.

The Man For example.
I've shown a marked preference for coffee.
Even though they offer tea here.
But that's not very English, is it?
To drink coffee?

Anna Well, these days . . . I don't know. I drink coffee
myself and I'm English. Well, as I say, Welsh.

The Man Welsh.

Anna Yes.

The Man If you hadn't said, I'd never have guessed.

Anna People don't.

The Man Where from in Wales?

Anna You wouldn't know it.

The Man I suppose not.

Anna To be honest, I say I'm Welsh, my father came from Wales. I was actually brought up in Essex.
So . . . whatever that means.
And then I went to school in Yorkshire.
Nuns.
And then I went to university in Brighton.
And then I joined the Diplomatic Service, so I've lived in Tel Aviv and in Gaberone and now here I am in France.
But if pressed
I think of myself as Welsh.
Whatever that means.

Something of a pause.

Let's carry on.
I mean, there isn't much more to do.
I think we've established that you're English.
Quite possibly from the West Country.
Probably middle-class, professional.
At some point you may have worked on the sea.
We have some material on tape for the forensic experts to study. I think it's a safe bet that you're the responsibility of the British Embassy.

The Man I can't argue with that.

Anna All I need to do now, really, is to establish some details about your arrival here. And then I have everything I need.

The Man Whatever you need.

Anna Now, the report from the gendarmerie –

The Man Bernard-Marie.

Anna Yes.

I received a copy of his report.

He says that you were found in the snow in one of the high passes near here on the pilgrims' way to Santiago de Compostela. Two climbers on their way down from the pass saw you slumped in the snow, apparently unconscious. They approached you, found you were alive, and carried you down to here.

The Man That's my memory of events as well.

Anna They say you were found wearing a suit, and a coat. The coat was labelled 'Abercrombie and Fitch', the suit was labelled with a Geneva tailor's mark. Does any of that mean anything to you?

The Man Not in the slightest.

Anna Me neither.

The climbers also say that close beside you was a briefcase and that when you were brought back here they opened the briefcase with your permission and they saw it was filled with money, in euros. There was no other documentation in the case.

The Man Yes, that's right.

Anna And finally we know that in your hand, when you were found, you were holding a scallop-shell medallion.

The Man That's correct.

Anna The doctor who examined you found nothing physically wrong with you except things that could be explained by prolonged exposure to the cold and injuries to your feet consistent with having walked a long distance in inappropriate footwear.

You have a scar on the left side of your forehead.

The Man Yes.

Anna But the doctors say that's from a previous injury.

The Man Having rested, I have to say I feel fine.

Anna So that's all we know from the reports.
  What I wondered is if you could add to this stuff . . .

The Man Not really.

Anna What do you remember about the snow?

The Man I really remember the moment.
  Very intense.
  Of waking up – in the snow.
  That moment's where I start from. Now. New.
  A moment in the snow and being born, I suppose.

Anna This was when the climbers found you?

The Man Oh, before they found me.
  When I woke up.
  Amongst the snow.
  Something happened to me.

Anna Like waking up from a terrible dream?

The Man I saw – not saw, felt – experienced . . .
  I . . .
  I . . .
  Can't describe it.

Anna Was it . . . you must have been . . . you just woke
up, amongst snow?

The Man Yes.

Anna With no memory of how you got there?

The Man None.

Anna Cold? Afraid?

The Man The opposite of afraid.
  The opposite of cold.

Anna Warm? Safe?

The Man More. More than that. Something . . .

Anna Like – like what?

The Man Like having been scourged.

Anna Gee-whizz.

The Man Not being scourged – having been scourged.
No memory of the scourging itself – only the raw
afterwards –
   Put your bare skin against snow for long enough.
   That feeling.
   Burning.

Anna And did you know that you'd forgotten who you
were?

The Man No.
   It was the opposite.
   I had an intense understanding of exactly who I was.

Anna What do you mean?

The Man I was everything.
   Everything was me.
   There was no 'me'.

Anna One-ness?

The Man Doesn't capture it.

Anna Connection?

The Man No, more and . . .
   No.

Anna A religious feeling? A sense of the presence of
God?

The Man Maybe –

Anna Look.

I'm wondering. I may be way off beam here . . .
Do you have any history of epilepsy?

The Man How would I know?

Anna Of course. I forgot.
It's just – some of the symptoms.
In the immediate moments before a fit.
I've felt . . .
It's called an aura.
An enormous intensity of sensation.
With me it's smell.
Or, more accurately, a memory of a smell.
And then, coming round afterwards.
It's . . .
A sense one has been made aware of another world.
Is it like that?

The Man Do you mind if we . . .?
Can we . . .?
I feel quite tired.

Anna Of course. I'm sorry. We have plenty of time.

The Man I find it, all this, I suddenly find it terribly
burdensome.
I'm sweating like a pig.

Anna It's warm.
It's definitely warm.

The Man There was a scallop-shell medallion in my
pocket.
Look.

He takes out the scallop shell.

That means I'm a pilgrim.
To be given shelter.

Anna The proprietor told me about it. I know.

The Man So obviously.
    Whoever I am – was. Was.
    Was on a pilgrimage.
    And whoever I was I – found –
    I had an experience.
    And –
    So . . . I don't really see what business the British
Embassy has – deciding who I am.
    I'm sorry, I was overtaken by a feeling.
    I'm sorry.

    Something of a pause.

Interrogating me.

    Something of a pause.

Implying that I'm mentally subnormal.

    Something of a pause.

It's not you.
    You're fine.
    It's the whole . . .

    *He makes a gesture with his hands suggesting that the
    world is jumbled up.*

Clanjamfrie.

Anna I'm sorry?

The Man Clanjamfrie.

Anna I don't understand.

The Man Jumble. Noise. Mess – you know.

Anna Clanjamfrie?

The Man Don't you know the word?

Anna No.

The Man It's like 'palaver'. Or . . . 'shenanigans'.

Anna Is it Welsh? It doesn't sound Welsh.

The Man It's an old word.
  Everybody knows it. It's an old word people use with children.
  Your mother comes into your bedroom and looks around and says –
  'Goodness me, what a clanjamfrie.'

Anna Is it to do with Edward Lear?

The Man Look it up.
  There must be a dictionary.
  I don't know.
  It may well be Old Cornish.
  Given the West Country connection.

Anna It could be a clue.

The Man You keep picking up on words. It's just a word.
  It doesn't mean anything.

Anna You said your mother used it.

The Man Did I?

Anna She would come into your room.

The Man I don't really remember.

Anna It's OK
  I've noted it.
  I'll look it up.
  It's probably nothing.

The Man I'm sorry for being difficult.

Anna It's all right.

The Man I seem to be quite a volatile person, don't I?
  Quite stormy.

Anna It's perfectly understandable in the circumstances.

The Man The world seems so beautiful.

Anna You nearly died.

The Man Quite volatile.

> *There is a catch in The Man's throat.*
>   *He starts to cry in the manner of one for whom*
> *crying is not at all easy.*
>   *He may well not have cried for over thirty years.*
>   *It's a sort of cracking.*

Quite unlike myself.

> *Anna holds his hand again across the table.*
>   *He manages to control the noise of his crying.*
>   *But he still weeps.*

I don't know why I'm crying.

> *He laughs.*

Anna It's good.

The Man It's good.

Anna Let it out.

> *Very abruptly the crying has stopped.*

Let it all out.

The Man Sorry about that.

Anna You just cry all you like.

The Man I'm fine now.
  I don't know what came over me.

Anna Let it go.

Something of a pause.
*Anna seems to expect him to continue crying, but
he doesn't.*
They are still holding hands.

The Man Look.
Is it possible we've met before?

Anna I don't think so.

The Man No.

Anna But I know what you mean.

The Man Do you?

Anna I think so.

The Man A sense.

Anna Yes.
Quite dim but –

The Man I feel more comfortable with you than seems . .
.

Anna Exactly.

The Man You sense that.

Anna More comfortable, very suddenly comfortable.
Which one doesn't normally feel.

The Man No.

Anna Certainly not in these circumstances.

The Man A strong sense that I like you.
I feel that.
Quite strange.

Anna It isn't that strange because I have the same feeling.
The same –

The Man I don't mean anything by it. I don't – but –

Anna You have – I think you have something – some –
I believe people are – that we're – somehow that we have a –
You know – a – something spiritual almost.

The Man I know it's silly.

Anna No, it isn't.

Something of a pause.

It's getting dark.

The Man It gets dark quickly here.
The sun goes behind the mountain.
It gets chilly quite quickly.

Anna I booked a room for the night.
So I'm . . .

The Man Right.

The Proprietor enters.
He is dressed in a formal black waiter's uniform.
He puts candles in bottles on the tables and lights them.

The Proprietor Good evening, sir.
Good evening, madam.

Both Good evening.

The Proprietor A beautiful evening.

Anna Yes.

The Proprietor We're very lucky.

Anna Yes. About before . . .

The Proprietor Madam?

Anna When I – I offered you a tip –

The Proprietor I don't remember, madam.

Anna Before.
  When you came out here.

The Proprietor It must have been one of the other staff.

Anna No, it was you.

The Proprietor I'm the waiter, madam.
  My shift only begins at six.

Anna It was you and – anyway I wanted to apologise . .
.

The Proprietor Do you think we all look the same,
madam?
  Wogs begin at Calais?
  Is that it?
  Is that what you're suggesting?

The Man Pedro.

Anna Of course not.

The Man Pedro's the waiter.

Anna Right.
  Obviously I made a mistake.
  I do apologise.

The Proprietor There's no need to apologise, madam.
  A lot of English people make the same mistake.
  I like to – you would call it – 'wind them up'.
  Like a clockwork toy.
  I was born in Africa. We Africans think it's fun to
tease you bwanas.
  I don't mean anything personal by it.

Anna I see.

The candle is on the table and lit.

The Proprietor Can I bring you something to drink? An aperitif?

Anna and The Man look at each other.

Anna Yes, please.

The Man Wine.

Anna A bottle of the house red.

The Man Thank you.

The Proprietor You're welcome.

The Proprietor leaves.

Anna Oh God.

The Man What?

Anna I've offended him again.

The Man You shouldn't have mentioned the tip.

Anna I wanted to apologise.

The Man It was forgotten.
When you offered to tip him, he saw you were embarrassed. Pedro wants to make everyone feel comfortable. He's a natural host.
And he decided to pretend the incident never happened.
He pretended to be someone else, so you would feel comfortable again.
But you mentioned it.
He couldn't back down – because that would have drawn attention to his motives and made you feel even more uncomfortable. So he turned it into a joke.

That's all.
It's best to leave it.

Anna God.
Why can't he just –

The Proprietor comes back in with the wine.
He uncorks the bottle.
Pours a little into Anna's glass.

Anna tastes it.

That's fine, thank you.

The Proprietor pours the wine into both glasses.
He places the bottle back on the table.

He stands a little back from the table, hovering.

Cheers.

The Man . . .

The Proprietor exits.

Anna What?

The Man He was expecting a tip.

Anna But –

The Man He thought that, given the fuss you've made about it, tipping made you feel comfortable.
He was waiting for a tip.

Anna Oh, for God's sake.

Anna laughs.

The Man Cheers.
. . .
It's nice to hear you laugh.

Anna I'm just – how ridiculous.

The Man You don't feel so bad now, do you?

Anna No.

The Man You don't feel awkward?

Anna He's the one with a stick up his arse. Not me.

The Man You're more relaxed.

Anna Yes.
  Thank God.

The Man He's a tremendously good chess player.

Anna He's a character.

The Man Very interesting man.
  Very interesting life.

Anna Like you.

  Something of a pause.

The Man Do you mind if I say something which might seem
  quite personal.

Anna No.
  Sun's over the yardarm.
  We're off work – aren't we?

The Man I think so.

Anna I think so too.

The Man So I can speak personally?

Anna Depends what it is.

The Man You strike me as quite a delicate person.
  I don't mean you're not strong.
  I just mean you're delicately balanced.

Anna Go on.

The Man And I think that when you say things like –
you have a weight problem. When obviously you don't.
You're quite slim. Or when you – you apologise for
yourself.
  I feel.
  You're uncomfortable with yourself.
  You don't like yourself.
  And that makes you unhappy.

Anna Gosh.
  Whoo.

The Man I'm sorry if I've offended you.

Anna No.
  God, you're right. No.

The Man You're aware of it?

Anna I'm aware of it – when am I not aware of it?
  . . .
  I'm just unnerved.
  A person saying it to me.

The Man Since my experience in the snow.
  I see some things more clearly.
  And I –
  For what it's worth.
  I sensed you wouldn't mind me saying it.

Anna Not at all.

  Something of a pause.

The Man There's something else.

Anna Hmm.

The Man Something I've noticed.

283

Anna Gosh.
Something else.
. . .
Mephisto.

The Man I think the undertow . . .
The sense
Between us.
I might be wrong.
But I think it's sexual.

Something of a pause.
    Anna sips her wine.

The Man I know there's something unlikely about it.
I'm older than you.
And I'm not –
And you're –
But nonetheless, it's what I sense.

Anna I need more wine.

*Some music starts to play from a speaker hung above
the terrace.*
    It isn't played loudly.
    But after its absence it is momentarily intrusive.

The Man Pedro's tape.
He plays tapes in the evenings.

Anna pours more wine into her glass.
    The music playing is 'Africa' by Toto.

I love this song.

Anna So do I.
I haven't heard this song for years.

The Man I wonder if I knew it before.

Anna There's something terribly poignant about this song.
Something so sad.

The Man Perhaps there's a clue in it.

They listen to the song.
  For quite a period of time.
  They search for a clue.
  Anna takes his hand.
  The music continues.

Anna There is something . . .
  Between us.
  Isn't there?

Vivienne enters.
  The music stops.
  Vivienne is dressed for walking in the hills.
  She is wearing heavy boots.
  She stops.

Vivienne Evening.

Both Evening.

Vivienne clomps across to a nearby table.
  She sits.
  She starts taking her boots off.

Vivienne Lovely evening.

Anna Isn't it just?

Vivienne It was hot earlier on.

Anna Yes.
  Where were you walking?

Vivienne Oh, up through the forest.
  I was following the pilgrims' way.

Anna Lovely.

Vivienne (*introducing herself*) Vivienne Sutherland.

Anna Anna Edwards.
  I work for the British Consulate in Marseilles.

The Man has stood up to shake Vivienne's hand.

The Man Nice to meet you, Vivienne.

A slightly awkward moment.

Anna This is Bob – Abercrombie.
A friend of mine.

Vivienne Bob.

They shake hands.
Vivienne sits back down and continues to take her boots off.

It's absolutely beautiful in the pine forest.
It took me the whole morning walking before I reached the snow.
I saw a deer.
Drinking at the burn.
Caught in the sunlight.
Just idyllic.

Anna It sounds lovely.
Would you like to join us?

Vivienne Are you sure?

Anna We were just – we're – we were – We're only having a drink.
Please.

Vivienne I've been walking all day.
I'll just go up to my room.
Wash the dust off.

Anna Lovely.

Vivienne leaves.

I felt I had to invite her.

The Man It's all right.

Anna I didn't mean to spoil our . . . whatever.

The Man Of course.

Anna I was just being polite.

The Man Look.
  I – what I said before.
  It's best if we forget it.

Anna Why?

The Man You're younger than me and –
  I'm sorry.
  I got a bit 'spazzy'.

  Anna laughs.

I should have kept my big mouth shut.

Anna No.

The Man Stupid. Stupid. Oh God.

Anna Please don't be like this.

The Man I feel sick.

Anna Please.

The Man I'm actually going to have to be sick.
  I'm sweating like a pig.

Anna I wish I knew your name.

The Man Why?

Anna I want to say it to you.
  I want to say your name to soothe you.

The Man I'll tell you one thing.
  It isn't fucking Bob.
  Bob fucking Abercrombie.
  Sort of fucking name is that?

The Man leaves.

Excuse me.

The Proprietor enters with another glass.
He puts the glass on the table.

The Proprietor Can you still see in the dark?
Out here in the dark?
Would you like some coloured lights?

He switches on some coloured lights.

Is that better?

Anna That's fine.

He tries a different combination.

The Proprietor That any good?

Anna Fine, thank you.

He tries another.

The Proprietor How about that?

Anna Fine. Fine it's –

The Proprietor Just trying to catch a mood.

He tries another combination.

That do you?

Anna That's fine. Only I get headaches if lights go on
and off –

The Proprietor Everything has to be just so. Fussy.
Pernickety. Is that it?

Anna Sorry.

The Proprietor Typical woman.

Anna I'm sorry.

The Proprietor I was talking about me.

Vivienne enters.

Vivienne Evening, Pedro, what a lovely night. Haven't you done a good job with those lights?

The Proprietor The snow's melting, the forest's full of water, the earth is unbinding itself – who knows what spirits are abroad, Mrs Sutherland?
The lights confuse them, keeps them hiding in the dark.
All part of the package.

Vivienne notices the empty chair.

Vivienne Where's . . . Bob?

Anna He wasn't feeling very well.

Vivienne Oh dear, that's a pity.

Anna Probably something he ate.

Vivienne Poor man.

Anna Mm.

Vivienne indicates the third chair.

Vivienne May I –

Anna Of course.

Vivienne sits.
Silence.

The Proprietor remains, hovering.

Look, do you mind?
He said he was feeling sick.
I think I'll just go up to his room.
Check that he's all right.

Vivienne D'you know, Anna,
  I don't think that's such a good idea.

Anna I'm sorry?

Vivienne I think we should leave him for now.

Anna I'm not clear what you're getting at.

Vivienne Perhaps you should have a look at this.

  Vivienne puts a photograph on the table.
    She opens it.
    Anna looks at it.

Anna Is this . . . This is –

Vivienne Yes. It is.
  I don't know what he's told you about himself, Miss
Edwards, but I know who he is. I know him.
  Oh, by the way, Pedro. The hairdryer socket in my
room isn't working.
  Would you see to it for me, please?

  End of Act One.

Act Two

The next morning.
  Vivienne is sitting on the terrace.
  The Man enters.
  Something of a pause.

The Man Apparently you're my wife.

Vivienne Keith.

The Man Keith.

  . . .
  Keith.

Vivienne Keith Sutherland.

The Man Pedro said you had a photograph.

Vivienne Sit down.

  Something of a pause.
  The Man sits down.
  Vivienne pushes the photograph to him.
  He looks at the photograph.
  After a time:

It was taken at the Fisheries Department ball.
  At the North British. Four Christmases ago.
  With the McColls.
  D'you remember?
  We went with the McColls.

The Man . . .

Vivienne That's Gavin, that's Trish, and that's you.
  We were all a bit tipsy.
  Your cheeks are red.

The Man This is Keith?

Vivienne That's you. That's right.

The Man This man. There's a superficial resemblance
but I don't think –

Vivienne It's you.

The Man I'm sorry, Mrs Sutherland.
I really have no memory of this event.
Of you.
Of any of this.

Vivienne Keith.
I know this can't be easy for you.
I didn't want to have to just come out with it.
That's why I waited.
I booked in to the hotel and I thought, I won't
introduce myself.
I'll just wait till he's ready.

The Man You've been watching me?

Vivienne I was waiting for you to come to yourself in
your own time.
I knew it wouldn't be easy for you.
And I wanted to be there when it happened.
To help you through.

The Man Don't you think that's a bit –

Vivienne But when I saw the woman from the Embassy.
I thought –

The Man I think this is a little bit sinister.

Vivienne I thought I ought to – because she was –

The Man Stalking me.

Vivienne She was clearly forming a bond.

The Man Which is none of your business.

Vivienne I am your wife.

The Man So you say.

Something of a pause.

You and your husband –

Vivienne Keith.

The Man Have you been married long?

Vivienne Twenty-eight years.

The Man Really.

Vivienne Twenty-nine in June.

The Man Right.

A pause.

Any children?

Vivienne No.

The Man Where is it that you said you live?

Vivienne In Edinburgh.

The Man I don't know Edinburgh.
It's supposed to be very nice.

Vivienne It's home.

The Man Your husband, is he a – what is he?

Vivienne A civil servant.
In the Fisheries Department.

The Man Really. How interesting.
. . .
Is he 'Edinburghian'?

Vivienne From Aberdeenshire originally.

The Man Fascinating.

Vivienne Near Aberdeen. A little place called Fyvie.

The Man Och aye the noo.
It's a braw bricht moonlicht nicht the nicht.

Vivienne Don't mock, Keith.

The Man I'm sorry.

   Something of a pause.
     The Man looks at the photograph.
     The Man takes out a cigarette, lights it, smokes.

Vivienne You've started smoking again.

The Man Was Keith a smoker?

Vivienne Keith had given up.

The Man Look, do you mind if I ask you a personal question?
You and Keith.
Were you – happily married?

Vivienne We were married. It wasn't unhappy.
We are –
Happy is probably not the most appropriate word, given the circumstances.

The Man I mean – whoever this Keith is –
He's run away, hasn't he?
He's run off.
Disappeared off the face of the earth.
So, you can see what I'm saying.
He can't have been –

Vivienne I think you were unhappy.
I think you'd probably been unhappy for some time.

I didn't know anything about it – everything seemed
normal right up until the day you disappeared.
But it seems that normal for me was unhappy for you.
You were having an affair with a young woman in
London.
After a time you broke it off.
And you faked your own death.
You made it appear that you had walked into the sea.
. . .
That was quite hard for me.

The Man It must have been.

Vivienne We never talked, Keith.
We sat in that room night after night.
We sat quietly.
And we never talked.

The Man Really.

Vivienne If we'd only – if I'd only read the signs, but –
One falls into a rut, doesn't one?
And . . .
Certain things get left unsaid.

The Man Like what?

Vivienne Things.
Affectionate things.

The Man Affectionate things get left unsaid?

Vivienne I think they do. Sometimes.

The Man You've come here and I . . . Superficially I . . .
Is it it all possible that you're . . .

He makes a gesture of searching.

Do you think it's fair to say that you could be
Clutching at straws?

Vivienne You're still my husband, Keith.

The Man Really?

Vivienne Despite everything.

The Man Well that's . . .
An admirable sentiment.

Something of a pause.

Vivienne We've both changed.
We're not the same people.
I think –
I know we can . . .
I think it's worth trying at least.
I'm not putting any pressure on you to come back.
But for what it's worth.
I've forgiven you.

The Man Oh. Well. Right. Thanks. Thank you.
I'm glad that I'm forgiven.
Thank you for that.
That's certainly a weight off my mind.

Vivienne This isn't easy for me either.

The Man You see what I'm thinking is – this 'Keith'–
Because I don't deny that you think I am Keith.
And so – you know – it's only right that I take that
quite seriously –
But you see – I look at you and –
I think, well, is this a woman I could have . . . is it
possible that I was married to this woman? And then
I think –
I apologise for being so blunt.
I don't find you attractive.
I'm not –
. . .
It's nothing personal.

You're a very good-looking woman.
You're just not my type.

Vivienne Keith, I'm old.
Your type, for the past couple of years,
Has been rather younger than me.
Girls who were playing you along.
Girls who didn't know any better.
Quite frankly, you made yourself look a little bit pathetic.
I'm not being personal, Keith.
Many men make fools of themselves at your age.
You're no different.

The Man Even if I was Keith, and I'm not.
But even if I was.
It sounds from what you say that Keith's having quite a nice time on his own, thank you very much.
Money, girls.
It sounds to me like perhaps
You ought to take a hint.

Vivienne takes another photograph from her pocket.
She puts it on the table.
The Man looks at it.

Who's this?

Vivienne This is just before we were married.
In the country, near your mum and dad's house.

The Man This is Keith again.
Good old Keithy.

Vivienne That's you. That's me. That's your mum and dad.

The Man laughs.

What?

The Man That beard.

Vivienne I liked your beard.

The Man I would never have a beard like that.

Something of a pause.

The landscape in the picture.
    That's where Keith is from?

Vivienne That's where you were brought up.

The Man That's not Scotland.
    Scotland has mountains.

Vivienne Not in the Howe of the Mearns.
    It's a farming area. Rolling hills, no mountains.
    Your dad was a teacher in the high school.
    He died about ten years ago.
    Your mum went just after.
    They were proud of you, Keith.

A pause.

This is us on a walking holiday,
    With the University Labour Club.
    This is somewhere near Glastonbury, I think.
    I must be about twenty.
    That's where we met. One day you just started
walking with me.
    We walked together.

The Man You're very beautiful.

Vivienne Aren't I?

A pause.

The Man I'm terribly sorry, Mrs Sutherland.
    I don't –
    I've listened to what you have to say and –

Thank you for being so –
But –
No.
No, this is not –
I'm afraid I just –
I do hope I haven't been a disappointment.

Vivienne I'm not in a hurry, Keith.
I'm not going anywhere.
Keep the pictures.
I wanted to go for a walk before lunch anyway.
You know where I am.

Vivienne stands up.
She prepares to leave.
Anna enters.

Anna Don't mind me.
If you're –

The Man Anna, good morning. I hope you slept well.

Anna I didn't want to interrupt.

The Man You're not interrupting anything.

Anna Do you mind if I join you?

Vivienne I was just going for a walk.

Anna It's a lovely morning.

Vivienne Isn't it.

Anna Look, if I'm in the way –

Vivienne No.
You must have some – administration to do.
I'll leave you to it.

Vivienne leaves.
Anna hesitates.

Anna sits.
She looks at the photographs.

Anna How do you feel?

The Man Oh, you know.

Anna It's a lot to take in.

The Man I'm not her husband.

   . . .
Look,
Any woman could turn up here –
Could get wind of my situation and just turn up out of
the blue.
And lay claim.
You know.
Just blah blah blah – there you go – that's it.
It's a good deal more complicated than that, don't you
think?

Anna Of course.

The Man She was persuasive, I'll give her that.

Anna Well, the photograph does look like you –

The Man It looks like me. Looks like. Like.
But –
It's hardly evidence.

Anna Well . . .

The Man I was sitting there. Trying to be reasonable.
And she was talking about this man.
And how he ran away.
And what a bastard he was.
And I was feeling, you know, this tug of guilt.
You know.
Gnawing away.
Horrible taste in my mouth.

And oh – just – awful.
And then I thought,
How dare you?
After everything I've been through.
How dare you make me feel –
Exploit my situation for your own neurotic –
To satisfy your own sad fantasies.

Anna She is odd.

The Man Odd? She's – she's . . .
Certainly odd.

Anna And this business of staying here.
Having been here all this time and –

The Man It's pretty suspicious, isn't it?
Quite a lot of time to concoct . . .

Anna Yes.
. . .
Poor you.

The Man No. Honestly, I'm fine.

Anna What did she say your name was?

The Man Keith.

Anna laughs.

Anna Keith.
It is a bit ridiculous.

The Man laughs.
Something of a pause.

The Man About last night. I'm sorry.

Anna It's all right.

The Man No I . . . I was . . . I behaved quite badly.

Anna You were upset.

The Man I know, but –
I had no right to swear at you.

Anna I've heard worse.

The Man It wasn't right.

Anna I was worried about you.
I was about to follow you up to your room, to see if you were all right – and then she –

The Man She what?

Anna She showed me the picture.

The Man She showed you this?
She had no right to –

Anna Yes. Well.
And I . . . saw it and I thought –

The Man And you didn't come up to my room because she showed you the picture?

Anna Well. I suppose so.

Something of a pause.

The Man The bitch.

Anna I only wanted to see if you were all right.

The Man I was in my room.

Anna Because I knew you were upset.

The Man I was in my room and I –
I have to be honest.
I felt terrible about what I'd said to you.

Anna Honestly, I was fine about it.

The Man I hoped – I didn't think you would but I hoped –

I watched BBC World.
Lay on the bed with the remote.
I actually didn't let myself fall asleep until after three because –
I hoped you would come to my room.

Anna I was thinking about it.
I was watching BBC World, thinking – should I . . .?

The Man I kept thinking, 'There'll be a knock.'

Anna I very nearly did.

The Man Of course there wasn't, and I –

Anna That ridiculous programme about Lech Walesa.
So annoying.

The Man Just absurd. Lech Walesa.

Anna And we were both lying there.

The Man And we could have been –

Anna So silly.

The Man I felt terrible about the way I'd spoken to you.

Anna You musn't.

The Man Because that isn't what I'm like.
I'm not – I don't want to be like that.

Anna You're not like that.

The Man But yesterday night. That woman's presence.
It was – baleful.
It upset me.

Anna The way you're coping with what's happened to you.
It's brilliant. It's hardly surprising you get upset.

The Man I was waiting for you.

Anna I wanted to come.

Something of a pause.

The Proprietor enters.

The Proprietor Good morning, Miss Edwards.

Anna Good morning, Pedro.

The Proprietor Good morning, pilgrim.

The Man Good morning.

The Proprietor Can I bring you anything? A coffee?
Aspirin?

The Man A coffee would be nice, thank you.

The Proprietor And for Miss Edwards?

Anna A coffee, thank you.

The Proprietor You look like you need one.

Anna laughs but not with pleasure.

The Welsh – there's no stopping a Welsh darkness, is
there?
  The Celtic twilight – I'm part Galician on my
grandmother's side
  I know about the Celtic twilight. The great black
cloud that comes rolling in off the sea as darkness falls.
'The great fog' my grandmother called it. Sat on her
chair looking out the window knocking back the brandy
and weeping.
  'Do not go gently into that good night.' Isn't that right?
You Welsh – 'Rage rage against the dying of the light.'

Anna Ah, right. Dylan Thomas. Right.

The Proprietor I don't presume to pass comment, Miss
Edwards.
  We all self-medicate, don't we?

Some of us with chess.
Some of us with the minibar.
I'll get your coffee.
Strong.

The Proprietor exits.

Anna That was actually rude. He was rude to me.

The Man Pedro's OK.
He gets lonely up here, out of season.

Anna I'll have to interview the woman.

The Man It's an inconvenience for you. I'm sorry.

Anna Oh God. It's not your fault, it's hers.
I'll interview the woman.
I'll finish up my notes.
I'll take another sample of your speech,
And then I – have to go back to Marseilles.

The Man You have to leave today?

Anna I . . . well, unless – I don't like driving in the dark
so . . . if it all takes time then –

Something of a pause.

What you said last night.
About the undertow.

The Man Yes.

Anna I feel it too.

. . .

So yes, last night I got drunk – of course he has to
make something of it. He deliberately tried to upset me.
But last night after you went,
I felt very very alone.
And yes, I got drunk in my room.
Because I wanted to be with you.

305

The Man Anna.

He touches her hand.

Anna When I'm with you I catch a glimpse of a possibility.
That I might be truly connected with someone.
And it's taken me by surprise.
Because I had stopped allowing myself to feel that possibility.
Just a few too many mistakes and one learns:
Shut that back in its box.
But you –
. . .
And last night I felt that witch was stealing it away from me.
I got drunk.
. . .
I was going to walk out of here this morning and forget the whole thing.
. . .
It's all right if you don't want any more to do with me.
Quite all right.
I understand perfectly.
I'm hardly a catch but –
. . .
I don't think possibilities come very often.
I had to say.

The Proprietor enters with coffees.
He puts them on the table.
He has a small pair of binoculars round his neck.

The Proprietor What a morning I'm having.
Evangeline's wailing like a baby in there.
She's supposed to be waitressing this shift.
But her boyfriend the climber told her this morning that he was going up the hill. To try a new route.

Evangeline's convinced he's going to die.
She dreamt it.
Honestly, I said to her – 'There are plenty more fish in the sea.
Do your work and put it out of your mind.'
But she refuses to come out on to the terrace.
She doesn't want to see him fall.
I said – keep your eyes on the customers.
But she's lying on the chaise longue clapping her hands and moaning like a bereaved seal.
I gave her the morning off.

The Man Poor Evangeline.

The Proprietor I brought you an aspirin and a glass of water anyway.
And some tincture of ginkgo biloba.
Helps you think straight.

Anna Thank you.
I'm actually fine but –

The Proprietor Evangeline says he's 'the one'.
She actually believes there is such a thing.
Poor naive child.

The Man Where is the climber?

The Proprietor looks through his binoculars.

The Proprietor He's on the long traverse before the second chimney.
He's making an attempt on the chimney.
At this time of year the ice is melting and the rocks come pinging down the chimney like bowling balls in an alley.

He gives The Man the binoculars.
The Man scans.

The Man I've got him.
He's on his own.

The Proprietor Solo.

The Man If he falls . . .

The Proprietor We're all on our own when we fall,
pilgrim.

The Proprietor takes the binoculars back.

I need the room cleared by twelve o'clock, Miss
Edwards.
It's going to seem so quiet here when you're gone.
After all the hustle and bustle.

The Proprietor leaves.

The Man You don't know who I am, Anna.

Anna I don't care about that.

The Man I could be anybody.

Anna I'm falling for you.

A pause.
Anna touches his face.
They kiss.
Briefly.
Anna stops kissing.
A pause.
Anna is a little embarrassed.

I'd better go up to my room.
Collect my things together.

She takes the aspirin and drinks the water.

I still have an hour or so before check-out time.
I'll just be in my room.

Anna leaves.
  The Man remains.
  He looks at the photographs.

The Proprietor comes out.
  He looks through the binoculars.

The Proprietor HE'S STILL ALIVE, EVANGELINE.
YOU'RE ALL RIGHT FOR NOW.

He puts the binoculars down on the table.

She wants to go to the toilet.
  Can't move from the chaise longue in case she catches
sight of him through the patio doors.
  Where's Morgana?

The Man She said she was going to pack.

The Proprietor I've heard that one before.

The Man What do you mean?

The Proprietor 'Going to pack'.

The Man That's what she said.

The Proprietor 'Just in case you wondered where I
might be.'

The Man Do you think she wants me to go up to her?

The Proprietor I'm the proprietor of a hotel, pilgrim.
  I understand the psychology of these English women.
  It's the same every time.
  The dusk, the mountains, and always, always a pilgrim.
  It's the scallop shell.
  It's a powerful aphrodisiac.

The Man Maybe she just didn't want to miss check-out
time.

The Proprietor Pilgrims are seekers after truth. Some people like to think they're truths waiting to be found.

The Man Do you think I should go up to her?

The Proprietor If you want to have sex? Yes.

The Man There's no need to be crude.

The Proprietor Crude.
 Unsentimental.
 I'm from New York.
 I don't got time for bullshit.

The Man She's attractive.
 I think there's a connection between us.
 After what happened to me in the snow.
 She's damaged. Fragile.
 I want to –

The Proprietor Yes yes.
 Saddle up yo hoss, cowboy, save da lady.
 Indulge the fantasy.
 Go on.

The Man You don't think I should?

The Proprietor God's given you the soul of a child, pilgrim.
 He's washed you clean.
 If you want to plash about in the muddy fens of sexual desire.
 Be my guest.
 Just don't be surprised if the stains don't wash out.

The Man I don't think love has to be a staining thing.

The Proprietor You love her?

The Man I may do.

The Proprietor Ask yourself what was so intolerable that you decided to walk across the Pyrenees in the snow, pilgrim?
  What skin did you want to shed?
  I like you. I think of myself as your friend.
  If you start looking for yourself in her arms
  You don't know what horrors you might find.
  . . .
  Bernard-Marie's here – you need to sign your daily sheet.

The Man Send him out.

The Proprietor You'll have to go in.
  He won't come out here.
  Evangeline's spooked him.
  He doesn't want to see the climber fall.

  The Man gets up.

The Man Listen, thanks, Pedro.
  You've been very helpful.

The Proprietor Don't mind me, pilgrim.
  I'm quarter Basque on my dad's side.
  We're a shit-stirring people.
  We like to throw spanners in works.

  The Man leaves.
    The Proprietor looks through the binoculars again.
    Vivienne enters.

The Proprietor How's your eyesight?

Vivienne All right.
  I need glasses to read.

The Proprietor There's a climber on the face.
  He's solo.
  Very likely to fall.

If you don't want to see a man fall.
Look away.

Vivienne I hadn't noticed.

The Proprietor puts the binoculars on the table.

The Proprietor Can I bring you anything?

Vivienne A herbal tea.

The Proprietor You look gorgeous today, Mrs
Sutherland.
   The mountain air must suit you.

Vivienne Thank you.

The Proprietor You know, when you arrived,
   You struck me as elegant and dignified. A good-looking
woman.
   But you seemed weary, pale.
   These past few days you've blossomed.
   There's a bloom in your cheeks.
   Mountain air and camomile tea.

Vivienne Pedro, I'm a Scotswoman.
   You won't win my custom with flattery.
   But if you supply me with a working hairdryer socket
and clean bathroom towels I promise you, Pedro, your
name will be spoken of in whispers in all the secret
places where my countrywomen gather.

The Proprietor The handyman's on holiday.
   I'll look at it myself today.

Vivienne You said that yesterday.

The Proprietor Yes, but I mean it today.

The Proprietor leaves.
   *Vivienne looks over her shoulder to see if she can
see the climber.*

She can't.
She turns back.
She puts her hand on the binoculars.
She takes her hand from the binoculars.

The Man enters.

The Man You're back.
Did you enjoy your walk?

Vivienne Very much.

The Man Good.

. . .

That's my coffee.

Vivienne Why don't you sit down?

He sits.

Pedro's bringing me a camomile tea.

The Man Calming.

Vivienne I find it is.

The Man A stressful time.

Vivienne For both of us.

The Man What is it you said you do, Mrs Sutherland?

Vivienne Vivienne.

The Man Vivienne.

Vivienne I'm a speech therapist.
Was.
I gave it up.

The Man Why?

Vivienne To look for you.

The Man I see.
Did you enjoy speech therapy?

Vivienne Very much.
   But I wasn't unhappy to leave.
   It was quite liberating really.
   I sold the house.
   Our house.
   Made rather a lot of money.
   You were always good with property.

The Man Vivienne.
   I seem to have an accent.
   Anna – from the Consulate – she noticed.
   'A lilt,' she said.
   She couldn't place it –
   Do you . . .?

Vivienne A lot of people confuse speech therapy with
elocution . . .

The Man I know.
   I know what speech therapy is.

Vivienne Of course you do.

The Man I was just asking whether you heard anything
in my voice.

Vivienne You have a Scottish accent, Keith.
   It's very light.
   But it's there.

The Man I wondered if it might be West Country.

Vivienne No, it isn't West Country.
   It's posh Edinburgh.
   With a tiny amount of residual Aberdeenshire.
   . . .
   Your father was a schoolteacher.
   He was keen you spoke properly.
   When we lived in Africa, our friends were all English.

We both unconsciously tempered our accent.
But it's there.

The Man Africa?

Vivienne For a few years.
Nigeria.
Lagos.

She brings out a photograph.

That's us.
Outside Lagos Yacht Club.

He looks at the photograph.

The Man Keith's a yachtie?

Vivienne You were.
Never had enough money to buy a boat.
When we moved to Edinburgh.
You tried it a couple of times.
Gave it up.
Took up golf.

The Man Oh God.

Vivienne Once, at a car-boot sale, you bought a pair of cross-country skis for twenty pounds. They sat in the garage for years.

The Man He sounds like a bit of a sap.

Vivienne You wanted to ski.
I could understand that.
I wanted to want to play the piano.
And speak French.

The Man Do you speak French?

Vivienne *Fermez la porte, s'il vous plaît.*

The Man laughs.

The Man Same as me.

Vivienne We bought a cottage in the Highlands.
   At weekends we would go there.
   And for a couple of weeks in the summer.
   You were fond of it.
   I kept it on.
   I couldn't bear to sell it.
   I went back last Christmas, on my own.
   I didn't know how to switch the water on.
   I had to drive to the shop and buy a crate of Evian.
   I sat by the fire and read the *Perthshire Advertiser* and
–
   You see; you had always done the water.
   I did the fire, and you did the water.
   I was a bit lost without someone to do the water.

The Man This Keith, he sounds like –
   He sounds like he should have got out more.

Vivienne It's easy to fall into habits.

The Man Still.
   What a sap.
   What a mediocre . . .

   Something of a pause.

So according to your theory. Keith – somehow – he has
what?
   An affair?

Vivienne With a stripper.

The Man Good God.

Vivienne Yes, I was somewhat taken aback by that
detail.

The Man He breaks off the affair. He fakes his own
death – he ends up wandering in the Pyrenees clutching
a scallop shell?

. . .
From what you say it doesn't sound very 'Keith'. Does
it?

Vivienne No.
But then Keith died, didn't he?
You killed him.

The Man Isn't it possible that Keith really is dead?
That he didn't fake it?
That he walked into the sea and he drowned?
Because he couldn't bear how unbelievably mediocre
he was?
How little he'd done with his life?

Vivienne We were both so innocent, Keith.
The things I've seen since – the things you've seen.
Things we didn't know before.
We've changed.
Really.

The Man How do you know what I've seen?

Vivienne I've been following you.

The Man You followed Keith?

Vivienne It took some time. After that Christmas I
decided to look for you.
I tracked you down to the Western Isles. You were
staying on a croft on Benbecula. I found you.

She takes out a collection of photographs.
She puts the first one down on the table.
He picks it up.

I watched you walking on the beach one morning, in the
wind and the rain. I remember thinking about how
you'd often said we should buy a dog. I remember
thinking – 'Why don't you buy a dog, you stupid man, to
walk along that beach with you?' And I thought, 'Well,

he's working things out. He needs space to work things out.' So I didn't confront you, I just kept an eye on you.

The local barman phoned me every day.

And then one day he called and said you'd disappeared again.

And I thought – oh no, this time he's actually walked into the sea.

But in fact you'd come into some money. The barman didn't know how. But you'd gone up to Stornoway and bought yourself a motorcycle. And you'd taken the ferry to Ullapool. Fifteen thousand you spent on that bike. I very near wept, because you'd had a bike when we were courting and you'd sold it when we got married.

She shows him another photo.

You rode that bike down the motorway, Keith, and I was driving behind you in the Volvo desperately trying to keep up. Weaving and bobbing through the traffic. I was worried you would crash.

I thought, his balance won't be good enough. He'll wobble and fall. But it was as if you'd never been off that bike, Keith.

As you drove into Fife my heart was in my mouth because I thought you were coming home.

But you turned off at Rosyth and caught the ferry to Zeebrugge.

The Man Good old Keith.

Sorry.

What happened next?

Vivienne On the ferry you fell into company with some Norwegian Hell's Angels and spent the next three months on amphetamines riding with them across Europe.

Another photo.

Torsten, Karl, Jonny, Gogoboy and Mickey Finn.

Poor Keith, you never stopped. The Norwegians and the drugs pushed you on.

More photos.

Hamburg and Berlin and Leipzig and Munich and Prague and Vienna.

The Man looks through the photos.

All the time, me following you in the old Volvo.

We took the grand tour. You stayed in the filthy city campsites and drank beer with the Angels. I stayed in B and Bs and visited cathedrals. Torsten was my spy. I begged him to keep an eye on you. I think they adopted you – the 'Old Man', they called you – '*gammle gubben*'.

You were happy.

I saw you one night sleeping with a young Slovenian girl by the fire in a campsite in Bratislava.

I couldn't bear to break your spell.

You broke away from the Hell's Angels not long after.

They stole your bike. I think there was a fight. That's how you got the cut on your forehead. A biker's chain tore your head open and they left you for dead in a hedge. I patched you up with the first-aid kit in the car and I called an ambulance. When they came to pick you up they asked me who I was and

I said I was just passing.

When you came out of hospital, the walking started. You walked through Austria, through Switzerland into France. Now you insisted on staying in the best hotels. It was easy to follow you. I would drive to the next five-star place and wait for you to turn up dusty from the road and take a room. I'd take a room next to yours.

It was late summer. You'd sit on your balcony and I'd sit on mine and together we'd watch the sunsets in the evening. You didn't know I was there, of course, but I think you sensed something – I think you sensed –

One night a hotel barman told you about the pilgrims' way to Santiago de Compostela.
And you became a pilgrim.

The Man You've had an adventure.

Vivienne It had to stop eventually.

The Man Keith, who'd have thought it?

Vivienne I think you sensed something.
I think that's why you became a pilgrim.

The Man Sensed what?

Vivienne I'm ill, Keith.
I'm not well.

Something of a pause.

I've been angry, and sad . . .
Scared, very scared sometimes.
I've spent the night with conference delegates
And
Yet – there has been lightness, Keith. Joy, even. In moments.
Everything I was has fallen away from me.
My house, my work, my friends, my life.
Even the old Volvo died at the foot of the valley.
All that's left of me is here.
And I still . . .
You're the only person I have, Keith.
We shaped ourselves around each other.
If that's what love is.
I love you.
. . .
I don't know any other way to say it.

The Man This Keith.
This man Keith.

You . . .
The way he's behaved.

Vivienne I know, it's silly, isn't it?

The Man You never abandoned him.

Vivienne Perhaps I should have.

The Man Why didn't you?

Vivienne I have nowhere to go back to.

The Man I do sense something from you, Vivienne.

The Man looks at Vivienne.

There's an undertow.
It's – (*The Man tries very hard to identify what he is feeling.*) There isn't a word for it I can think of in English.
It reminds me of the snow.
The snow.

Something of a pause.

The Proprietor enters.
He is carrying a pot of camomile tea.
He puts the tea on the table.
He picks up the binoculars.

The Proprietor STILL ALIVE, EVANGELINE.
WAIT. HOLD ON!
. . .
NO! JUST A WOBBLE. YOU'RE ALL RIGHT. HE'S FINE.
There's your tea.

Vivienne You took your time.

The Proprietor That'll be your hairdryer socket fixed.
And Evangeline's seen to the bathroom for you.

Vivienne Thank you.

The Proprietor No need to thank me.
   If people moan about something,
   I take action.
   Most of my customers are moany old cows.
   So, you know,
   It's better to pander to their whims.
   Keeps them off my back.

   Vivienne puts some money on the table.
      Anna enters.
      She has a very small suitcase.

Thank you, madam.

Vivienne You're welcome, Pedro.

   The Proprietor takes the money.
      He returns inside.

Anna Hello, Mrs Sutherland.

Vivienne Hello, Anna.

The Man Come and join us.

   Something of a pause.
      Anna comes over to the table.
      Pulls up a chair.
      Sits.

Vivienne Tell me, Anna, in your room, does the hairdryer socket work?

Anna Yes.

Vivienne Ah.

Anna Why?

Vivienne Just something I've got going with Pedro.

   Anna touches her hair.

Anna I ought to be leaving soon.

Vivienne Is it a long journey?

Anna A fairly long journey.

The Man To Marseilles.

Anna Back to – all the usual.

Anna laughs.
   Something of a pause.

Vivienne Keith said you'd noticed his accent.

Anna Who?

Vivienne Keith.

The Man I mentioned it.

Anna Did you?

Vivienne He did. It's Scottish.

Anna Don't worry. We'll be sending the tape to experts in London.
   So it should all be cleared up then.

The Man You did say you needed to interview Vivienne.

Anna Yes. I do. Just routine. For the records.

The Man Would you like me to . . .?

Anna Yes, if you don't mind.

The Man I'll just – I'll just go and say hello to Bernard-Marie.
   Do you mind if I take these photographs.

Vivienne Not at all.

The Man He's depressed.
   Don't tell him I told you.
   I'll just –

Some of these pictures will give him a laugh.
This one with the beard.
I'll just see if I can
Cheer him up.

The Man leaves.
Something of a pause.

Anna So.

Anna opens her little suitcase.
Takes out her tape recorder.
She puts it on the table.

Last night, you gave me your file on your husband.
Thank you for that.
I'll send that back to England with the other material.
I'm sure it'll be given due consideration.
All I need now is to take a short statement from you.
. . .
Before I switch this on.
Off the record.
Mrs Sutherland.
What's your game?

Vivienne I'm sorry?

Anna I think you know what I'm talking about.

Vivienne I don't understand.

Anna You're here. You're watching him. He has money.
You don't say anything and then last night – just when
you've gathered enough information you –
Move in.
So what's your game?

Vivienne Is this the interview?

Anna Never mind what it is.
Answer the question.

Vivienne He's my husband.

Anna Really?

Vivienne I have photographs.

Anna We all have photographs, don't we?

Vivienne I don't know what you mean.

Anna Computers.
  We all have photographs of ourselves next to . . .
whoever we want.

Anna takes a photograph out of her filofax.

Here's me with Bill Clinton. So don't give me
photographs.

Anna puts the photograph back.

Vivienne That man is Keith Sutherland.
  I know my husband.

Anna There's no point lying, because this is all going to
be verified by experts.

Vivienne He's Keith.

Anna I don't know what you expected, Mrs Sutherland.
  Some idiot, perhaps.
  But you've got me.
  And I don't believe you.
  And even if I did believe you.
  Even if you were married to him.
  He's changed. He's . . . new.
  What's your game?
  Did you come back to see what you'd done?
  Flying in here like a raven.
  To peck over his bones.
  You vampire.
  I sense people and I sensed you the moment I saw you –
  I smelled blood.

Vivienne I'm not entirely certain that a British diplomat ought to be talking to a British citizen with quite your tone.

Anna Tone? Whose tone? Mine – what about yours?
Winding me up.
Talking about my hair.
Setting the proprietor onto me.
I've watched every step you've taken.
I'm onto you.

Vivienne I don't need to sit and listen to this.

Vivienne is about to rise.

Anna Stay there, you old witch.
I found him first.
And he likes me.
And you can't bear that, can you?
Seeing chances slip away time after time?
Back against the wall to stop you falling down.
Looking out at the dancers like Medusa.
Cold stare.
Turning everything into stone.
Every man you touch goes cold on you.
Well, I'm out on the parquet, witch.
Whirling about,
And you can't bear to see me.
You just can't bear it.

Vivienne stands.

Vivienne I think you should be aware, Miss Edwards, I will be talking to the Consul about this.

Anna Your perfume.
Do you smear it on or what?
Cloying. Roses.
My mother used to wear that perfume.

It's actually overwhelming.
It's – overpowering –

Anna pauses.

Could you put me on the floor, please?
Could you loosen my top?
Would you mind?

Anna's left arm begins to jerk uncontrollably.
Anna's face becomes blank.
She is about to slump.
Vivienne catches her.

Vivienne Are you all right?

. . .

Miss Edwards?

Vivienne puts Anna on the floor.
Anna's arm continues to jerk, rhythmically.
Vivienne pauses.

PEDRO!

Vivienne loosens Anna's top button.
Anna's arm continues to jerk.
Vivienne watches.
The Proprietor and The Man enter.
They see what's happening.
Anna's arm stops jerking.
Stillness.

The Man What's wrong with her?

The Proprietor kneels.
Puts his hand on her lips.

The Proprietor She's breathing.

Vivienne I think she's had a fit.

The Man She said, she told me she was epileptic.

The Proprietor Stand back. Let her breathe.
Get me a cushion.

Vivienne takes off her jacket, folds it up to make a pillow.. She puts it under Anna's head.
Anna opens her eyes.

Anna Thank you.

. . .

The sun's in my eyes.

She shields her eyes.

I'm terribly sorry if I've caused any embarrassment.
I appear to have had a fit.
How long was I out?

Vivienne Only moments.

Anna Could somebody hold me?

Vivienne takes Anna's arm.
Anna gets to her feet. Slowly.

Vivienne Slowly.
Sit her down.

Anna sits.

Anna Please don't be alarmed.
I know what's happened and why.
I'm sorry if my behaviour was erratic immediately
before I fitted.
That happens.
I do apologise if I did anything embarrassing.

Vivienne Don't. Please. Don't worry.

Vivienne sits, opposite Anna, puts her hand on Anna's hand.

Anna It's entirely my own fault.

The hangover.
I pushed myself beyond a limit.
I should have known better.

The Proprietor Can I bring you anything?
Water?
A doctor?

Anna No.
I'll just sit here for a moment.
If that's all right.

The Proprietor Of course.

Anna Could you take my things back to my room?
Would you mind?
I don't think I can travel to Marseilles today.
I'll travel tommorow.

The Proprietor Certainly, Miss Edwards.
And, Miss Edwards.
There will be no charge.

The Proprietor whispers something to Keith.
The Proprietor leaves, taking Anna's suitcase with him.
The tape recorder and the binoculars remain on the table.
Vivienne's hand remains on Anna's hand.

Vivienne How are you feeling?

Anna Tired.

Vivienne Perhaps you should lie down.

Anna In a moment.
It's a beautiful afternoon.
You're very kind, Vivienne.
Can you smell the thaw?
Gorgeous.

The Man What was it like?

Anna The usual.
Terribly dark.
Then clear.
Then nothing – which is the opposite of nothing.
Then gorgeous.
Then sad.

The Man Gorgeous.

Anna Now, it's sad. Only now.

The Man Did you sense –? Did you have a sense of –?

Anna Yes.

The Man Maybe that is what happened to me in the snow.
What happened to you.

Anna A fit.

The Man Maybe.

Vivienne I think Anna has had enough questions.
Don't you, Keith?

The Man Yes. I'm sorry.

Anna What did Pedro say to you?

The Man He said . . .
I'm not sure if you –

Anna Tell me.

The Man He said you were a visitor from the world of spirits.
You could bring us good luck or bad luck.
We had to placate you with gifts.

Anna laughs.

Anna I'm going to go up to my room now.
  To lie down.
  That's where I'll be.
  If anyone wants to find me.

  Anna leaves.
    The Man sits.
    Anna, just as she is about to exit, looks back at The Man.
    The Man is looking at her.
    She exits.

Vivienne Poor girl.

The Man Poor girl.

Vivienne Well,
  My bathroom's clean, or so I'm told.
  I'm going to wash, and rest.
  Perhaps you'd like to join me for dinner.

The Man I need to think.
  Maybe I should go for a walk.
  A walk up through the pines.
  By the burn.

Vivienne Perhaps you'd like to join me for dinner, after your walk.

The Man I should go to her.

Vivienne You must do what you think is best.

The Man A walk up through the pines.
  By the burn.

  A pause.
    Vivienne makes to leave.
    The Man remains still, looking away from her.
    He begins to cry.

*The following words are a response to his tears and
each word provokes tears.*

The Man Burn.
Burn.
Burn.
It's such a gorgeous word, Viv.
Burn.
She's . . . I've . . .
Burn.
. . .
What would Keith do in this situation?

Vivienne Keith walked into the sea.

Vivienne leaves.
The Man presses play on the tape recorder.

*The tape recorder: 'Five languages and it doesn't make
sense in any of them.'*
The smallest of laughs.

He rewinds.
Presses play again.

*The tape recorder: 'Five languages and it doesn't make
sense in any of them.'*
The smallest of laughs.

The Proprietor comes out.

The Proprietor Why didn't you tell me she was a spirit?
For God's sake, pilgrim.
You've visited the realm of angels.
You must have spotted it.

The Man I sensed something.

The Proprietor You don't fuck about with the spirits.
Jesus. Don't you know anything?
We could be in big trouble.

This is an avalanche-prone area, you know.
Good God.
You could have landed us right in it.

The Man I'm sorry.

The Proprietor It's too late for sorry now.

The Proprietor looks through the binoculars.

Damn.
I knew it.
I can't find him.
Damn.

The Man The climber.

The Proprietor He's not there.

The Man Maybe he's reached the summit.

The Proprietor It's nearly dark.
Oh God.
Look.
This is all your fault.
Don't tell Evangeline. It'll kill her.
You don't want that on your conscience as well.

The Man I'm sorry, Pedro.
I'm really sorry.

The Proprietor OK. This is what we do.
We tell Evangeline he reached the summit.
OK.
But before he left he told us he had to go back to
Germany.
Right.
He told us to tell Evangeline he loved her.
But he'd lied.
And he was married.
And he had to go back.

333

And he loved her so much he couldn't bear to tell her.
But he waved, from the summit.
We saw him wave.
That's what we tell Evangeline.

The Man What if he did reach the summit?

The Proprietor Then he can do what the fuck he wants.

The Man Evangeline will know we've lied.

The Proprietor You and your sorry conscience.
Learn – idiot.
Carry the lie.
Put the stone in the old rucksack and add it to the rest.
Good God.
There's no vanity like an Englishman's concern for his conscience.
Let the poor girl pick up her own stones when her time comes.
I live in the mountains, pilgrim.
We've all been in the snow.
You're not so special.
Not round here.

The Proprietor leaves.
The Man picks up the binoculars.
He looks through them.
Anna enters.

Anna You didn't come.

The Man No.

Anna I hoped you –

The Man I know.

Anna I need to know where we stand.

The Man I see.

   . . .

  Sit down, Anna.

Anna doesn't sit down.
  Something of a pause.

I like you, Anna.

Anna Come to Marseilles with me.

The Man Anna, I'm . . .

Anna You're what? What are you?

The Man I'm . . .

Anna Come with me.

The Man I'm too old for you.
  I'm a damp towel over a flame.

Anna I see.

The Man You're so alive.
  We made a connection.
  I even love you. In a way.
  But it's impossible.

Anna Do you know how tiring it is?
  Sensing?
  Moving back and forth between worlds?
  How it wears you down?

The Man No.

Anna Waking up from that, so many times, back to this?

The Man No.

Anna No. Of course you don't.
  You've only done it once.

The Man I'm sorry.

Anna You could have come with me.
  You could.

The Man I'm too afraid.

Anna Yes.

The Man I'm too weak.

Anna Yes.

The Man It's my fault I –

  Something of a pause.

Would you like to join us for dinner?
  It's a lovely evening.

Anna No thank you.
  I'm quite tired.
  I need to sleep.
  After a fit I tend to sleep very deeply, for a long time.
  If you could ask Mrs Sutherland to send a statement
to Marseilles.
  That would be quite helpful to me.

The Man I will.

Anna What happened to the climber?

The Man He made the summit.
  I saw him waving.

Anna I'm glad.

The Man Yes.

Anna Well.
  Goodnight.
  I won't see you in the morning.

Something of a pause.
  Anna leaves.

The Man You've forgotten your tape recorder.

Anna comes back.
  She picks up the tape recorder.
  She takes the tape out.
  She stands on it.
  Stamps it into small pieces.

Won't the experts need that?

Anna You don't need an expert to tell you who you are.
  You know who you are.
  You live with it.

Anna leaves.
  The Man remains.
  The Man rises from the seat.
  He goes to the edge of the terrace.
  He lights a cigarette.

The Proprietor enters.
  As he speaks he puts a tablecloth over the table.
  He puts a candle down.
  He lights it.
  He puts down a bottle of wine and two glasses.

The Proprietor Beautiful evening.

The Man Gorgeous.

The Proprietor Warm still.

The Man Yes.

The Proprietor It's veal tonight.
  Do you like veal?

The Man I don't know.

The Proprietor I love it, myself.
But then I'm Spanish.
I'll eat anything that bleeds.

The Proprietor leaves.
As he leaves he passes Vivienne entering.
Vivienne is wearing an evening dress and climbing boots.

The Proprietor wolf-whistles.

It is now night.
The Man turns round and sees her.

Vivienne I left my heels in the Volvo.
I kept the dress.
Don't know why.

The Man It suits you.

She approaches him and stands beside him.

Vivienne It's warm tonight. The snow's melting.
The pass will be open soon.

The Man I'd like to see the pass. Everything above the forest has been hidden in cloud since I got here. The cloud never seems to rise.

Vivienne It will.

The Proprietor switches on the coloured lights.

The Man I was never at sea, was I?

Vivienne No.

The Man No.

Vivienne You had a cousin.

The Man A cousin?

Vivienne He had a fishing boat.

The Man Oh.

Vivienne Up near Peterhead.

The Man A cousin.

Vivienne But not you. You were never at sea.

The Man Poor Keith.

She holds her hand out.
  He takes her hand.
  They are quite self-conscious about it.

Vivienne Poor Keith.

Music comes on: 'Africa' by Toto.
  A moment between them of embarrassment.

The Man Did Keith like this song?

Vivienne I don't think so. I don't know. He never said.

The Man I like this song.

There is a moment in which they experience many emotions.
  None of which they express.

The moment passes.

It would have been nice if there could have been dolphins.

The End.

THE AMERICAN PILOT

For Linda MacLean

The American Pilot was first performed by the Royal Shakespeare Company at The Other Place, Stratford-upon-Avon, on 27 April 2005. The cast was as follows:

The Pilot David Rogers
The Farmer Tom Hodgkins
The Trader Jonathan Slinger
Sarah Bridgitta Roy
Evie Sinead Keenan
The Captain David Rintoul
The Translator Paul Chahidi
Soldiers Peter Bankolé, Stewart W. Fraser,
    Geoffrey Lumb, Chris McGill

Director Ramin Gray
Designer Lizzie Clachan
Lighting Designer Phil Ash
Sound Tim Oliver
Fights Terry King
Costume Supervisor Christopher Cahill

Characters

The American Pilot

The Farmer

The Trader

Sarah
the Farmer's wife

Evie
the Farmer's daughter

The Captain

The Translator

American Soldiers

Setting

A small farm high up in a rural valley,
in a country that has been mired in civil war
and conflict for many years

Act One

Farmer The American pilot was the most beautiful
human being I had ever seen. His skin was the colour of
sand flecked through with gold. He was tall and he was
strong and his eyes were as blue as the sky he fell from.
Every time I looked at him a cloud of unbidden thoughts
would rise in my mind like insects from disturbed grass.
He might have been in the same room as us but he
wasn't like us. He seemed of a different kind entirely. All
the time he was with us, I kept sensing I was only a
moment away from a moment when I would suddenly
kiss him.

. . .

The American pilot was unsettling.

As far as I was concerned, the sooner he was gone
from my shed, the better.

TWO

A rough agricultural shed, built to house animals.
It is dark.

*The American Pilot is sitting in a corner. He is injured
and in pain. His leg is clearly badly damaged and his
flying suit is torn and bloody. He is listening to music on
some earphones. He sings along. His voice is weak and
tired. The song is 'Gin and Juice' by Snoop Doggy Dogg.*

The door is noisily opened.
Bright morning sunlight pours into the shed.

347

The Farmer and the Trader enter. The Trader is carrying an old rifle.

The Pilot stops singing.

They look at him. The Trader goes over to the Pilot and looks at his uniform. He examines it carefully. He finds a Stars and Stripes badge on the uniform.

He smashes the Pilot in the face with his rifle butt.

He stands back.

Farmer For God's sake.

Trader What?

Farmer Steady on.

Trader What?

Farmer Nothing.

. . .

I just didn't expect you to hit him.

Trader He's American. On his uniform – that's the American flag.

Farmer Fine.

Trader He needs softening up.

Farmer Right. Whatever you say.

Trader I'm a village councillor. When the Captain comes he's going to ask me if the prisoner's ready to talk. What am I supposed to say to that?

Farmer Well, now you'll be able to that you've softened him up.

Trader Anyway, it's as well for him to be afraid. We don't want him trying to escape.

Farmer What do you mean, 'escape'?

Trader He could run away.

Farmer Away where?

Trader Into the mountains.

Farmer His leg's broken.

Trader He's American. You never know what to expect.

Farmer So, why not hit him again?

Trader Once is enough. I've made my point.

Farmer I've known you a long time, my friend. You're a trader. You've seen a bit of the world. I'm just a farmer. I respect your experience.

Trader I know how these things go.

Farmer But I've never seen you hit a man who couldn't hit back.

> *They both look at the Pilot for some moments.*
> *The Trader is a little ashamed.*
> *He goes over to the Pilot and examines his face.*

Trader Where did you find him?

Farmer Out by. About half a mile.

Trader Last night?

Farmer Just at dusk. I was taking the sheep back over the river. I saw a man standing by the frog stone. It was dark but I could see by his shape he was a stranger. So I shouted: 'Ho!'
  'Ho!'
  He just stood, leaning on the stone. He didn't say anything. So I went up to him. I held up my stick in case it was someone I needed to give a thump to.

Anyhow, he didn't move and as I got closer I could see that he was some kind of a soldier.

Trader He's a pilot. That's a pilot's uniform.

Farmer Pilot.
I could see he was hurt. His face was blue. His body was cold. He looked in a bad way. He looked to me like he'd been out on the hill for a couple of days. I don't know what he's eaten. It's been cold this week and his leg's broken. When he tried to walk it dragged behind him. I was surprised he wasn't screaming, to tell you the truth. So I put him on my back and carried him here. Sarah came in last night and had a look at his leg. As soon as the sun was up this morning I sent one of the boys to fetch you.

Trader Who else knows he's here?

Farmer Well, with the kids knowing, I suppose pretty much everybody by now. I didn't really put my mind to keeping it a secret.

Trader Hmm.

Farmer What do you mean – 'Hmm'?

Trader This sort of thing is very complicated. There are all kinds of things . . . all manner of potential complications.
This is a serious situation for us. That's all I'm saying.

Something of a pause.

Farmer I'm beginning to wonder if you should have hit him.

Trader I didn't hit him very hard.

Farmer You hit him quite hard.

Trader It was a forceful push as much as it was anything.

Farmer There's a bruise.

Trader He's been wandering in the hills for God knows how many days. He's covered in bruises.

Farmer He's in pain. He needs a doctor.

Trader I don't think we should move him.

Farmer Why not?

Trader Security.

Farmer Your house is more secure than mine.

Trader You found him.

Farmer What does that mean?

Trader Nothing. I just mean . . . this is as good a place as any.

Farmer The man's wounded. I don't think he ought to be kept in a shed.

Trader We should wait and see what the Captain wants.

Farmer Look. You're on the village council. Something like this is the council's responsibility.

Trader All right. I'm a councillor, and I'm saying he should stay here. At least until the Captain arrives.

Farmer For goodness' sake.

Trader We don't know what the Captain wants.

Farmer What am I supposed to do with him in the meantime?

Trader Just make sure he's all right.

Farmer How? By giving him dunts on the jaw?

Trader I did not give him a dunt on the jaw. I was moving his face so I could see what his badge said.

Farmer Does he need more softening up, for example? Should I give him a kick? I'm sorry to be pedantic, but I don't want to get in trouble with the Captain. I'd like some clear instructions.

Trader Use your common sense, for crying out loud.

Farmer Common sense tells me he needs a doctor.

Trader Just make sure he doesn't die.

Something of a pause.

Farmer I have fed him.

Trader Good.

Farmer And he'll want some breakfast.

Trader Good thinking.

Farmer It hasn't been the best year for me, you know.

Trader No.

Farmer Just so as the council are aware.

Something of a pause.
The Trader goes over to the Pilot again.
The Pilot flinches.

Trader DON'T RUN AWAY. YOU. DON'T RUN AWAY.

. . .

IF YOU RUN AWAY I WILL KILL YOU. UNDERSTAND?

Farmer I think he only speaks English.

The Trader mimes a man running away. The man gets killed.

Trader UNDERSTAND?

They both look at the Pilot.

I don't know, my friend. I don't have much experience
of dealing with a thing like this. I'm not happy about it.
A lot depends on us marking a path through this because
we don't know. It could be very good for us or it could
be very bad. We just don't know.

Farmer No.

*The Trader gives the Farmer a few crumpled and filthy
banknotes.*

Trader This will pay for his keep.

Farmer Thank you, my friend.

Trader God bless you.

Farmer Go well.

Trader Go well.

The Trader leaves.

The Farmer remains. He stands looking at the Pilot.

Pilot I'm thirsty. Mister. Water. Water.

The Farmer doesn't understand.

Farmer It's no use talking to me, Pilot, I have no idea
what you're saying.

He takes out a cigarette. He lights it. He smokes.

You want some? (*He offers it to the Pilot.*)

Pilot I don't smoke.

The Farmer continues to offer.

Shit. Why not?

*The Pilot takes the cigarette, takes a draw and then
coughs.*

The coughing hurts the Pilot's other wounds.

Goddam! (*He hands back the cigarette.*)

The Farmer takes another draw.
He offers it to the Pilot again – as a joke.
The Pilot looks at him – realises it's a joke.
They both laugh.
The laughing hurts the Pilot.

Shit.

They both laugh again.
They stop laughing.

Water.

The Pilot mimes drinking.

Farmer Water.

THREE

Sarah The story of everything, my life from its beginning
to its end, the lives of my three sons, the life of my
daughter, the life of my brother and the lives of my sisters,
the lives, thank God, of my father and mother and husband
– all of our stories from their beginning to their end, are
contained in God's mind. It is a mind that I have no
possibility of ever understanding. I can only know that
God's is a mind of infinite mercy and compassion and
I can be sure that my story and the story of every man
and woman in this village occupies no more space in
God's mind than a single blade of grass occupies in the
mind of a woman contemplating an endless meadow in
high summer. So all I can say about the American pilot
is that our encounter was simply a moment in the
unfolding – a light breeze that shakes the grass a little in

one part of the meadow – the passing of a thought. His arrival neither worried me nor did it make me happy. I simply took it that it was my duty to do what hospitality required of me, that's all. I cleaned his wounds and I bandaged his leg. I fed him. I brought him water.

FOUR

The Pilot is drinking some water. Sarah and the Farmer stand watching him.

Farmer He's thirsty.

Sarah He would be.

Farmer Trader gave me some money for his keep.

He gives Sarah the money.

Sarah What do you want me to do with it?

Farmer See what you can get for it. Maybe get some meat. See if you can find any painkillers.

Sarah Where will I find painkillers?

Farmer Maybe someone's got some.

The Pilot looks at Sarah. He smiles.

Pilot It's good. Good food. Thank you, ma'am.

Something of a pause.

Wait –

The Pilot reaches into a pocket of his flying suit and takes out a small wallet. In the wallet is a photograph. He holds the photograph out to Sarah.

Pilot Here. My wife. Francesca. My kid. Carl. Carl. This is the Georgia State Show. See? That's Carl with Daffy

Duck. Daffy Duck?

She doesn't take the picture. He puts it on the ground in front of her.

I guess you guys don't get Daffy Duck.

Sarah picks it up.
She shows it to the Farmer.

Farmer Looks like Daffy Duck.

She looks at it.

Sarah They're so young.

She gives the picture back to the Pilot.

Sarah I don't like him being here.

Farmer I know, love.

Sarah I'll see if I can get a chicken from someone.

Farmer That's a good idea.

Sarah I don't think it's worth buying meat.
We don't know how long he's staying.

FIVE

Evie I had a dream once where the sky was torn open and there was a different world behind it. I had a dream once where I was walking behind our donkey through the village just following where he led, and the village didn't ever seem to stop, it just went on and on for house after house after house for ever until I woke up, so I'm quite used to thinking strange things, stranger things than most people think. That's why it was no surprise to me to find out that I had been marked out by God for an astonishing purpose. I've known ever since I was little that I was special and I always knew that some day my specialness would be revealed, probably in the nature of me being a saint, a martyr, a film star, an acrobat or possibly a teacher. I didn't expect what happened, though – that took me by surprise, I have to admit. Because of my specialness I have always taken a note of things I find myself thinking – what I find myself liking and what I find myself not liking – because it might be important. One day I might be called upon to teach these things, or sing about them or outline them for the less well informed. So during the days that the American pilot was with us I decided the following: that I don't think people ought to be beaten; I don't like seeing blood; I don't like seeing blood coming from a goat. I don't like the smell of blood. I don't like the smell of my own blood, or goat's blood or anybody else's blood. I don't like just being lifted up to Heaven without so much as a 'please' or 'thank you' and I don't like wetting myself. I don't like those things. Not at all.

. . .

But I liked the American pilot.
I liked him fine.

SIX

The Pilot is asleep.

Farmer He's asleep.

Evie Poor man.

Farmer This man is American.

Evie He glows. He seems to glow.

Farmer Now, Evie, America is a country far away.

Evie I know that, Dad. Goodness me.

Farmer I suppose you do.

Evie I know acres of stuff about America.

Farmer Do you?

Evie From the television.

Farmer Where do you watch television?

Evie There's a television at Ruthie's house.

Farmer I didn't know that.

Evie They haven't had it for long.

Farmer What do you watch?

Evie Goodness me, Dad. You see television in the shop.

Farmer I see television. I see television in the shop. I'm just not sure I like what I see.

Evie Cars. Music. Indian girls dancing. That sort of thing.

Farmer How did Ruthie's dad get a television?

Evie I don't know.

Farmer Well, look, despite what you might have seen on television, America is an extremely powerful country with a very mighty army. They also have a president. The people there have fabulous riches, but you know they're also devils who have no respect for women and – look, they go around the world encouraging all kinds of debasements and wickednesses and – anyway – this is one of them.

Evie He glows.

Farmer He doesn't glow.

Evie Yes, he does.

Farmer It's just the way the sun happens to be shining on him.

Evie God arranged the sun that way.

Farmer All right.

Evie So he glows.

Farmer He's just –
Anyway I thought it would be educational for you to see him.

Evie Can I speak to him?

Farmer I don't think that's a good idea.

Evie I can speak English.

Farmer Can you?

Evie My name is Evie. What is your name? I can speak English.

Farmer What does that mean?

Evie It means 'My name is Evie. What's yours? I speak English.'

Farmer I'm not sure what I think about you watching television at Ruthie's house.

Evie How else am I going to understand the world?

Farmer Don't mind me. I'm just a jealous old man.
When I was your age –
You don't want to know, do you?

Evie I do.

Farmer When I was your age, I had an idea that I would be an engineer. It was a pretty stupid notion but I thought I would quite like to build a dam. Anyway. One day I was told I was to marry your mother and that would put paid to being an engineer. So I said no.

Evie I know this story.

Farmer Oh well.

Evie You thought one day you'd take a look and see what you were missing so you spent all night walking down the valley and through the forest until you got to the town where you found her house and you climbed the wall and spied on her in the courtyard and you thought she was more beautiful than any dam.

Farmer Well, the point is that I couldn't be a student and support a family. To support a family I needed some land. So I gave up the idea of being an engineer and I set about – and – so, well, I didn't become an engineer in the end. That wasn't God's idea for me. But you – well – things – things could be different for you.

. . .

Just be careful around the television.

Evie I never watch it alone.

Farmer You're a good girl, Evie. I hope we sort you out with a good man.

We've been looking, you know.

Evie You haven't found one, though.

Farmer They're all terrible. I haven't seen one I like. I'm going to hate it when you go. Sons are sons. They're fine but – I shouldn't say this – you can't talk to them.

Daughters are –

Well, I'm going to hate it when you go.

Evie He's waking up.

The Pilot stirs in his sleep.
He opens his eyes and groans.

Pilot Owwww.
  Fuck me . . .
  Jesus.

Evie My name is Evie. What is your name? I speak
English.

Pilot You speak English? My name is Jason Reinhardt.
I am an officer of the United States Air Force. Do you
understand. OK?

Evie OK.

Pilot If you arrange for me to be safely transported to
the nearest telephone or radio I will personally ensure
that you and your family are well rewarded by the
United States government. OK?

Evie OK.

Farmer What did he say?

Evie I don't know. (*She speaks to the Pilot again.*) My
name is Evie. What is your name? I speak English.

Pilot Miss. My name is Jason Reinhardt. Do you
understand?

Evie This is hopeless. He doesn't understand.

Pilot Jason Reinhardt. Jason.
  Telephone.

  The Pilot mimics the sound of a telephone.

Telephone. OK?

Evie OK.
  He wants to use a telephone.

Farmer I don't think that's a good idea. Tell him it isn't
possible.

Evie There's a telephone at the shop.

Farmer Just tell him it isn't possible.

Evie All right. (*She mimes a telephone. Shakes her head.*) No. OK?

Pilot (*realises this is pointless*) OK. OK.

> *The sound of a jeep pulling up outside.*
> *A horn toots.*

Farmer The Captain? Best behaviour.

Evie What does the Captain want?

Farmer Who knows?

Evie What's he going to do?

Farmer I don't know, Evie. Just tell the pilot everything will be all right. Tell him in English.

> *The Farmer leaves.*
> *Evie goes to the Pilot.*
> *She is solemn.*

Evie OK.

Pilot OK?

Evie (*sings/dances*)
I don't know what it is that makes me feel like this,
I don't know who you are
But you must be some kind of superstar.
'Cos you got all eyes on you no matter where you are.

> *The Pilot laughs.*

Pilot OK. OK.

Evie OK.

SEVEN

Captain This is my district. I am the authority. When I arrive in a village I give out money. When I eat with a farmer I talk to him about his crops. I learn the name of each man's eldest boy. Wherever I go I wear sunglasses – even on overcast days. I do these things because people expect it. If an American turns up in my district, the people expect me to know what to do with him. If I don't know what to do, the people become nervous. Personally, I had nothing against the American pilot. In another world we could have been friends. But he and I were not in another world. We were not, for example, walking together on the streets of Oslo looking for a bar. The American pilot had fallen from the sky into my district. He was my prisoner. I had to decide what to do.

EIGHT

The Captain, the Translator, the Farmer, the Trader and Evie.
   The Captain is carrying a Kalashnikov.
   The Captain languidly points the barrel of his gun at the Pilot.
   They all look at the Pilot.

Captain Has he been searched?

Trader I don't know. Did you search him?

Farmer No. (*to the Trader*) Did you?

Trader Of course I didn't search him. I just assumed –

Farmer You didn't tell me to search him.

Trader For goodness' sake! I shouldn't need to tell you something like that.

Captain (*to the Trader*) You search him.

Trader Yes, sir.

Captain Matthew – help him.

Translator Right. (*to the Trader*) You – you hold his arms. Let's see what he's got on him.

The process hurts the Pilot.
After some moments:

Evie That hurts him.

Captain Is this your daughter?

Farmer This is Evie.

Captain Good afternoon, Evie.

Evie You're hurting him.

Captain This is no place for a girl.

Farmer I know, but she speaks English.

Captain Matthew is my translator.

Farmer Evie, go and bring tea for the Captain.

Evie They're hurting him.

Farmer Do as you're told.

Pause.

Evie.

Evie leaves.

Trader The American has been searched, Captain.

Captain So. Let's see.
Some family photographs.

A dog tag.
A knife.
What's this?

Trader It's a computer, sir. It plays music.

Captain How does it play music?

Trader It's a computer, sir.

The Captain studies the machine, amazed.

Pilot Sir. My Name is Jason Reinhardt. I am an officer of the United States Air Force. There is a reward for my safe return. On the other hand. If you harm me. The United States will hunt you down and kill you. Tell him that. Make sure he understands that.

Captain What did he say?

Translator It's complicated.

Captain What's the gist of it?

Translator He wants to go home. The Americans will hunt you and kill you. Some other things I didn't catch.

Captain What's been going on here? Why is the American here?
Farmer – who have you been talking to?

Farmer I don't know what you mean.

Captain WHO HAVE YOU BEEN TALKING TO?

Farmer Nobody.

Captain Why has the American come here? Are you a spy for the Americans?

Farmer No, sir.

Captain An American pilot lands right in the middle of my territory. Everybody knows the government are taking money from the Americans. Everybody knows the Americans are training the government army. You want me to believe it's a coincidence?

Farmer I don't want you to believe anything. I just found him in a field out by.

Trader The government have no friends in this village, Captain.

Captain I'm not talking to you. You've handled this situation very badly, Councillor. Everybody in the district knows about the American. The government will know about the American by now. By now, even the Americans probably know about the American. I could do without this.

Where did you find him?

Farmer A little way up the river. There's a big stone in the shape of a frog.

He was sheltering from the wind.

Something of a pause.

Captain Why couldn't you just leave him to die?

Trader We knew you'd want to speak to him, Captain.

Farmer He was alive.

Captain Translate for me, Matthew. (*to the Pilot, shouting in his face*) WHAT ARE YOU DOING HERE?

Translator He says, what are you doing here?

Captain WHO'S YOUR CONTACT?

Translator He says, eh . . . eh . . .

Where is the betrayal?

Pilot My name is Jason Reinhardt. I am an officer in –

Captain SHUT UP.

The Captain slaps the Pilot hard.
The Pilot reacts with pain.

Captain Shut your mouth.

Translator He says –

Captain Don't bother translating that, Matthew. I need to think. Where is the wreckage?

Trader What wreckage?

Captain The plane, for goodness' sake. He's a pilot – where's his plane? Where is it?

Trader I don't know.

Farmer He's been in the hills for days. It could be miles away. It must be up higher. If it was anywhere nearby someone would have seen it.

Captain You're right. Whoever has seen the wreckage of a plane will know there's an American. He'll have a transponder somewhere, broadcasting a position. The Americans will look for him. They'll find him eventually. Hell. Hell. Hell. What's on the computer? Let's find out what's on the computer.

The Captain tries to open up the MP3 player.

Pilot Hey, man, be careful. That's my music.

The Captain kicks the Pilot.

Captain Shut up.

The Captain puts the earphones on.
He listens.
He gives an earphone to the Translator.
They both listen.

Translator I think it's just music, sir.

Captain It's not music it's – I don't know what it is.

Translator It's hip-hop, sir.

Captain It could be code, you bespectacled vole. God God God.

You're supposed to be educated, Matthew. Switch it off, it's intolerable. If it's a code we'll never understand it. I don't care.

I'm tired. Go and get some rope from the jeep. Get the prisoner secure.

The Translator exits.

Trader Is there a cassette player in the jeep?

Captain Of course there is.

Trader I've got some stock in the shop. It just came over the border. It might be compatible. We could play it over the jeep's stereo.

Captain You have this sort of equipment?

Trader I have a contact in Dubai.

Pilot It's got my entire fucking record collection on it, man.

Trader Would you like me to to take the computer, sir? I could see if it's compatible with what I have in the shop.

Captain Yes.

Trader What do you want me to tell the village, Captain?

Captain Tell them the American has died of his wounds. Don't let anybody come up here. Send someone up to the stone. And send some men up to the high pass to see if they can see the plane.

Trader Yes, sir.

Captain It's very important that everybody does the right thing. Do you understand?

Trader Yes, sir.

Captain Good man. Now go.

The Trader exits.

He doesn't understand.

Farmer Captain. If you'll forgive me for speaking.

Captain Forgive you? For what?

Farmer I don't understand either.

Captain No.

Farmer This is my house. I would like to understand what's happening in my house. That's all.

Captain America has happened to you.

Farmer I'm afraid I still don't understand.

Captain Look at him, Farmer. He's weak – a half-jar of life. If it was a fire it would barely sustain a flame. But that tiny quantity of life is easily the most powerful force within a hundred miles of here. You may as well have picked up a stone and found yourself with a handful of uranium.

Farmer What are you going to do with him?

Captain Whatever I can.

The door opens.

Translator The farmer's wife has made us some food, sir.

Captain Bring it in.

369

Translator (*to Evie, off*) He says bring in the food.

Evie enters, struggles to hold the door open and balance her tray.

Captain Hold the door for her, Matthew, you barbarian.

Translator Sorry.

The Translator ties the Pilot to an animal tether. He also ties his hands. The Pilot has some scope for movement but not much.

Evie Cake, sir, and tea.

Captain Thank you, Evie. (*He takes a bite*) That's good cake. (*to the Farmer*) Your wife makes good cake.

Farmer Thank God.

Captain Thank God, indeed.
I knew your wife's father. He fought beside me during the revolution.

Farmer Her father was well known.

Captain He was a good man.

Farmer He was a good man, thank God.

Captain So, Farmer. How's the farm?

Farmer Well. It's not easy.

Captain No. It never is.

Farmer The winter's been mild so far, thank God. It was cold, but none of last year's lambs have died. Not yet.

Captain Let's hope for a good summer. Have there been any attacks here?

Farmer Not this year, thank God. Only one last year.

Captain The government soldiers are at the foot of the valley. It isn't easy to keep them out but they haven't entered the valley. Not yet.

Farmer I'm too old to fight. Of course, my youngest son will join you. When he's old enough.

Captain I hope it never happens.

Farmer I'm sure you'll prevail, Captain.

Captain Tell me about your daughter.

Farmer Evie.

Captain She speaks English.

Farmer Apparently so.

Captain Do you send her to school?

Farmer As often as I can. If we have something for the teacher.

Captain Do you have a husband for her?

Farmer We're still looking.

Captain Bring her over here. I want to talk to her.

Farmer Evie. Come here.

Evie comes over.
She sits.

Captain How old are you, Evie?

Evie Sixteen.

Captain Are you obedient?

Evie To whom?

Captain She'll never find a man with a tongue on her like that.

Farmer I think it's a reasonable question.

Captain I had a daughter your age, Evie, she was called Belle. She was an exasperation to her mother. Are you an exasperation to your mother?

Evie No.

Captain Now, why don't I believe you?

Evie I don't know. I don't know what thoughts are in your head.

Farmer Evie.

The Captain laughs.

Captain Your voice is so like my daughter's. It's very strange. Isn't she like Belle, Matthew?

Translator She's very similar.

Captain Matthew was fond of Belle.

Evie I'm sorry about what happened to your family.

Captain Thank you.

Evie You'll see them again when you go to Heaven.

Captain Unfortunately, Evie, I'm not a religious man. I'm afraid I won't get to Heaven.

Evie Not if you keep hitting people, sir.

The Captain laughs.

You shouldn't laugh at Heaven.

Captain Your hand's a fist, Evie. Do you want to hit me? (*The Captain laughs, slightly.*) Is there something in your hand you don't want me to see?

What are you holding, Evie? Show me.

Evie It's for the pilot.

Captain What is it?

Farmer It's a painkiller. I asked for it to be brought to him.

Captain A painkiller? Did he seem to you to be in pain? Let me see.

. . .

Excuse me.

The Captain gets up. He goes over to the Pilot. He plants a well-aimed boot on the American's leg. The Pilot screams in agony.

You're right. He does seems to be in pain. Matthew, give him the painkiller.

The Translator goes over to the Pilot.

Captain I decide. Is that clear?

Farmer Yes, Captain.

Captain I decide.

Translator Open your mouth.
This is aspirin.
Look.
It says so.
Aspirin.
Drink the tea.
It's only tea.
Drink it.
Open your mouth.

The Pilot opens his mouth. The Translator puts the aspirin on his tongue. Then he pours the tea gently into the Pilot's mouth.

Captain Ask him what his mission is. Tell him I'll know if he's lying. Tell him he'd better talk fast or I'll flay him alive.

Translator He wants you to explain your purpose. If you don't speak with vigour he will . . . take? Is it take? Separate! your skin from your muscles – you know – pull the skin away – what's that word, there is a word – flay? Is that a word?

Pilot My name is Jason Reinhardt –

The Captain kicks him again.
The Pilot groans.

Evie Stop it. Stop. Stop it. Stop!

Farmer Shush, Evie, please.

Evie I will not shush.

Captain QUIET.

He points his gun at Evie.

Does nobody understand that I cannot solve this situation unless I know what the landscape is, I must know the landscape.

Something of a pause.
He turns the gun away from Evie and towards the Pilot.
He takes off the safety catch.

Pilot My name is Jason Reinhardt. I am an officer of the United States Air Force. If you harm me you will be hunted down and brought to justice.

Translator This is pointless. He's just saying the same things again and again.

Captain Farmer, take the girl and go. Attend to your farm. GO. GO.

Farmer Come on, Evie.

Evie Get off.

The Farmer takes Evie outside.

Captain Now, Matthew, at last. It's just him and us. Three military men together. Tell him he has nothing to fear.

Translator That's not true, is it?

Captain Tell him anyway.

Translator The Captain tells you not to be afraid.

Pilot OK, look. Tell your Captain my guys will be looking for me. My guys are out there right now. OK? Tell him to get me out of here and down into some place where I can be picked up. Tell him that. Tell him if he doesn't do that he will be regarded as an enemy combatant of the United States of America and he will be treated as such if there is any contact between our forces.

Translator The Captain is already regarded as an enemy combatant of the United States. Have some respect for the Captain. Tell him what business you have here.

Pilot Listen, man. Listen to me just one second. You can do what you want to me. I don't know anything. OK? I don't know anything about this shit hole or whatever the fuck war it is you're fighting here. I just crashed into a fucking mountain. OK. I crashed. This situation is an accident. Do the right thing here, man. You know what you gotta do. We all know what you gotta do – so do it. OK. Quit wasting time and get me to a phone. If I die here. All hell will break loose for you. Tell him. Tell him that.

The effort of this speech has exhausted the Pilot.

Translator He won't talk.

Captain Of course he won't talk.

Translator Maybe we should torture him. Make him talk.

Captain What could he possibly say?

Translator I don't know. What he's doing here. What they're up to.

Captain We wouldn't understand.

Translator We're not fools.

Captain Whatever information he has will make no sense to us. Because it doesn't refer to us. The information he has is about another world.

He wouldn't even understand our questions. We may as well interrogate a word about the meaning of a sentence.

Translator The Americans will be looking for him. They'll find him eventually.

Captain Do you think I don't know that?

Translator I'm just saying.

Captain One day, Matthew, I'm going to be captured by my enemies. A rabble of government conscripts will beat me. I will be trussed up like a chicken, spat at, urinated upon and mutilated. I'll be taken to some field of rubble and weeds. I'll be made to kneel in the dust. I will have the briefest of moments to reconcile myself to God and consider the pointlessness of everything I've fought for. The last sensation I will experience will be the taste of my own broken teeth. That is what will happen to me one day, Matthew.

. . .

An American satellite will witness my death.

The pictures will be filed in a computer along with pictures of empty desert and pictures of the sea.

. . .

Do you understand?

Nothing we can do will make any difference to our fate.

Translator The Americans fund and arm the government. The government are our oppressors. We should take this chance to aim a blow at our enemies. The people will expect that.

Captain What if we hand him back? Perhaps then the Americans will fund and arm us instead.

Translator I don't think so. The Americans support the government for the same reason I hate them. Because they will do anything for money. Even betray their own people. The Americans are afraid of you.

Captain Do you think so?

Translator They're afraid of you because you represent the legitimate aspirations of your people. You can't be bought.

Captain Maybe I can. They've never asked.

Translator You know it's pointless.

Captain All right. We'll keep him as a hostage. Make demands.

Translator They'll never pay.

Captain We'll negotiate a price.

Translator America never negotiates. They don't make bargains.

Captain Everyone in the world makes bargains. It's rational to make bargains.

Translator It's not rational for an elephant to bargain with an ant.

Captain So what do you suggest?

Translator There are people who are offering a million dollars for the head of an American. We'd probably get more for a pilot.

Captain Those people are terrorists.

Translator We're all terrorists now.

Captain I'm a soldier.

Translator You no longer have the power to decide what you are.

Captain We could certainly do with a million dollars.

Translator With the money, we'd be able to arm ourselves better.

Captain It might buy us a year or two, a chance to build up our strength.

Translator We'd have to get a video camera.

Captain When you say the 'head', Matthew. What precisely do you mean –?

Translator I mean we contact these people. Come to an arrangement. A form of words. Then we kill him. Then these people send the video to a satellite station.

Captain I don't want to kill him. He's a prisoner. It's uncivilised. Prisoners should be ransomed.

Translator If you do this my way. Our struggle will be on the front page of every newspaper in the world.

Captain At the moment our cause is misunderstood by a handful of diplomats. Now we have the chance to be misunderstood by the entire population of the world.

Translator What do you think we should do?

Captain I think whatever we do the outcome will be the same.

Translator It's your decision.

Captain I like you, Matthew. Why do you stay with me?

Translator I trust you. I think you're a good leader. I also believe that in the circumstances you're our only hope.

Captain Of what?

Translator Of being able to determine our own destiny.

Captain Do you think that'll ever happen?

Translator Probably not.

Captain But you're still with me?

Translator I'm just trying to do the right thing.

Captain I'm tired, Matthew. I've been fighting in this valley for thirty-five years. Do you know how much I long to be in exile again. Do you know how much I want to go back to Oslo? To get myself a room in the Hilton and drink myself stupid – arrange for some girls . . .

Translator We need you here.

Captain Do you know how much I wish I was in Norway? With a Norwegian wife beside me? With Norwegian babies playing in my Norwegian garden listening to Norwegian jazz? Do you know how much I wish I was Norwegian?

Translator I know.

Captain I wish I'd never come back.

Something of a pause.

I feel weak, Matthew. His presence makes me feel weak.
    Maybe I'm too weak to kill him. If you're so keen on killing him why don't you do it?

Translator I would find it very difficult. I think I would be sick.

Captain You've been on operations with me. You've killed before.

Translator I'm always sick.

Captain You break my heart, Matthew.
    Go – leave me alone. Wait for me in the jeep. I need to decide what to do.

The Translator leaves.

The Captain picks up the Pilot's photograph. He picks up the Pilot's knife. He opens it and exposes the blade.

Lick my boot.

He lifts up his boot to the Pilot's face. The Pilot turns his face away.

Lick it.

Pilot No.

Captain I won't hurt you. I simply want you to lick my boot.

The Pilot's face remains turned away.

Please do it.

. . .

What's the worst that can happen? WHAT'S THE WORST THAT CAN HAPPEN? All I want is that you to taste the dust on my boot. Please do it. Please.

Pilot Fuck you, man.

The Captain lowers his boot.

Captain You would rather die, you child. You
unbearable child. Why did you come here? Why did you
have to come here?

*The Captain sits close by the Pilot. He looks at the
Pilot's photograph of his wife.*

She's very beautiful.
  Tell me something. Tell me something that will make
this better for us. Help me. Tell me the right thing to do.

The Pilot spits in the Captain's face.
  *The Captain cleans the spit from his face with a
handkerchief.*

Captain I'm sorry, son.

The Captain gives him his photograph back.

MATTHEW! MATTHEW!

The Translator runs in.

Matthew, tell him this:
  There is power in the world.
  And there is pain.
  And the one must always be equal to the other.
  If you cause pain.
  You have power.
  If you have power.
  You cause pain.
  In order for conflict to be avoided.
  Power must be equally distributed between people.
  Unfortunately.
  In order to redistribute the power.
  It is necessary to redistribute the pain.

Translator I can't translate that.

Captain Why not?

Translator It's too difficult.

Captain Then tell him the missile which killed my family was made in America.

Translator He wants you to know, an American missile killed his family.

Captain Go down to the town. Get a video camera. Gather twenty of the men. Be back here by tomorrow morning.

Translator Yes, sir.

The Translator leaves.

Captain FARMER. FARMER.

The Farmer enters.

Farmer Yes, sir?

Captain I'm leaving now. My men will guard the house tonight.

Farmer What will happen to the American? Are you taking him away now?

Captain Everything will be fine. The situation is under control.

Farmer Only I was hoping –

Captain He'll be gone tomorrow.

Farmer Oh. Well. That's good. Thank God.

Captain Farmer –
  Your daughter.

Farmer I'm sorry about all that. She's – hot-headed.

Captain I like her.

Farmer You do?

Captain The translator needs a wife. He's an educated man. He needs an educated wife. Most of the women in the district are illiterate. Would you consider Evie for him?

Farmer I'd consider – but –

Captain If I die without a successor. My men will fall apart. The district will fall into chaos. I want the translator to succeed me. He's educated and he's clever but he's also weak. He's unsure of himself. A woman like Evie would give him backbone. I want the translator to be strong. He'll have to be strong to succeed me.
I have no sons left.
I only have him.

Farmer I would like Evie to live a peaceful life.

Captain If you give me Evie, I won't ask you to give me a son. Consider it. Take your time.

Farmer I'll consider it.

Captain In the meantime, take this money.

Farmer What for?

Captain For finding the American.

Farmer I didn't do anything. I just . . . found him.

Captain Put it towards Evie's schooling.
Go well, Farmer.

Farmer Go well, Captain.

The Captain leaves. A jeep driving away.

Pilot Jesus. That guy is some kind of bastard, my friend. I feel sorry for you. Jesus. I feel sorry for you people. You people are so fucked.

The Farmer looks at the Pilot.

Farmer I know how you feel.

Sarah enters.
She is carrying a blanket.
She puts the blanket down.

Sarah It's cold tonight.

Farmer Yes.

Sarah There are soldiers all along the road. I don't like it.

Farmer They'll be gone soon.

Sarah The boys were excited about seeing a jeep. I had to tell them to stop climbing on it. They were sitting in it. Pretending to drive about. Pretending to fire the big gun.

Farmer They're just playing.

Sarah I don't like it.

Farmer The Captain gave me some money. (*He shows her the money.*)

Sarah That's a lot.

Farmer Yes. (*He gives her the money.*) It's late. You go in. I'll come in a while. I should take some feed up to the pasture before it gets dark.

Sarah looks at the Pilot.

Sarah He brings in an income, this one.

Pause.

Almost as good as having a cow.

Sarah leaves.

The Farmer waits a moment.

Farmer Why did you come here?
Why did you have to come here?

The Farmer exits.
The Pilot looks up.

Pilot Where are you?

He prays.

End of Act One.

Act Two

Morning.
  The Pilot is asleep.
  The sound of Evie and the Farmer arguing outside in the courtyard.

Evie No!

Farmer Evie, wait.

Evie No.

Farmer Will you just listen for one second?

Evie No.

Evie enters, carrying a tray of breakfast for the the Pilot. She shuts the door behind her.

She puts the tray down near the Pilot. She watches the Pilot sleeping.

The Farmer enters.

Farmer Will you stop just saying 'No'?

Evie No.

Farmer I'm only asking you to meet him.

Evie Quiet, you'll wake him.

Farmer (*more quietly*) The translator is an educated man. Quite reasonable-seeming, I thought.

Evie You told me I could say yes or no to any marriage suggestions.

386

Farmer I know.

Evie So 'No.'

Farmer But you haven't even met him properly. You're saying 'No' before you've even given him a chance.

Evie His glasses fall down his nose. He slurps his tea like an animal. He thinks he knows it all.

Farmer If I had glasses they might fall down my nose.

Evie I don't care.

Farmer I'm sure I've slurped my tea from time to time. If your mother had taken your attitude, she might never have agreed to marry me.

Evie Well, that would have been good. Because if you'd never married, I never would have been born.

Farmer Evie. He'll be here shortly. I want you to have breakfast with us. I want you to be polite. That's all. I'm not asking you, I'm telling you. Is that clear?

Evie How can you do this to me?

Farmer Do what?

Evie Sell me off.

Farmer Don't exaggerate.

Evie How much? Eh? How much am I worth? How much?

The Pilot groans. He wakes up.
  The Farmer and Evie draw back from their argument, slightly sheepish.

Pilot Oh, man.
Woah.
Hey.

Good morning.

Evie Good morning, Mr Jason.

Pilot Is this for me?
This is for me?

Farmer Tell him to eat.

Evie I am breakfast, Mr Jason. Eat me up.

Pilot What?

Evie Eat me up. I am breakfast. Eat me up.

Pilot OK. OK. I'll eat you up.
I'm a big bad wolf. I'll eat you up.

The Pilot laughs.

Evie He has a nice laugh.

Farmer He's just American. Don't be too impressed.

Outside, the arrival of a jeep.
A very loud tuneful blast of the horn.
The jeep stops.

Farmer The translator is back.

The Farmer exits.

Evie I know who sent you.
Last night I prayed.
You're here to save us.
I'm here to save you.
I know.

Pilot You're a nice kid, Evie. I like you.

Evie I know you understand me.

TWO

Translator Belle evaporated. A drop of water hits a hot pan. You forget a thought. There was a river once and now there is a dry bed. There was a wedding, there was a missile and Belle evaporated. She sang beautifully. Me, I have a bone in my throat. I loved Belle when she sang. I loved Belle. Not a particle of her body was left to me. My heart is made of leather, my stomach is a sea, my mind is a landscape of pain – I long ago became a ghost. When I saw the American pilot I found, to my surprise, that I wanted to hurt him. I felt as though hurting him might bring me some small relief. And when I stabbed him I felt relief – a sudden communion, as though in some way I was with Belle again. Not a particle of her body was left to me, not a particle, Belle evaporated – but when I stabbed the American pilot, I could see her in his eyes.

THREE

The Translator enters with the Farmer.

Pilot Holy shit, the nerd's back.

Translator Good morning, Jason Reinhardt.

Farmer He survived the night.

Translator It would seem so.

Farmer I suppose you'll want to be taking him away.

Translator He can stay here for today.

Farmer Right. I see.

Translator He needs further interrogation.

389

Farmer Right-ho.

Translator You can go now. I'll take over.

Farmer I wondered if you would like to have breakfast with us. With my family.

Translator Thank you, but I should be here, with him.

Farmer Surely you can you spare an hour? I'm sure he won't run away.

Translator I'd prefer to be here.

Farmer We could bring breakfast to you here?

Translator Really, there's no need.

Farmer It's no trouble. I'll just go and tell my wife to bring the food here.

Evie leaves.

Pilot Hey, mister. I got to pee.

The Translator exits.

Pilot Hey! Hey, come back, you fuck.

The Translator re-enters with a rusty old powdered-milk can, probably used to water animals. He puts the can down in front of the Pilot.

Translator Piss in this.

The Pilot struggles to his feet. The Pilot leans against the wall to brace himself. It causes him great pain to stand. The Translator doesn't help him. The Pilot pisses.
   It causes him enormous pain. He tries to hide the pain, but it is impossible. The Translator doesn't react. The Pilot sees his face.

Pilot You motherfucker. You enjoy this, you motherfucker.

The Pilot is finished. Exhausted.

There's blood in it.

The Translator exits with the tin to dispose of it.
The Pilot collapses to the floor.
He is in tears.

A moment of loneliness.

The Farmer returns.

Farmer Breakfast's ready.

He sees the Pilot. He pauses. Sees the situation.
The Translator enters.

He seems . . .

Translator He's all right now.

Sarah and Evie enter, carrying a tray of food and a carpet.
Evie unrolls the carpet.
They put the food in front of the Translator.

Farmer This is my wife, Sarah.

Translator Good morning, Sarah.

Farmer Sarah, this is –

Translator Matthew.

Sarah Good morning, Matthew.

Farmer Of course you know Evie already. Evie?

Evie Morning.

Farmer Sit, Matthew. Eat.

Sarah Evie made this breakfast,

Farmer It's a pleasure to have a guest. We don't have guests very often. Sit.

> *The Translator sits. They all sit.*
> *The Translator eats.*
> *When the Translator drinks tea he slurps like an animal.*
> *His spectacles fall down his nose.*

> *Sarah, Evie and the Farmer watch him eat.*

Translator I don't get meat very often.

Farmer Is it good?

Translator It's good.

Farmer Evie's a good cook.

Evie Mum cooked it.

Farmer She's modest.

Evie No.

Sarah So. Tell me, Matthew. What does your father do?

Translator My father's dead. God rest his soul.

Sarah God rest his soul.

> *A pause.*

What did he do – before he was dead – your father?

Translator He was an architect in the capital. He built houses for wealthy families.

Farmer An architect. Did you hear that, Evie?

Translator He died when I was in America.

Evie You were in America?

Translator I got a scholarship to travel in America when I was eighteen.

My father was involved in politics. During the revolution the regime had him executed.

Sarah How awful.

Farmer Evie's very interested in America. Tell us about America.

Translator I spent three months in New York. Then I took a train to San Diego. I spent three months in San Diego.

In San Diego I walked along the side of wide roads. I saw, in a shop, a wall bigger than your house, stocked only with different types of orange juice. One man took me to his house. He had a television in every room. Every person has a car. In the cars they play music. I didn't know anybody. The man who took me into his house tried to molest me. I was very lonely in San Diego. I spent all my money on drink and cigarettes and pornography.

Sarah God forgive you.

Translator God forgive me.

An American train is more like a palace than a train.

New York is a very dangerous place. Personally I was never robbed, but people told me that I should expect to be robbed. In New York I addressed a political meeting. A lot of people came.

They wanted to send money to help our people, but I didn't know who to send it to. I spent it on pornography. I loved America. America is the most perfect society on earth. You can't deny it. How do you explain it? Almost every day there was a moment when I sat on a bench and wept. Maybe I would have been happier in Moscow. I was a communist then.

Sarah God forgive you.

Translator I'm sorry. I shouldn't talk like this. I've been uncivil. You make a good breakfast, Evie, thank God.

Farmer Thank God.

A pause.

Sarah Tell me, Matthew. Is your mother alive?

Translator My mother lives with my brother in the capital. I have no contact with her. God willing, I'll see her again before she dies. But it's difficult.

Sarah I'm sure she prays for you every day.

Translator The Captain's men will be arriving soon. If it's possible, I want to buy a goat from you to feed them. Can you show me your animals?

Farmer Of course. I'll take you to the pasture.

Translator Thank you for breakfast.
Nice to meet you, Evie.

The Translator and the Farmer leave.
Sarah starts to collect together all the things that need to be taken back to the kitchen.

Sarah Well?

Evie Never.

Sarah I know what you mean. Perhaps he's learned too much. His movements are too gentle. His eyes are too thoughtful. He doesn't look like he can turn his hand to much that's any use.

Evie Never ever.

Sarah He has a big appetite though. That's good. It's hard to love a man with a small appetite.

Evie No.

Sarah The Captain recommends him. A man changes when he gets married. Your father ate like a bird when we first met. He's more solid now.

Evie I don't want him.

Sarah He's sad. You tend to be happy. Both of you need a dose of the other. If he becomes an important man, so much the better for everyone.

Evie Never in a million years.

Sarah He will save me a son, Evie.

> *Sarah leaves.*
> *Evie remains.*
> *A moment.*

Pilot OK?

Evie OK.

Pilot OK.

Evie When I'm with you, everything is clear.

Pilot Evie. Tell your father. America wants to help you. America wants your freedom. Tell your father. If they kill me – bombs come here. If they don't kill me – money comes. You understand? (*He points up.*) My guys are looking for me. My guys will find me. You gotta do the right thing, Evie. You gotta do the right thing.

Evie How can you be here? You're from America.

Pilot OK.

> *He reaches out his hand towards her.*
> *She lets him touch her.*

Evie How can you be here now?

Pilot Hey. Hey. Don't cry. It'll be all right. Just tell your dad – get me a telephone. It's gonna be all right, kid. Get me a telephone.

She moves back, away from him.

Evie I can't. I can't do it. I can't.

Evie leaves.

FOUR

Trader For me the American pilot just meant more work. The Captain was throwing money around the village, which caused arguments which I had to sort out. As usual. There was all sorts of business about finding food and lodging for his men. Who arranged all that? Me. These are my burdens. All the time I walk a thin line. All the time I'm treading on petals. I don't court popularity. I have a stomach ulcer that won't go away, but I hide the pain. I'm always thinking three steps ahead. Where's the margin? Every situation contains a margin, if you know where to look. I can find the penny under the snow. There is a pilot. He is an American. These are the circumstances. Where is the margin? It's my job to find the margin.

FIVE

Early evening.
   The noise of music playing from the jeep.
   The music is from the Pilot's tape. The song is 'Burn, Motherfucker, Burn' by Metallica.

Pilot TURN IT UP.
   BRING A GUY A BEER.

BRING IN THE BITCHES!
LET'S PARTY.

The Pilot laughs.

The Trader enters. The Farmer follows.

Trader Four thousand songs. The adapters cost five dollars apiece from my contact in Dubai. He got them for two dollars from his contact in America. I sold the whole lot, player and adapter, to the Captain's men for a hundred dollars. Ha ha. Four thousand songs. That's America, Farmer. You don't have to keep anything in your head. Not even a song.

The Pilot is silent again.

Farmer I'm not sure you should be in here.

Trader It's fine.

Farmer The Captain said –

Trader Here.

The Trader reveals a bottle of whisky he has been concealing. He passes it to the Farmer.

Take some.

The Farmer takes a swig.

Farmer You've had most of this already.

Trader There's plenty more.

Farmer Do you know what's going to happen to him?

Trader Don't trouble yourself. These things are like the movements of the clouds. They take place high above us. There's sun, there's rain. That's all we need to know. Have you got a knife?

Farmer Why do you want a knife?

Trader Never mind why. Have you got one?

Farmer Yes.

Trader Can I borrow it?

Farmer I suppose.

Trader Keep watch. Tell me if anyone's coming.

Farmer He doesn't need any more softening up, for goodness' sake.

Trader Will you just guard the door?

Farmer What?

Trader Do it.

The Farmer goes out.
    The Trader goes over to the Pilot holding the knife.
He grabs the Pilot's uniform.

Pilot Get off me.

Trader Shut up.

The Trader slaps the Pilot.
    He takes out a folded piece of fax paper.
    Gives it to the Pilot.
    The Pilot opens it and reads it.

Trader America knows you're here. I told my contact in Dubai. They want proof before I get my money. You stay here. They come here. This is your proof. Now I take my proof.

The Trader cuts the Pilot's name badge and number from his uniform. He puts the name badge in his pocket.

Farmer You're all right – they're all drinking round the fire – nobody's coming in.

    . . .

What on earth are you doing?

The Trader gives the knife back to the Farmer.

Trader The village was here before the American pilot and the village will be here long after the American pilot has gone. We have to look after ourselves.

Farmer They're going to kill him, aren't they?

Trader The clouds move above us, we experience the weather.
   Keep the whisky. Don't tell the Captain.

The Trader leaves.
   The Farmer remains, holding the whisky and the knife.
   He takes another swig.
   He goes over to the Pilot.
   He cuts the rope that is binding the Pilot to the post.

Farmer Go. They're going to kill you. They'll probably kill me for this. Go.
   They won't see you. Go. Go on. They're killing a goat out there. You can get a couple of hours ahead of them – maybe a whole night – go – GO –

The Pilot doesn't move.

Farmer For God's sake!

Pilot I have to stay here.

Farmer Go.

He tries to push the Pilot. To help him to his feet.

Pilot No! No! It's OK. I'm OK.

Farmer Not OK. Not OK. They're going to kill you.

Pilot My guys are looking for me. (*He points up to the sky.*) This is where they'll look. They'll find me. Your guys are having a party. They killed a goat. They won't

399

do anything tonight. My guys will be here very soon. Very soon. It's OK.

The Farmer looks out of the door.

Farmer It's too late.
Too late.

He ties the Pilot up again.

Too late.

When he has finished:

Pilot It's OK. Everything's OK.

Farmer OK.

Pilot OK.

The Translator enters.
He is carrying a video camera on a tripod.

Shit.

Translator You can leave now. I'll take over.

The Farmer leaves.
The Translator sets the camera up in front of the Pilot.

Translator You're going to die, but you don't seem afraid.
Are you afraid?
. . .
I'm always afraid. My mind is a desert of fear and grief. All my thoughts, even gentle ones, have to survive in that landscape. Mostly they die.

The Translator finds the knife on the floor.
The Translator looks at the knife.

The men are celebrating. Whisky and a killed goat. I don't

like to be around celebration. I don't like the singing.
I can't stand the smell of roasting meat.

. . .

You try translating these thoughts. I have to translate
your thoughts into my language. I would like you to
translate my thoughts into your language.

Pilot I don't understand. Speak to me in English. I don't
understand you.

*The Translator stabs the knife into the Pilot's broken
leg.*
The Pilot screams.
The Translator withdraws the knife.
The Pilot reels in pain.

The Translator goes outside the door.
He is sick.
*He re-enters, takes his glasses off and wipes them
on his shirt.*

The Captain enters.

Captain Is he all right?

Translator I stabbed him in the leg.

Captain Why did you do that?

Translator I wanted to see if I could bring myself to do
it.

Captain You've been sick.

Translator Yes.

Captain There's still hope for you.

Something of a pause.

It's cold.

Translator Yes.

Captain I think it's going to snow tonight.

Translator The video camera is ready, sir. Have you written something for him to say?

Captain No.

Translator The message is important.

Captain I know.

Translator The whole world's going to hear it.

Captain I know.

Translator We can tell them what we're fighting for.

Captain Remind me what that is, Matthew. It eludes me.

Translator We're fighting for the chance to –

Captain We're fighting for small tactical advantages in a war that we'll never see the end of. It's hardly a compelling message.

Translator We still need something.

Captain We're a poor people, in a poor country, and we can muster only a very small, very poor army. In the scheme of things. We're nothing.

  If we identify ourselves, the Americans will destroy us.

Translator At least can we attach a message about –

Captain What?

Translator Justice.

  The Captain laughs.

Captain Imagine a family with a hundred servants, Matthew. They live in unimaginable luxury. One morning they wake to find the youngest son has been murdered in his bed. They know a servant did it.

They just don't know which one. In their search for a culprit they must examine the motives of every one of the hundred servants. As they sit around their dining table investigating, they must enumerate to themselves a hundred wrongs they've done, a hundred guilts.

Let America enumerate its guilts.

Let it haunt them.

Is the camera ready?

Translator Yes.

Captain Switch it on.

Pilot What are you going to do?

Translator We want you to record a message.

Pilot What sort of message?

Translator OK, I think it's on.

Pilot What sort of message?

Translator Will you shut up?

Captain Are we ready?

Translator Yes.

The Captain raises his gun. Points it at the Pilot.

Pilot Tell me what's going on.

Translator Wait. I'm just thinking. We should check it's working. Hold on.

The translator rewinds the video. He presses 'play'. He looks to see if the thing is recording.

It's just blue screen.

Captain What?

Pilot What's going on?

DAVID GREIG

Translator Something's wrong, it isn't recording.

Pilot Put the gun down, OK?

Captain I can't stand this. Never mind the video.

Pilot OK? OK?

Translator There's no point killing him unless we've got the video.
I think I can fix it. I just need to look at the manual again.
Give me a minute.

Pilot Don't shoot, OK?

Captain Give me another choice, American.
I swear to God you seem to glow.
Give me something.

Pilot Please.

Captain He's pissed himself.

Pilot WHERE ARE YOU?

Translator Will you shut up?

Pilot WHERE ARE YOU?

Captain We could be in Norway.
Drinking aquavit.
Discussing our troubles.
No tears between us.
. . .
You're wet.
Yet still you diminish me.

The Captain raises his gun.

Translator What are you doing?

Captain Aiming.

Translator I honestly won't be a minute.

> *Evie bursts in.*
> *She runs to the Pilot.*
> *She throws herself down on her knees beside the Pilot.*

Evie DON'T KILL HIM. YOU CAN'T KILL HIM.
If you kill him you have to kill me.

Translator Evie.

Captain Take her away, Matthew.

Evie Listen to me.
He was sent to us.
I know this.
He was sent to us for a reason.

Captain Go back to your father, child.

Evie America sent him to save us.

Translator He crashed.

Captain FARMER.

Evie America sent him.

Captain FARMER!
COME HERE!

Evie He's come to save us, Captain.
He's a messenger. Can't you see?
He was sent here to test us.

Captain That's enough now. (*He raises his gun.*)

Evie America is on our side.
He told me this.
America is watching us.
America sees us, Captain, just as surely as if we were on television.

All the attacks.
All the awfulness.
America has seen it.
All the hunger.
All the fighting and stealing.
America has seen it.
He told me this.
We had no hope left.
We were full of dust and sorrow.
We were lost but America sent him to tell us, we don't
have to be alone any more.
We can save ourselves.
We can be found.
We can be American.

The Farmer and Sarah enter.

Farmer Oh, Evie, for God's sake.

Sarah Evie! Get up off the floor.

Captain Leave her.

Evie I know this, Captain. I know because I prayed and
I can pray harder than anyone else because I practise
every day. I went to the pasture just right now and I had
a vision – a vision, Captain.
  I saw a vision of a new road winding up the valley,
Captain, I saw a road and a car driving up the road,
going fast, and I saw a dam and I saw helicopters in the
valley like a flock of geese and I saw people with
beautiful clothes and a bridge – and when the vision was
over I heard him calling.

Captain It sounds nice, Evie.

Evie That's what America wants for us, Captain.
  But we have to believe.
  We have to do the right thing.

Translator Sir. We have work to do.

Farmer Evie, please.

Sarah I'm so sorry about this, Captain.

Farmer Come on, girl.

The Farmer grabs her by the arm.

Evie I saw a dam, Dad, a huge dam curving at the head of the valley. A dam.

Farmer EVIE, SHUT UP.

The Farmer slaps Evie.
The slap is surprisingly hard.
Evie is utterly shocked.

Farmer I'm sorry. I'm sorry, Captain.

Captain How like Belle she is.

Translator Oh no.

Captain How like Belle.

Translator You don't believe her?
For God's sake, Captain.
You don't believe her?

SIX

Sarah She was like her father. She dreamed things. He was never really a farmer, he was too fond of concrete. He dammed the river one summer out by the frog stone and made a pool for the sheep to drink at. Eventually the council complained that the village houses were losing water so he had to take it down, stone by stone. He built outbuildings. He put a new storey onto the house. Every year he would spend a half of the feed money on mortar. He dreamed. He drew up his plans without reference to God. If God has given you a house with no running water, don't make plans for a bathroom. If God has given you a time of war, don't daydream about visiting the city. God gave us an American pilot. God asked that my daughter be taken away from me. God decided that I should be left alone. This was God's plan for me. It is painful and unnecessary to dream of a life in which it could have been otherwise.

SEVEN

Night.
   The Captain is stripped to the waist.
   The Captain is shaving using a milk tin of water and a disposable razor.
   The Translator is polishing the Captain's boots.

During the scene the Captain oils his hair, his moustache. He dresses in a pressed, clean uniform. He doesn't wear sunglasses.

Captain Pass me the glass.

   The Translator passes him a small glass mirror.

Translator You know this is absurd.

Captain I want to look like a respectable officer on camera.

Translator You can't possibly believe her.

Captain I'm not some shabby provincial warlord, some unshaven hoodlum, Matthew, I am a Captain – a parade-ground commander.

Translator No one will believe her.

Captain On the contrary, Matthew – she will be a sensation.

A video message from a girl to the world. A message carried by a rescued pilot. What a story. A girl leading an army. What a story.

Like you said, Matthew. She'll be on the front page of every newspaper in the world. The Americans will be forced to support us. Are you sure the camera works now?

Translator I've tested it.

Captain She's got the fire of something inside her.

Translator She doesn't know anything about the world.

Captain She's innocent. Being in her presence – it's like feeling thirty-five years of dirt being washed off my body.

Translator What you're proposing is suicidal. You'll be killed. She'll be killed. Twenty of our best men will be killed.

Captain You're probably right, Matthew, but I feel twenty-five again. Full of heat and light. Invincible.

Translator No man will join an army led by a girl.

Captain She's a saint. A visionary. And besides, who better than a girl to lead us in this time of corruption? Who else can we believe in? Besides, when the people see me following her, they'll believe – they'll believe and they'll join us and every new recruit to Evie's army will bring two more in the next town.

Translator It's hopeless romanticism.

Captain It's a story. You're clever, Matthew, but you don't understand stories.

Translator I understand that the Americans haven't the slightest concern for us. I understand that government troops will massacre you before you reach the valley bottom.

Captain The government spies will see me walking down the valley openly – an act so patently insane that I would only do it if I knew something they didn't. They'll assume I must have air support. They'll assume I have some magical power. They'll assume all sorts of things. They'll hear a rumour that the girl is a saint. They'll be scared. They'll come to us. I'll negotiate with the government. By the time we reach the capital we'll have three thousand men marching with us.

Translator She's a child.

Captain In the first years of fighting, I dreamed of a ministry, Matthew. That was all. That I would wear a suit and I would be in charge of transport. That I would procure a loan for the building of a road. That I would employ contractors who were not corrupt. That the road would bring a small measure of development to a village in the interior. At the time I mocked myself for the smallness of my ambition. I haven't dreamed of that desk for years. My dreams have been full of a half-mile gained in the valley. A trench defended. Evie is water on a dry field to me, Matthew.

Translator She's not a saint. And she's not Belle.

Captain I'm ready. I'll go and fetch her.

The Captain leaves.

Pilot What's going to happen to me?

Translator You're going to be released.

Pilot OK. You need to get me to a phone. My guys will be looking for me.

You're a military outfit. You must have a SAT phone or something.

The Translator unties the Pilot.

Translator Jason Reinhardt. Do you see me? Look with eyes. I am wearing bad clothes. I am a civilised human being. In nineteen eighty there was poetry in this country, and jasmine trees and I am training to be a teacher. I am teaching Marxism-Leninism to the children. I am in a village telling people build an irrigation system. You kill my president. You don't want any more Marxism-Leninism. I want my country. I want walk in my own shoes. You want sell me cigarettes. You want me to bring you a telephone.

. . .

You bring telephone to me.

The Captain returns with Evie.
Evie is dressed in battle fatigues.

Captain All right, Evie. Stand there.

Evie Where, here?

Captain That's it, don't look at me. Look at the camera. Is it switched on?

Translator It's on.

Evie What do I say?

Captain Just say what you said before. Just how you said it before.
About America.
Only this time, say it to the camera.

EIGHT

Trader You could call it betrayal, but I'm a trader. A trader doesn't really have enemies as such, nor do we have, exactly, friends. It's not in our nature to think that way. We have competitors, of course, and we have clients, but an enemy is someone that you refuse to deal with and a trader wouldn't last long if he refused to deal with people. The margin exists in the deal and the deal exists in the world as it is – not in a dream of the world, not in the world as you would like it to be. The margin exists in this world, not the next. So, it took time, it took me patience. But I have a telephone. I have a fax. I have contacts. I am connected to the internet. So yes – in retrospect you could call it betrayal, but my loyalty is to no country. My loyalty is to the margin. To the margin alone.

NINE

Music coming from the jeep.
'Signifyin' Motherfucker' by Schoolly D.
Laughter and shouts from outside.

Farmer Pilot. I brought you whisky. Drink it.
It'll help kill the pain.

He opens the bottle and gives it to the Pilot.
The Pilot takes a drink.

Pilot Gut rot. Jesus.

Farmer They're eating the goat. They're drunk. They're listening to your music. Apparently my daughter's a saint. I'm supposed to take you over the high pass to the border.
Drink.

He passes the bottle to him again.
The Pilot drinks again.

Pilot Man, that stuff's got a kick.

Farmer You'll need to be drunk. With a broken leg, on a donkey, on the hill tracks. You'll suffer.

Pilot Man.
One minute you guys are gonna kill me.
Now it's a party and bottles of moonshine.

Farmer Put these on.

Pilot What?

Farmer Warm clothes. Put them on.

*The Farmer gives him a warm coat, a blanket, a hat.
The Pilot wraps the blanket around him.
He puts the hat on.
The Farmer helps him. The process is painful.*

Pilot OK.

Farmer OK.

The Farmer takes out a cigarette. He lights it. He takes a drag. He offers a drag to the Pilot. The Pilot takes a drag. Coughs. Laughs. They both laugh.

Pilot OK.

Farmer OK. (*The Farmer smokes.*)

Pilot Now I look like you. What do you think of the hat?

Farmer Good. Very good.

*The Pilot sings along with a small section of the music. He performs the actions.
Both men laugh.
They drink.*

Farmer OK. OK.
See what you make of this.
This one's a lament.

From this valley.
See what you make of it.

The Farmer begins to sing.
    He sings a lament.

The lament is over.
    A pause.
    They drink.

The Trader enters.
    The Pilot continues to get dressed.

Trader I brought a gun for you. The Captain said you were to have a gun for the journey.

Farmer Right. I don't know anything about guns.

Trader It's just for show. Sling it on your back. Be careful with it.
    It's my gun.

Farmer I don't know how to use it.

Trader It's for show. There aren't any bullets.

Farmer What?

Trader The Captain said you should have a gun. Didn't say anything about bullets.

Farmer What's the point of me having it if I don't have bullets?

Trader The American doesn't know it's empty.

Farmer I suppose you fancy giving him another whack? Well, bad luck. The American's our friend now. I'm taking him to the border.

Trader Bandits won't know it's empty either.

Farmer All right.

Trader Don't break it.

Farmer I won't. Don't worry.

Trader This business with Evie –

Farmer Yes.

Trader It could be very useful for us, you know?

Farmer How?

Trader Evie has been blessed with visions. Visions
attract people.
  If she gets on television saying that stuff – we could
have the world on our doorstep. Television brings
people.

Farmer Tourists – here? I don't think so.

Trader Pilgrims.

Farmer Pilgrims? Dear God.

Trader You don't have any experience of these things,
Farmer.
  Perhaps I ought to manage things for you.

Farmer Manage things?

Trader It's right that the whole village should benefit
from a stroke of luck like this.

Farmer Yes, well, thank you, when the first pilgrim turns
up I'll let you know.

  The Trader leaves.

Pilot Shh.
  Shh.
  Listen.

Farmer What?

Pilot Do you hear that? Do you hear? I'd know that sound anywhere.

Trader What's he saying?

Farmer It's no use talking to me, Mr Jason. I don't understand a word you're saying.

Pilot That's it. That's it.

Farmer EVIE! Come here a minute.

Something of a pause.
   Evie enters.

Evie Yes, Dad?

Farmer I think he's trying to tell us something.

TEN

The sound of helicopters.
   In the distance.
   Getting closer.

Farmer Evie, do you hear something?

Evie I hear something.

A sound like a rush of air.

Trader What the hell is that?

Pilot GET DOWN.

A massive explosion nearby.

The Farmer's compound is under sudden and overwhelmingly massive and violent attack. Explosion follows explosion, suddenly, incredibly loudly.
   The pauses between the explosions are dark and quiet.

Evie is screaming hysterically.
   The Pilot protects her. Holds her.

IT'S GOING TO BE ALL RIGHT.
   HOLD ON TO ME. OK? OK?

Now a helicopter is hovering directly overhead.
   A hole is blown in the shed roof.
   The brightness of a searchlight above.
   A winch comes down through the roof of the shed.

Three Soldiers burst in.

Soldier 1 WHERE'S THE AMERICAN?

Pilot I'M THE AMERICAN. JASON REINHARDT US
AIR FORCE.

Soldier 2 CAN YOU WALK?

Pilot MY LEG'S BROKEN.
   YOU GOTTA CARRY ME.

Soldier 2 COME ON.

Soldier 1 Go go go.

*The Pilot is raised up on the winch. Taking Evie with
him.*

Farmer Stop. Please. Stop.

He runs towards the Soldiers.

Soldier 3 Fuck fuck fuck fuck fuck.

*Soldier 3 sprays gunfire at the Farmer and the Trader
and kills them both.*

*The Captain, the Translator and the Captain's men
storm into the shed.*

Captain Evie!

They fire at the Americans. The Americans fire back.

The last American throws down a grenade.

The Captain and the Translator are both killed in the explosion.

The American Soldiers leave.

The Mother calls for Evie.

The Mother sees the bodies.

The bombing continues.

The gunfire continues.

The End.

BEING NORWEGIAN

Being Norwegian was recorded in a live performance at the Traverse Theatre, Edinburgh, on 5 October 2003. It was a Catherine Bailey Ltd/Traverse Theatre co-commission for BBC Radio Scotland, and first broadcast on 30 December 2003. The cast was as follows:

Sean Ewan Stewart
Lisa Vicki Liddelle

Director Philip Howard
Producer Marilyn Imrie

The play was first performed for the stage, in a co-production between A Play, a Pie and a Pint and Paines Plough, at Òran Mór, Glasgow, on Glasgow, on 22 October 2007. The cast was as follows:

Sean Stewart Porter
Lisa Meg Fraser

Director Roxanna Silbert
Designer Rita McGurn
Producer David MacLennan

Characters

Sean
Lisa

Setting
A room

A key turns in a lock.
A door opens.
A light is switched on.

Sean I'm sorry about the mess.

Lisa I don't mind.

Sean I only moved in – not long ago.
I haven't really unpacked yet.
The whole room's in boxes.

Lisa That's OK.
I know what it's like when you're in a new place.

Sean I wasn't really expecting –
I would have tidied up a bit.
I haven't even got any furniture.

Lisa There's a sofa.

Sean That was already here. I didn't choose it.
I just –
Anyway.

Lisa You're so lucky.
This flat's right high up.
You can see the whole city from up here.

Sean You can.
It's one of the advantages.

Lisa I live in a basement.
My window has bars on it.
I answered an advertisement.

My flatmates are all students of beauty therapy.
They lead such a dizzy sort of a life.
They can be quite tiring sometimes.
I'm glad we decided not to go to the club in the end.
Aren't you?

Sean I never wanted to go the club.
I just thought you'd want to go.
With your friends, you know.

Lisa Just think, we could have been shouting at each other.
Flailing our arms about trying to make ourselves understood.
Feeling hopeless and tired.
That's what they're doing right now.
But not us. We're here.
Tucked up on the sofa out of the rain.

Sean Well, as long as you're sure.
We could still catch up with them if you –

Lisa Look at the city.
You can see as far as the hills from here.

Sean It doesn't look so pretty in the daytime.
On a rainy day you wouldn't want to look at it.
But at night. The dark hides the grey.
At night it's quite . . . You can sit and look at it.

Lisa The sea. The dark hills. The city all shimmery lights.
It reminds me of Oslo.

Sean Oslo? Really?

Lisa Oslo in winter.

Sean Oslo. Is that a place you – are you – have you been?

Lisa I'm Norwegian.

Sean Oh. I see.

Lisa Did you not realise?

Sean No.
 I –

Lisa It's all right. Most people don't at first.

Sean What am I doing?
 Standing here like a –
 Can I take your coat?

Lisa Thank you.

Sean Would you like something to drink, Lisa?
 Can I get you something?
 What would you like?

Lisa I don't mind.
 Whatever you're having.
 Have you got any wine?

Sean Sit down.
 Make yourself comfortable.
 Just ignore me.
 I'm not –
 I'm –
 Whisky I've got.
 A couple of cans of beer?
 I think I've got gin somewhere.

Lisa Whatever you're having.

Sean Wine.
 Right – it's ridiculous because – if I'd thought –
 I could easily have bought a bottle of wine at the pub
but –
 I wasn't thinking.

I just didn't use my brain.
Idiot.

Lisa I don't mind. Beer is fine.

Sean Wait – I have got wine.
I think.
In one of these boxes.

Lisa It's OK.

Sean No – I'll find it.
It'll be in a box somewhere.
A bottle of red.

Sean looks inside boxes.

Is that where you're from then, Lisa?
Oslo?

Lisa No.
I've been to Oslo.
I love Oslo, of course, being Norwegian.
But in fact I come from Trondheim.
In the north.
You've maybe heard of it.
It's in a place called the Land of the Midnight Sun.

Sean Oh, right.
I've heard about that.
It's sounds –
It must be –
I'd like to go there one day.

Lisa That's where I come from.

Sean Lisa.
Is that a Norwegian name?

Lisa It's quite a common name in Norway.
In fact it's short for Liselotte.

Sean Right. Liselotte.
Your English is –
You speak it really well.

Lisa Thank you.
Actually I've lived here so long.
That's how I've got the accent.

Sean Right.

Lisa Most people don't realise I'm Norwegian at first.
They don't even notice.
But I can tell they're thinking – there's something
different about her. And they can't put their finger on it.
Usually I tell them.
Put them out of their misery.

Sean If you hadn't said I wouldn't have –
Because you don't expect – I didn't think.

Lisa But you noticed I was different, didn't you?

Sean I suppose I did.

Lisa Your sofa faces your window.
You can sit, and look out of the window at the city.
Did you know
That's a very Norwegian furniture arrangement?

Sean Is it?
I didn't really think – I just –
I didn't know that.

Lisa Most people here make their sofa face the television.
But not you.
You don't even have a television.

Sean I have one somewhere.
It's in one of the boxes.
A portable one.

Lisa I've noticed that people here watch television all the time.

In pubs they have the television on even when you can't hear the sound. When I visit people they have the television switched on.

Even the streets have televisions in shops and there are great big televisions attached to buildings.

And people talk about television programmes to each other.

I don't even understand what they're saying most of the time.

People talk about television programmes right up against your face –

I feel like they're punching me or something.

I feel winded.

Sean I nearly unpacked it.

I opened the box.

But then I looked around and I thought.

If I start with that I won't stop.

So I mostly don't.

Mostly it lives in it's box.

Lisa In Norway people very rarely watch television.

Only important events.

When Norway are in the World Cup, for example.

Or if King Haakon is making a speech.

Then they'll gather together and watch.

But mostly Norwegians talk gently to each other in the evenings.

Sean Here we go.

Wine.

I knew I had this somewhere.

It's red, is that all right?

Lisa That's fine, thank you.

Sean It should be good, this wine.
  It's ten years old.
  I don't have glasses.
  Is a mug OK?

Lisa I think it's fine to drink wine out of a mug.
  It's more real.
  It's just a container.
  Just a flipping container so the drink doesn't spill all over your hand.

Sean I know – who needs crystal?
  Not me anyway.

  Sean pours the wine into two mugs.

Here.

Lisa Thankyou.

Sean Is it OK?

Lisa It's fine.

Sean It's supposed to be very good, this wine.
  I've been waiting for the right occasion.
  I remember when I bought it the man in the shop –
  He said – in ten years time this'll be a peach.
  So, you know, it should be good.

Lisa I like it.

Sean I don't know anything about wine.
  I wish I did.
  It's supposed to be a real – you know – special.
  But to me it just tastes like red wine.

Lisa It's perfect.

Sean I'll – why don't I – here we go. I'll sit on this box.

Lisa Why don't you sit here? Beside me.

Sean Right. On the sofa. A bit cosier.

Lisa Sit down.

Sean I'll just – it's a bit bright.
I have a dimmer switch – can you believe that!
Whoever had this flat before me must have installed
a dimmer switch.
It's a bit . . . James Bond. A dimmer switch.
Here we go.
Lights up – lights down.

Lisa 'So, Mr Bond, we meet at last.'

Sean That's it.

Lisa And you would be tied to a chair.
I would have captured you.
I would say – something like –
'I like a man who . . .'
'I like a man with . . .'
I don't know . . .

Sean Yeah.

Lisa I can never think of these things.

Sean Me neither.

Lisa I could be the Norwegian Bond girl.

Sean Yes.

Lisa Is there one? I don't really know the films.

Sean I don't know. Probably there is.
I don't know.
. . .
You tell me when the light's right.

Lisa Darker.
There.

There is a small electrical buzz.

432

Sean That's better, isn't it?
Things can be too bright.
I forget that sort of thing.

Lisa Sit down.

Sean sits down.

Sean Hoo.
Here we are.
Chez moi.
Welcome to my humble abode.
Lick of paint.
Put a few knicknacks out.
Soon be home.

Lisa Sean. Why don't you put your arm around me?

Sean Why not indeed?
The old arm around the old shoulder.
That's what you're supposed to do, isn't it?
I haven't done that since I was –
Actually I was waiting to do it surreptitiously, you know . . .
Like in the cinema with your first girlfriend.

Lisa Can I ask you something?

Sean Sure.

Lisa Have you ever read Knut Hamsun?

Sean I haven't actually – no – I haven't read anything by him.

Lisa You remind me of him.

Sean Oh – I hope that's a compliment.

Lisa I think that's what it was that made me want to talk to you in the pub.

Sean Right.

Lisa When I read the novels of Knut Hamsun –
I felt a very strong connection.
Something spiritual.
And when I saw you in the pub.
Sitting alone. Watching everything.
You seemed apart and yet
Something about you connected with me.
And that doesn't happen very often.

Sean Lisa, I . . . you probably should know I . . .

Lisa Shh.
This is perfect.
The two of us.
So late at night.
The city asleep at our feet.
Alone together and hungry.

Sean Would you like something to eat?
I've got toast.

Lisa No – I mean hungry in the Norwegian sense.
'Hungry', you know
With a needing in us.

Sean As a matter of fact – there's a buzz.
The dimmer switch is buzzing.
It sometimes does that – anywhere in between
completely dark and completely light – it buzzes.
It's a bit maddening.
I'll just see if I can fix it.

Lisa Why not just switch the light off, Sean?

Sean Do you think I should?

Lisa There's a moon.
And the light from the city.

That's enough.
Our eyes can adjust.

Sean You're right.
That's what we'll do.
Switch it off.

Sean switches the light off.

That's just the job.
We'll have the moon for a lamp.

Sean stumbles.

Oww.

Sean falls over.

Shit. Ayahh.

Lisa Are you all right.

Sean I'm fine. Box. Stubbed my foot.
Stupid.

Lisa Have you hurt yourself?

Sean No. No.
I'm fine.
Shit.

Lisa Sean.
Why don't you sit down?

Sean Yeah.
I'll sit.

Sean sits.

There we go.
Here I am – inviting you back –
You must think I'm a right dipstick.
Falling about.

Lisa Your heart's beating awful fast, Sean.
Like a wee mouse's heart.

Sean Is it?
What am I?
Am I a man or a mouse?
As a matter of fact this wine is quite good, isn't it?
You can tell it's good.

Lisa Look at the moon.

Sean I know.

Lisa Fat and calm.

Sean Full.

Lisa Full up.
I'm always at my best with a full moon.
When it's waning I find myself just sitting in my basement sometimes.
But when it's waxing I'm out and about.
I'm a social butterfly virtually.

Sean I'm sorry I'm not a better talker. I don't often –
I hardly ever in fact –

Lisa I think talking is overrated.
In Norway people don't speak much.
They're more comfortable passing time in silence.

Sean That's like me.

Lisa Put your hand on my heart.
Here.
Feel that.
My heartbeat.

Sean I can feel it.

Lisa Everything moves so fast in this country.
Everybody shouts – everybody lies – everybody spends

time running – that's what makes your hearts beat so
fast.
  Look out there.
  This is winter.
  It's time to hibernate.

Sean Lisa, you're –

Lisa What am I?

Sean You're –
  In the moonlight.
  You're gorgeous.

Lisa But not in the daylight.

Sean No I didn't mean –
  Shit.

Lisa I'm teasing you.

Sean Oh. Right.

Lisa I have quite a Norwegian sense of humour.
  Sometimes it puts people off balance.
  I'm sorry.

Sean No. No. It was – you got me.

Lisa Look out there.
  If we were in Trondheim now.
  We could sit here for months and the sun would never
rise.
  The whole city, the hills would be covered in snow.
  The only sign it was day would be a glow behind the
horizon.
  And a blue light on the snow.
  In Trondheim in midwinter.
  We stay inside all the time.
  We switch the heating on.
  And we sit at the window.

Just like this,
Watching the winter go past.

Sean What about eating and things?

Lisa We eat crisps mostly.
You don't need to eat so much because you don't spend much energy.
Your heart slows down. Your mind becomes still.
You just pull a downy over you and sit.

Sean I could live like that.

Lisa I knew you would think that.
Isn't that amazing.
I think that proves we're connected.
I knew you would understand about winter.

Sean I could hibernate. Just shut down for a while.

Lisa That's it.

Sean In Trondheim, in winter –
Don't your muscles sort of shrivel up?
What about daily exercise?

Lisa For exercise we dance.
And we have sex.

Sean Oh.

Lisa People think that in Norway there's a very high suicide rate.
But in fact that's a myth.
The suicide rate is quite low,
Because, being Norwegian, we know how to live with the dark.

Sean gets up again.

Sean Would you like some music? Shall I put a cassette on?

I've got a few cassettes?
What would you like?

Sean starts looking through some cassettes in a box.

Madness. Everybody likes Madness. Do you like
Madness?

Lisa I don't know.
I've never heard them before.

Sean Never heard Madness?
Everybody's heard Madness.
'Baggy Trousers' – da da da da.

Lisa I don't know it.
Put it on if you want.

Sean Maybe not.
It's maybe a bit lively.
Gary Numan.

Lisa I really don't mind.

Lisa gets up, goes over to him.

Sean I don't know what people like these days.

Lisa The woman in the photograph – on the windowsill?
Who is she?

Sean She's – my ex-wife.
She's – quite a long time ago.

Lisa Is that your boy in the picture?

Sean Yeah.
That's why I have the picture out.
Because it's a picture of him.

Lisa Do you still see them?

Sean No.

Lisa That's a shame.

Sean Yeah.

Lisa What's his name.

Sean Conor.

Lisa That explains your tattoo.

Sean That's right.

Lisa 'Conor Forever'.

Sean Yeah.
A bit stupid.

Lisa I don't think it's stupid.

Sean I tried to have it burned off.

Lisa Why?

Sean Because –
Anyway, I couldn't afford the treatment so it's still there.

Lisa I think it's nice.

Sean Yeah.

Lisa What's your wife's name?

Sean Catriona.

Lisa At least you didn't get a tattoo which said –
'Catriona Forever'.

Sean Yeah.

Lisa Why did you split up with her?

Sean Lisa, I don't really want to talk about it, OK?
If that's all right.
I wasn't very clever.

I was involved in some pretty grimy events and I
ended up fucking up her life, my life and my boy's life.
    So you know – there's not a lot to say.
    I try not to think about it.

Lisa Do you know
    When you talk, Sean,
    Your eyes dance?
    In all the time I've lived here
    I haven't met a man like you.

Sean I can't find any music.
    I can't find anything.
    I don't even know what half these tapes are.
    I haven't bought music for so long.

Lisa I don't mind about music.

Sean You probably like gothic music or something.
    Rap music.
    I don't – I haven't got any.
    I don't.
    Gangster rap, it's all a foreign country to me –

Lisa How old is Conor?

Sean He's ten years old.
    He's ten years old.
    And he's out there somewhere asleep.

Lisa You're thinking of him.

Sean I wasn't.

Lisa And he's thinking of you.

Sean Probably not.

Lisa I bet he is.

Sean I don't think so.

Lisa My father was a sea captain.
On a Norwegian container ship.
Can you guess what the ship's name was?

Sean I don't think I can, no.

Lisa It was called the *Liselotte*.

Sean So he named his ship after you. That was nice.

Lisa No. Silly.
I was named after the ship.

Sean Oh, right.

Lisa Anyway.
When I was small
He just went away.
Off on his ship.
And everybody said that was the end of that.
But I thought of him.
And I knew he thought of me.
And so I believe that out there in the dark
In the snowy forest
My thoughts and his thoughts meet like two ghosts.

Sean It's a nice idea.

Lisa And that's like you and Conor.

Sean Listen, Lisa, it's quite late.

Lisa Not really.

Sean You're probably tired.

Lisa I'm OK.

Sean I'm – I work shifts – in the car park –
I have to be – I'm on early tommorow morning –

Lisa Call in sick.

Sean I don't want to do that.

Lisa These moments don't happen very ofte, Sean.
Moments when people come very close to each other.
If I hadn't come to the pub.
If the moon had been waning.
If I hadn't seen you.
Just think.
We might have missed each other for ever.
But instead here we are.
Hungry and alone, together.
. . .
I don't know about you, Sean.
But I think that's a big turn on.

Sean Lisa – I don't feel exactly – at this moment – it's gone a bit –

Lisa Just play some flipping music.
We can dance.
Let's dance –

Sean No.

Lisa Come on. Take hold of me.

Sean It's all right. You're all right.

Lisa Put the music on loud and we'll dance.

Sean The neighbours – upstairs is an old woman, she sleeps like a bird.

Lisa It doesn't have to be loud then. Just hold me.

Sean Maybe we should have gone to the club.
With your friends.
It's stupid you coming back here.
Look at the state of the place.
Everythings in boxes.
I knew that. At the time.

I knew you would prefer the club.
Maybe it's not too late.
Your friends are there.
I'll take you down there.
I'll walk you.

Lisa They aren't my friends, Sean.
They were just women I was standing next to.
I wanted to come back with you, Sean.
I want to spend the night with you.

Sean You don't know me.

Lisa I do.

Sean You don't.

Lisa Not in the way people here 'know' people.
But I know you.
Let's kiss.

Sean Look just – Get off.

Pause.

I'm sorry.

Lisa What's wrong?

Sean I'm sorry.
Lisa – this is – this is not going – things like this don't
happen to me.
Someone coming back to the flat.
Meeting someone in a pub.
I just went for a drink – I didn't expect.
I don't really know how to handle it.
I'm not often entertaining a –
Someone like you.

Lisa Do you mean a woman, Sean?
Or do you mean, a Norwegian?

Sean I think I'd maybe better walk you home.

Lisa I see.

Sean I think it's probably for the best.
I know how this is going to go and it's not pretty.

Lisa You can tell the future, can you?
That's so typical.
Everybody here thinks they can tell the future.
Well, let me tell you a secret, mister.
Nobody knows.

Sean You're a really nice girl, Lisa.
You could have gone home with any bloke in that pub.

Lisa You asked me.

Sean I asked you. I never thought you'd say yes.

Lisa So much for your telling the future, then.

Sean A lot of drink, a clumsy fuck and then what am I doing here.
I don't think I can stand waking up to it.
I'm sorry.

Lisa OK.

Sean So I'll walk you back to – wherever.

Lisa I'll be fine. Just give me my coat, please.

Sean No.
You can't go on your own.

Lisa I'll be quite all right.

Sean This isn't a nice area, Lisa.
I'll walk you.

Lisa Piss off.

445

Sean At least let me call you a minicab.

Lisa I'm not a delicate flower.

Sean I realise that – I just think –

Lisa You don't know what you think.
One minute I'm gorgeous.
The next minute you don't want me in your house.

Sean It isn't that.

Lisa I'm sorry if I've offended you, Sean.
I know that – being Norwegian – I'm used to being quite open about sexual relationships.
I say what I feel.
I'm not going to apologise for that.
Men in this country – they're so – hypocritical.
They're either slathering dogs or whimpering puppies.
It makes me physically sick.
None of you are a match for a real Norwegian woman.

Sean You're right.

Lisa Don't smile at me.
You think it's funny.

Sean I'm sorry.

Lisa You can't help it.
It's this country.
It's not your fault.
I'm used to it.

Sean I'm not a good person for you to be with.
Believe me.

Lisa I've seen you before, Sean.
In the pub.
I had my eye on you.
Always sitting there.

On your own.
Reading your book.
In the dark and swirling lights all around you.
In your black suit.
All the noise around you.
And you still and dark and reading your book.
And I thought.
That man could be the last great hope of his nation.
But in fact.
You're no different from the rest.

Sean It was a detective novel, Lisa.
It's not exactly poetry.

Lisa It was a book.

Sean Lisa.
I'm not liked – OK?
I've been involved in some pretty grimy business and I'm not a liked person.
Everybody knows it and usually folk leave me alone.

Lisa You're forgetting I'm not from here.

Sean I've had a few incidents where I've fallen apart a bit.
You know – the floor's a bit shaky.
It's hard enough for me to stay standing
Without you barging in here – talking about souls.
I'm not mysterious or interesting, Lisa.
I'm a disaster.
I'm barely keeping my life together as it is.
The last thing I need just now is to have my head messed up
Because I find myself falling for a nutter. All right. I'm sorry. But that's how it is.

Lisa You're very judgemental.
Passing comments like that.
In Norway we don't –

Sean Will you just stop it with the Norway.
  You're not from Norway.
  I've seen you around.
  You're not from fucking Norway so stop going on about it.

Lisa Pow pow pow.

Sean What?

Lisa My electric shield of power sends your negative energy right back at you.

Sean What are you talking about?

Lisa You don't scare me.
  Show your teeth all you like.
  You don't scare me.

Sean I don't want to scare you.
  Shit.
  I really don't want to scare you.

Lisa Pow. Pow. Pow.

Sean Jesus Christ. Will you calm down?

Lisa Pow pow pow – coming right back at you.

Sean Calm down.

Lisa You can't touch me.

Sean Keep your voice down, will you?
  Oh Jesus. Shit shit.

Lisa You can't get me.

Sean I'm sorry. I didn't mean it. I didn't mean anything.

Lisa Onetwothreefourfivesixseveneightnineteneleven twelvethirteen . . .

  Lisa continues to count.

Sean doesn't speak for a few moments. Only the sound of her counting.

Sean It's OK.
It's all right.
I won't touch you.
I won't come near you.

Lisa still counting.

Just sit down.
That's it.
You just sit.
Yeah.

Lisa still counting, but slowing down and getting quieter.

OK.
I'm just here.
Just on the box, OK.
I'm here.

Lisa still counting but more controlled now.

That's it.
That's a girl.
I'm just here.

Lisa still counting.

You take as long as you like.

Lisa slowly comes to a stop.

SAre you OK.

Lisa I'm OK.

Sean I'm really sorry.

Lisa It's OK.
You couldn't know.

449

The most upsetting thing you can say to a Norwegian
Is to tell her she's not Norwegian.

Sean Of course you are.
Jesus.
I was way out of line.

Lisa I'm OK.
The counting always works.
I count and I think of home.
The forests and the mountains and the blue sea.

Sean I do that.
I do it as well.
They taught me that too.

Lisa They taught you too?

Sean Not in Norway.
I was in prison, Lisa.
I got let out a year ago. A year and I haven't even
unpacked my stuff. It's all I can do to sit in front of the
window and watch the clouds form and the day pass.
Do you understand?
So – you threw me – asking me to kiss you and that.

Lisa Poor Sean.

Sean And the wine – you know,
I bought that wine when my boy was born.
It was supposed to be drunk on his eighteenth birthday.
But I don't know where he is.
And anyway it tastes like pish.
And it threw me a bit.
The floor started to wobble.
You know what I'm saying?

Lisa Of course.

Sean So I sort of lashed out in my words to you.
But I know it was way out of line.

Lisa It's OK.

Sean And so, Lisa, if you want to leave
Which you probably do
I'll walk you home.
And I won't even say a word or ever mention anything
to anybody.
But if you want to stay –
I want you to stay.
I want you to stay.
It's quite dark up here, Lisa,
In the old head.
And – you're . . . so –
Light and gorgeous.

Lisa Like a very nice cake.

Sean No, I didn't mean –

Lisa I'm teasing you again.

Sean Right.
Norwegian humour – I'll need to get used to it.

Lisa In Norway we're used to darkness in people's heads.
We even prefer it.
Because if there is no darkness,
Then what in heaven's name are you thinking about?
How good you are or something?
How perfect? How wonderful?
That would be arrogant.
We Norwegians think people who are happy are
perhaps just a little bit above themselves, don't you?

Sean I do.

Lisa Where are you from, Sean?

Sean Me?

Lisa Yes.

Sean Here.

Lisa Were you born here?

Sean No – I was born up north.
    On the west coast.
    We moved here when I was little.

Lisa I thought so.
    Where?
    Where exactly?

Sean A little place called Kinlochleven.
    My dad used to work in the aluminium smelter there.

Lisa You may not know this, Sean, but in the tenth century
    The Vikings came here, from the west.
    A lot of people say they slaughtered and raped and burned.
    And they did – but only if people resisted them.
    Mostly they settled and farmed and married local women.
    What's your second name Sean?

Sean Macdonald.

Lisa I knew it.
    I knew it.
    That's a Viking name, Sean.
    Macdonald is a Viking name.

Sean D'you know.
    I think I'd heard that.
    I think I'd heard that once.

Lisa It's one-hundred-per-cent true.

Sean There you go.

Lisa You're a Norwegian after all.

Sean I suppose I am.

Lisa I could tell.

Sean Maybe that's why I turn my sofa to face that way.

Lisa Deep instinct.

Sean I suppose.
How are you feeling?
You're smiling.

Lisa I'm all right.

Sean Good.
. . .
Can I get you anything.
Some crisps.
More wine.

Lisa Put some music on.

Sean What do you want?

Lisa Let me look . . .
Let's see what you've got.

Sean It's all rubbish. Just the cassettes that were in the car when my wife left me.

Lisa This one.
This is Norwegian.

Sean God, yeah. I suppose it is.

Lisa Play this one.
And we'll dance.

Sean I wish we could, but there's no carpet down Lisa.
The guy downstairs, I swear he goes mental if I even just pace about.

Lisa puts the cassette in the player.

She presses play.
The volume is low.
The music is 'Aha – Take on Me'.

Lisa In Norway – what we do – is, we play the music quietly.

Like this.

And then we take our shoes off.

And we stand together like this.

And we hold each other like this.

You put your hand there.

That's it.

And then we rest our heads on each others shoulders.

So we don't have to look at each other in the eye.

And we just sway.

Like that.

That's it.

That way we can dance and no one is disturbed.

. . .

Just two Norwegians

Holding on to each other

In a foreign land.

Music plays quietly.

The End.

KYOTO

Kyoto was commissioned and co-produced by A Play, a Pie and a Pint and the Traverse Theatre, and first performed at Òran Mór, Glasgow, on 9 March 2009. The cast was as follows:

Lucy Vicki Liddelle
Dan Matthew Pidgeon

Director Dominic Hill
Designer Rita McGurn
Producer David MacLennan

Characters

Lucy

Dan

Setting

A hotel room

Lucy and Dan enter the hotel room.
  Lucy laughing.

Dan Shh.

Lucy I want you.

Dan I know.

Lucy I WANT YOU NOW.

Dan Someone might hear us.

Lucy No one can hear us.

Dan The walls in these places –

Lucy Everyone's in the bar.

Dan I know but – someone could be in the corridor.

Lucy Who?

Dan I don't know. France or Italy are both still awake

Lucy *Bonsoir*, France! *Buona notte*, Italy!

Dan Shh.

Lucy Don't shush me.

Dan I know but –

Lucy I don't care who's in the corridor.

Dan We don't want the world to know what we're up to.

Lucy The world's in the bar – the world's drunk.
  We're here.
  Alone.

Dan At last.

Lucy I thought today would never end.

Dan Fucking Russia –

Lucy And India going on and on.

Dan We could have been finished hours ago if you weren't so stubborn.

Lucy Me stubborn?

Dan Hope or desire. Hope or desire.

Lucy You could have agreed to desire.

Dan You could have agreed to hope.

Lucy You could have agreed . . .

Dan I don't want to fight you any more.

Lucy Then surrender.

Dan touches the wall, looking for a light switch.

What are you doing?

Dan I can't find the light switch.

Lucy Leave it.

Dan I want to see you.

Lucy You just want to see me naked.

Dan No – well, yes.

Lucy In all my glory.

Dan In all your glory.
Aha.
Found it.

Dan presses the switch.
Nothing.

He tries again.
And again.

It's not working.

He tries again.

Bulb must have gone.

Lucy Leave it.

He tries a bedside light.

Dan It's not working either.

Lucy Let's do without light.

Tries another.

Dan Hopeless.

Another.

Must be a fuse.

Lucy Let's just –

Dan Some sort of central fuse has gone and – I don't know – caused a short perhaps or an outage in the system. It's always the same in these post-communist places –

Lucy It's fine.

Dan Maybe I should call reception.

Lucy Oh for God's sake, Dan.
Let it be dark.

She opens the curtains.

Look out there.
Big fat moon.
Forest and lakes.
Who needs light?

Dan You're right.

Lucy We've got the whole night ahead of us.
Let's just be together. You and me.
The two of us drunk and in the dark at last.

Dan At last.

Kisses.

For God's sake!

Lucy What?

Dan How do I undo this dress?

Lucy There's a thing on the back –
Oww.

Dan Sorry.

Lucy Let me –

Dan No – it's OK it's just –

Lucy What?

Dan You today
You in that dress talking about desire and the
PowerPoint light catching your face in the dark

Lucy I saw you – putting me off my stride.

Dan I couldn't help it.

Lucy Looking at me – I was trying to talk about desire.

Dan I wanted to rip that dress off you.

Lucy I was trying to make a serious point and you were –

Dan A very serious point.

Lucy – ripping my dress off with your eyes.

Dan I'm sorry.

Lucy Don't be sorry.
   I spend my life in a kagoul.
   Sometimes it's nice to be looked at.

Dan Ten years I've waited for this moment, ten years thinking about it and now it's finally here and I'm stuck with a stupid clasp.

Lucy Rip it.

Dan What?

Lucy Rip the dress.

Dan It's Prada.

Lucy Do it.

Dan Have you got another?

Lucy I've got jeans.

Dan It's the plenary session tomorrow.

Lucy So.

Dan You can't wear jeans to the plenary session.

Lucy I don't care.

Dan What will you do for the plenary?

Lucy RIP IT!

Dan Right.
   Rip.

He rips the dress open.
   She laughs.

What?

Lucy Your face.
   Grr.
   Like a boy.

Dan Come on, let's get under the covers.
  It's cold.
  Are you cold?

Lucy Freezing.

Dan The heating must not be working.
  Let's get under the blanket.
  It's always the same in these ex-communist places.
They can do
  The fittings and the the food and the carpets but the
central heating. It's still the same awful plumbing they
had in the seventies.

Lucy We could go to my room.

Dan Best not.

Lucy Why not.

Dan I don't want to be wandering the corridors at night.

Lucy Why not?

Dan It's not very seemly, is it?
  For a *chef de délégation* to sneak round a hotel in his
stocking feet.

Lucy Seemly.

Dan You know what I mean.

Lucy Stocking feet.

Dan Socks. I mean – socks.

Lucy Very Victorian.
  Very Captain Scott.

Dan I'm just saying that there are certain standards
which I can't be seen to breach.

Lucy 'I am going down the corridor in my stocking feet.
  I may be some time.'

Dan Don't tease me.

Lucy You're too easy to tease.

Dan Besides, this room has a king-size bed.

Lucy Lucky you.

Dan Lucky me.

Lucy Dan?

Dan Mmm?

Lucy How come your room has a king-size bed?

Dan I don't know.

Lucy Did you ask for a king-size bed?

Dan No.

Lucy All our delegation have singles.

Dan Right.

Lucy Nigeria are all in twins. Sharing.

Dan I didn't realise.

Lucy And Holland.
I thought we were all given similar rooms.

Dan It's probably just alphabetical or something. You know what it's like.

Lucy Yeah, right.

Dan What does that mean?

Lucy Funny the way the alphabet always seems to favour certain countries

Dan Oh come on, you don't think –

Lucy Funny the way things end up –

Dan Don't read so much into what's obviously –

Lucy It just seems surprising

Dan I can't believe you're saying this.

Lucy I can't believe you're so naive!

Dan Naive!

Lucy The way this conference is arranged is not accidental.

Dan Beds – it's just beds –

Lucy The sleeping arrangements are a symbol of the underlying power structures.

Dan You search for signs –

Lucy I see signs.

Dan Everyone has bad intentions – that's what you think.

Lucy I just don't like –

Dan I can't believe you're so paranoid.

Lucy Paranoid – me!

Dan Yes.

Lucy Because I want to save the world.

Dan Because you think you're the only one who wants to save the world.

Lucy You didn't question the arrangements. You weren't curious about how the rooms were allocated. You just assumed. This is what you always do. You assume your comforts are – natural – that your comfort is your entitlement. And other people have to bear the consequences of your entitlements.

Dan Like who?

Lucy Like me?

Dan You're a polar scientist. You like being uncomfortable.

Lucy What about the poor?

Dan Polar scientists are poor?

Lucy No, but –

Dan You speak on behalf of the poor now.

Lucy I speak on behalf of the ice –
And the ice speaks on behalf of the poor.
Why are you smiling?

Dan I'm not smiling

Lucy You are smiling.

Dan I'm sorry.
It's just –
You – standing there in your underwear
Hands on hips.
Saving the world.
You look like
Wonder Woman.

Lucy You bastard.

Dan (*sings*) 'Wonder Woman.'

Lucy Stop smiling at me.

Dan (*sings*) 'All out hopes are pinned on you.'

Lucy I'm serious.

Dan (*sings*) 'In your satin tights. Fighting for your rights.'

Lucy That's it –

Fighting.

Lucy This is war.

Dan Get off.

Lucy Surrender.

Dan I'm too strong for you.

Dan Oww.

Lucy Surrender.

Dan You bit me?

Lucy Submit.

Dan Never.
Oww.
I submit – I submit.
I'm wrong. You're right.

Lucy Always.

Dan Always.

Lucy Good.

Dan Peace?

Lucy Peace.

Dan Am I bleeding?

Lucy I hope so.

Dan You're vicious.

Lucy It's funny.

Dan What's funny?

Lucy All those years of arguing with each other.
Calling each other all sorts of names across the table.

And all that time.
It turns out that we could have been doing this.

Dan Who knew.

Lucy Look at you –

Dan What?

Lucy I could wipe that smile off your face
I could leave marks on your skin
I could leave my pants in your suitcase
I could mess you up.

Dan Come here

Lucy I want to mess you up.

Dan Do you?

Lucy I want to fuck you up –

Dan I want to fuck you –

Lucy Do you?

Dan Don't you?
I mean – that's what – we are – aren't we?

Lucy We are

Dan Oh my God!

Lucy What?

Dan You hands are so cold.

Lucy Sorry.

Dan Your fingers are white.

Lucy It's normal for me.

Dan That's what your skin would look like if you were
dead.

Lucy I have poor circulation.

Dan You'll get frostbite. Put them against the radiator.

Lucy It's cold

Dan For God's sake. It's always the same in these ex-communist places – they can fix the menus but the mentality – they can't change the –

Lucy It's fine.

Dan It's not fine. It's freezing.

Lucy We'll just have to share our bodily warmth.
   In the Arctic I sleep with the dogs.

Dan Dogs?

Lucy Out on the ice. A full moon. Pack of huskies round me. Better than any man.

Dan Really?

Lucy Really.

Dan Woof. Woof.

   Laughs.

Lucy Dan.

Dan Yes.

Lucy When did you know?

Dan Know what?

Lucy Know about us? That we –

Dan Kyoto.

Lucy Even in Kyoto?

Dan After that dinner when you kissed me goodnight.

Lucy That was just a – just a formal – a formal peck.

Dan It was a peck but you held on to my arm for just a second longer than you had to –

Lucy No!

Dan Just a millisecond, a fraction of a millisecond, a nanosecond

Lucy A nanosecond?

Dan You kissed me and you held on to my arm and we made eye contact and I knew.

Lucy A nanosecond?

Dan Yes.

Lucy I'm such a slut.

Dan When did you know?

Lucy That same moment.

Dan How.

Lucy Your eyes gave you away.

Dan You never said.

Lucy Neither did you.

Dan I thought I must be wrong.

Lucy So did I.

Dan All those conferences.

Lucy Every time I promised myself I would make a move but –

Dan Me too.

Lucy But there was never a night.
   Or there would be a night but no room.

Or there would be a night and a room but no chance because the world was in the way.

Dan The world.
Always needing to be saved.

Lucy If it wasn't for the world needing to be saved we wouldn't be here at all.

Dan Let's have a drink. What do you want?

Lucy You have a minibar?

Dan Yes.

Lucy I don't have a minibar.

Dan It's locked.

Lucy Locked?

Dan Why the fuck is it locked? I can't believe it's locked

Lucy Was it locked yesterday?

Dan I don't think so. I don't know.

Lucy It doesn't matter.

Dan That's not the point –

Lucy We've got everything we need.

Dan It's the principle –

Lucy You, me and a king-size bed

Dan I'll see about that tomorrow.

Lucy Am I the first?

Dan What?

Lucy Do you do this often?

Dan What? Sleep with polar scientists?

Lucy You know what I mean?
    Am I your first affair?

Dan No.

Lucy Oh.

Dan Is that bad.

Lucy No. It's just –
    I wish this was ten years ago, that's all.

Dan Come on.
    The world won't be saved this time. Or the next time
either.
    There'll be plenty more conferences.
    Next time we can plan, we can –

Lucy No.

Dan What?

Lucy There won't be a next time.

Dan We're going to Copenhagen –

Lucy I'm not going to Copenhagen.

Dan I don't understand.

Lucy I almost didn't come here.
    I shouldn't be here.

Dan Why not?

Lucy I'm with someone –

Dan With someone?

Lucy A man.

Dan OK.
    Here?

Lucy At home.

He doesn't see me so often because of my work.
So – you know – I need to – be with him.

Dan Fair enough.

Lucy He didn't want me to come, but I said this would be the last time.

Dan Right,
A man.
Does he know you're here?

Lucy No.

Dan Does he know about me?

Lucy What is there to know about you?

Dan I just don't think the world needs to know about our – thing.

Lucy The world's down there in the bar now.
Drinking its troubles away.
Drinking to forget.
Nobody knows about our 'thing' except us.
And even we don't seem to know what it is.

Dan Do you want to leave?

Lucy No.

Dan Are you sure?

Lucy No.

Dan You really are cold.
This is ridiculous.
I'm going to call down to reception for a blanket.

Dan picks up the phone.

It's ringing.
Do you think they do room service?

Lucy Probably.

Dan Let's get some beer.
    Blankets and beer.
    And something to eat.
    Better than beer.
    If this is going to be our last – our final – then –
    Let's have champagne.
    And smoked salmon.
    A blanket, champagne, some candles and smoked
salmon and –
    Anything else you want.

Lucy I'm fine.

Dan It's still ringing.
    Every conference I dreamt of seeing you. Every time
the negotiations came round I asked to be part of the
delegation. I would even engineer the situation so that
I could be on the same sub-committees as you. Arctic
Research Policy. Deep-water Fish.
    I would spend all night studying reports and journals –
Fiona going mad with boredom – the kids shouting and
screaming – and me with my nose in a book about fluid
dynamics. I hated cold-water currents.

Lucy You said you loved cold-water currents.

Dan I hated them. But whenever I would study them I'd
imagine negotiating with you – and so in the end – it
actually began to turn me on. Can you believe it? The
phrase – 'Arctic water column' – actually used to turn
me on.

Lucy Arctic water column.

Dan Gulf Stream mechanism.

Lucy Greenland glacial outflow.

Dan Polar albedo feedback.

She laughs.

Look at you smiling.
  I hardly ever see you smile.

Lucy I smile a lot.

Dan I never see it.

Lucy I smile in the Arctic.

Dan Do you?

Lucy On the sledge, behind the dogs.

Dan You smile when there's no one there to see.

Lucy When there's no one there to see I'm happy.

Dan Do you smile with him?

Lucy Who?

Dan Your man.

Lucy I smile behind his back.

Dan You don't want him to see you smile.

Lucy No. It's just he has a nice neck.

Dan This is ridiculous, there's no answer from reception. It's just ringing and ringing and ringing. It's always the same in these ex-communist places –

Lucy Maybe they're off for the night.

Dan I'll go down to reception. It won't take a minute.

Lucy It's fine. Stay.

Dan We can't stay here.
  Cold and hungry.

You go to your room. I'll go down to reception and get us some beer and crisps.

Lucy Don't go.

Dan looks for his wallet.

Dan Can't find my wallet. Can't see a bloody thing.

Dan opens the door.

Hall lights aren't working either.

Lucy If there's no one answering it probably means there's no one there.

Dan I'll find a night porter.

Lucy We don't need beer.

Dan We need blankets.

Lucy We can use our coats to keep warm.

Dan Be sensible.

Lucy What if you can't find a night porter?

Dan Well then, I'll – I'll go out into the street and see what I can see.

Lucy Into the street?

Dan Yes.

Lucy Look out of the window. We're beside a lake. In a forest. The town is miles away. I don't think you'll find anything resembling a blanket shop.

Dan When the buses took us from the airport I distinctly remember seeing a street with shops and cafés and –
   It was distinctly suburban. This whole area is suburban.

Lucy Stay. We can eat shortbread – the shortbread that comes with the coffee.

One biscuit each.
And I have wine gums.
I bought them to suck on the plane.

Dan This is silly. I've got plenty of money. I'll go out and find a taxi and ask him to take me to the street I saw, the one with shops.

Lucy You don't even speak the language.

Dan The taxi driver will speak English.

Lucy There you go again – always assuming –

Dan I'm not assuming. I'll walk out on to the main road and then I'll keep going until I find an all-night garage – and then I'll buy some champagne and salmon and a blanket.

Lucy Do they sell blankets in garages?

Dan They sell everything in garages.

Lucy You have no currency.

Dan I have a credit card.

Lucy It might not work.

Dan It'll be fine.

Lucy How do you know?

Dan I don't know, I'm just saying it –

Lucy Just saying things will be fine does not make them fine.

Dan I hope things will be fine.

Lucy Hope! Always hope.

Dan Oh for God's sake, Lucy, for a polar scientist you're not very chilled out, are you?

. . .

Just – give me a chance – we have one last night, one night and a room and a bed and – please just give it a chance to be – comfortable.

. . .

This is what you always do – you look at the world and under your gaze the whole world turns into catastrophe. I don't know what might be out there, but that doesn't necessarily mean it's bad – I could go out there and meet a lovely man selling blankets – a kind man selling champagne – giving champagne away because he likes foreigners – why not? Somewhere out there in China right now there are a million boys and girls on computers somewhere and one day those kids – if only we give them a chance – those kids will give birth to a new world which we can't even imagine yet – a wonderful world full of smoked salmon and blankets and crisps that can teleport into your hotel room at the touch of a keypad on your phone – no, not your phone your wrist – we'll have keypads in our wrists – no – we'll just have to think – 'I want crisps' – and crisps will teleport into our hands – crisps which taste like crisps but are made of – of complex carbohydrates with no oil or fat – wonderful crisps – that make your stomach flat like it was ten years ago.

Lucy Do you remember in Kyoto? That meal. Where they seated us opposite each other.

Dan The plenary meal when the prime ministers came.

Lucy The signing meal.

Dan Yes

Lucy And you were sitting opposite me. We sat on either side of that long table. God, it was so long, wasn't it?

Dan Venison in a bramble jus –

Lucy Medallions of venison in a bramble jus.

Dan And that wine – do you remember? I've never tasted wine so velvety.

Lucy And because it was the plenary meal and all the dignitaries were there, they put out all the very best food and the very best wine and the table was piled up high with so much stuff –

Dan Towers of food.

Lucy I felt like a child.
   I felt like all around me were adults who knew what they were doing. Adults who expected to have venison in a bramble jus.
   At every meal.
   And I looked at you – and you smiled – a crazy smile like a boy.

Dan I was only just out of university. I couldn't believe I was wearing a tuxedo and sitting next to the *chef de délégation* of Estonia and drinking wine that tasted – actually tasted like velvet would taste if velvet were a drink – I thought it was ridiculous.

Lucy You smiled and you made a face. You imitated the *chef de délégation* of Estonia.

Dan I was showing off.

Lucy You made me laugh.
   I thought.
   I'm not the only child in the world.
   There are two of us.

Dan I should have said something.

Lucy Why didn't you?

Dan I was scared I'd screw it up. I thought – not tonight – I'm too drunk on this velvet wine and too full of this absurd food. I'll try tomorrow night at the summing-up talks. Tomorrow night at the summing-up talks I'll charm her, I'll make my move.

Lucy But I missed the summing-up talks and I went back to the ice instead.

Dan And I got drunk and I spent the night with Hungary.

Lucy And then at Bonn. I made sure I was on the delegation to negotiate deep-water fish and you were there and you said – in the bar – do you remember? You said, 'Do you mind if I smoke,' and I said, 'No I don't mind,' and you said, 'Good. My wife hates it when I smoke.' Do you remember?

Dan I noticed you noticing.

Lucy And then every two years we'd meet and each time I would swear to myself that I would ignore you and each time we would find each other, right across the table from you, eye to eye and fighting about words.
 And then in Poznan we got drunk –

Dan And – there was that night when we nearly –

Lucy And Geneva.
 And Caracas.
 And after every conference I would go back to the ice and every time a little bit more of the ice was melting.
 And then suddenly, this summer. The sea was open and black. Black sea sucking up heat. We hadn't expected that. And on the land where there had been permafrost there was melting snow and all the gas from rotting vegetation that had been locked up in the frost for thousands of years was being released up into the atmosphere and under the force of it the earth was cracking and sinking at crazy angles and when I looked around me at this new landscape I realised for the first time that I had been wrong at Kyoto.

There were never any adults. There was always only us. You and me and people like us. Stumbling about in the dark fighting about words.

Dan It's not going to happen, is it?
Us.

Lucy No.

Dan Ten years and finally we have a night.
Finally a room.
Finally a chance to be together.
And it turns out it's too late.
And it turns out we're freezing and hungry and naked and depressed and guilty and –
Anyway there's no future because the world's going to end.

Lucy Sorry.

Dan I'll walk you back to your room.

Lucy You don't have to walk me.

Dan It's no problem.
I'll put some clothes on.

Lucy You don't have to.

Dan Damn!
I can't see anything

Dan puts his trousers on.

Jesus, it's cold.

Lucy Are you holding your stomach in.

Dan No.

Lucy You are.

Dan No, it's natural, my stomach is naturally flat.

Lucy Let go.

Dan No.

Lucy Let go.

She laughs.

Dan You should have seen me ten years ago. In Kyoto. You should have seen me then. If this had happened ten years ago we could have had salmon and champagne and crisps and beer and we could have stayed awake all night and I wouldn't care what the world thought because we had a night and a room and time and –

Lucy I could have seen you.

Dan You could have seen me.

Lucy In all your glory.

Dan In all my glory.

Lucy Dan.

Dan What?

Lucy Maybe it's not too late.

Dan What do you mean?

Lucy It's cold,
It's dark.
There's only the moon.
We're in the middle of forests and lakes and out there – there isn't anyone moving – there isn't a car on the road – I can't even see any street lighting, never mind a town or shops.
Let's go out
See the frost on the trees.
See the lake – Look, can you see the moon on the lake?
It must have frozen in the night.

Dan Maybe that explains the power outage. Maybe the frost in the night took out a pylon or something.

Lucy It all looks so white and new like a page.
Let's walk out in the snow.
We'll make the first footprints.
And afterwards we'll slide across the ice.
I'll teach you how to slide on ice.
How to slide so you can keep going for miles.
And as we slide we'll throw stones across the ice.
The big stones that make that rumbling sound.
That big echo that comes all the way up from the bottom of the lake.
A big booming echo to wake up the world.

Dan That would be great.

Lucy We'll do it.

Dan When it gets light. Yes. When it gets light, we'll go out there.
That's what we'll do.

The End.

BREWERS FAYRE

Brewers Fayre was first performed at the Traverse
Theatre, Edinburgh, on 14 August 2009. The cast was
as follows:

Jennifer Black
David Greig
Andrew Scott-Ramsay
Ashley Smith

Director David Greig
PowerPoint Operator Natasha Lee-Walsh
Stage Manager Ange Thompson

A Note on the Text

Speech is unassigned in this play.
The voiced characters are

Christine

Elaine

Ian

Anthony

The Counsellor

The audience play the role of Elaine.
Her speech, in italics, is performed by them
as a chorus. An easy way to do this would be to use
PowerPoint as a prompt. However, any appropriate
method is fine. When the big speech arrives
an actress who has been sitting in the audience
should stand up and take over the role of Elaine.
Thereafter Elaine's speech is no longer in italics.

ONE

Imagine your worst fear
Imagine the worst possible thing that could happen to you.
Imagine your nemesis.

What?

Imagine Christine

What you looking at?

Sixteen, pale as snow with a red slash of a dress across her waist, black hair and a head full of snakes – here comes Christine hurtling out of the darkness riding not one of death's black horses no but the x52 bus from Halbeath to South Queensferry – a bolt of pure evil come down to earth to burn you up – her white forehead bumping against the vibrating glass of the bus window – eye to eye with herself.

Hello, Christine.

Fuck off.

Imagine meeting Christine in a car park somewhere.
Imagine it's cold.
Imagine she's walking towards you.
Your throat feels dry. Your stomach feels tight. Your knees feel weak.
Imagine that.
What would you say to her?

What are you doing here?

What do you think I'm doing here?

I don't know.

What are you doing here?

You seem angry, Christine.

Yeah.

Would you be willing to formulate your anger into a request?

I want to kill you.

That is not a reasonable request, Christine.

TWO

Do you feel as if your life is over?
   Are you stuck in a loveless relationship?
   Do you feel like your partner is more like your friend than your lover?
   How long it is since you felt that spark of lust light up inside you?
   Do you remember the thrill of finding out someone was interested in you?
   Do you remember that feeling of butterflies in your stomach?
   Do you remember that particular ache of wanting and being wanted.
   Do you sometimes wonder if you'll ever feel those feelings again?

Yes.

Have you ever considered having an affair?

Yes

You would be surprised how many people feel the same way as you. Right now there are

Four hundred and sixty-eight guys

Waiting to meet up with

Ladies (forties)

Like you. Sign up now. Fill in your profile. It only takes a moment. Chat. Send someone a virtual kiss. Soon you will be meeting real partners and entering a whole new world you never imagined was possible.

Welcome.

Elaine.

THREE

Apparently there are no puffins on the Isle of May this year.
    Elaine?
    On the radio it said.
    No puffins.
    No puffins on the Isle of May.
    Elaine?
    Elaine?

Are there usually puffins on the Isle of May?

Yes.

Oh.

Usually they're there in huge numbers.
    But this year they're gone.
    . . .
    This is how it ends.

This is the drift of it.

Not one awful thing but a slow accumulation of small
bad things just piling up and piling up until eventually
we can't bear the weight of it any more and the whole
thing just collapses.

. . .

Each day is jut a little bit worse than the last until
eventually some catastrophe that would have seemed
utterly unimaginable five years year ago suddenly seems
very likely and even normal today.

. . .

Once it was normal to see birds in a field.
Now you hardly ever see a birds in a field.
Our daughter has never seen a bird in a field.

. . .

Hurricanes. Waves. Wars. Diseases. Debt.

. . .

Children stabbing each other.

. . .

Twitter.

. . .

Human thought has been given the power to form
itself into words and be broadcast without reference to
the authority of any individual mind. All kinds of
thoughts can just bark themselves out into world as soon
as they happen – like a kind of cultural Tourette's.

. . .

Fuck.

. . .

We can't listen.
We can't think.
We feel overwhelmed.

Ian.
  When you say 'we'
  I think you mean 'I'.

I know.
    I know
    You're right.
    Sorry.

It's OK.

But it has to happen sometime.
    Eventually there has to be an end.
    What if this is it?

You have to stop listening to the radio, Ian.
    You have to open the curtains.
    You have to get out of bed.

I know.

Ian.

Don't touch me.
        . . .
    I'm just – I'm – I can't –
    I'm sorry.

Let's go for a walk.
    The grass in the field is covered in frost.
    Let's go for a walk in the field.
    They'll build on it soon.
    Let's walk in the field before they start digging it up.
    Maybe we'll see a bird.
    Come on.
    Please.

Tomorrow.
    I promise.

FOUR

Christmas is a good time to have an affair. Christmas parties provide an excellent excuse for being out at night and coming home late. Maybe you had to stay with a friend in town because you didn't want to drink and drive. Perhaps the party will end too late for you to get home.

Remember – if you use a Christmas party as cover – it's sensible to actually turn up at the party for a short period of time before going on elsewhere. Wear a distinctive dress or tie. Say hello to people. That way, if asked, colleagues will confirm you were where you said you were. When having an affair it's always best to tell as few lies as possible.

Although much has been written about the positive effects an affair can have on a marriage – remember an affair can be also be destructive for a relationship and cause emotional damage to other parties.

Please remember to enjoy your affair responsibly.

Elaine.

FIVE

Imagine a boy.

Twenty-two – jeans and a pink shirt – dark eyes.
　　Skinny and tanned with a face like a girl.

Imagine Anthony.

Anthony Likes: Running
　　Anthony Dislikes: Smoking.
　　Anthony is looking for: Fun.

Currently there are
    Twelve
    Ladies
    Looking for
    Fun
    In
    Fife.

Hottie1964, Whipmyass, Flaming Sambucca, Crazy-
nymphochick2, Partyanimal67, Analbabe, Fungal . . .
Fungal? Oh, Fun Gal, Princess21,
    Lonelylassie, and Elaine.

Elaine?

Elaine.

Everywhere I look I see unhappiness.
    My husband is unhappy.
    My daughter in unhappy.
    My colleagues are unhappy.
    Sometimes I would like to smile
    And touch
    And kiss
    With someone happy.
    Please don't send me a picture of your penis.
    Please just tell me what makes you happy.

Kiss.
    Elaine.

Hello
    Elaine.
    Running makes me happy.
    Anthony.
    Send.

SIX

I'd like to start with what we want.

   . . .

Sometimes when people ask us what we want, we say 'I don't know.' It's almost as if we want people to guess what we want. Or maybe even we want someone to tell us what we want.

Yeah?

Because we don't know.

   . . .

But I've found that deep down underneath every 'I want' is usually an 'I need'.

   . . .

I want a new dress equals I need to feel special.

I want sex equals I need intimacy.

Yeah?

   . . .

A good exercise can sometimes be to write down some of your 'I wants' and then work through them trying to find out what unmet needs lie underneath. Yeah?

   . . .

Would you be willing to take a moment and to write down some 'I wants' so that we can work though it?

   . . .

Would you all be willing to do that?

   . . .

Would you be willing to do that, Christine?

SEVEN

He
  Is
  Beautiful.

EIGHT

I want a black belt in Tae Kwondo.

I want someone to notice me.

I want a career in media

Or law

Or maybe media law.

I want to go to Bali.

I want to go a ball.

I want to go to a ball wearing a ball gown that makes me look perfect.

I want to be photographed.

I want to be caught up in an atrocity but survive it and be able to give the first eyewitness account of it on the news and when they cameras talk to me in the aftermath I want to be ash covered and tearstained and I want to say something surprising, I want to say something interesting and profound and new . . .

I want money.

I want fame.

I want love.

I want two children – I want a boy and I want a girl.

I want a husband.

I want interesting friends.

I want to sit on my bed all day wearing my socks and writing songs.

I want to write a song as good as 'Umbrella' by Rihanna.

I want to fall in love.

I want to smash the boundaries of art.

I want to write poerty and music.

I want to buy a helicopter and explode myself in the sky above Fife and I want to have what's left of me float down on Tesco's car park and coat the faces of the shoppers in an imperceptible film of glittering ash.

OK.
  OK.
  Let's . . .

I want things to go back to how they were before.
  I want to go back to before.
  I want before.

NINE

I like all kinds of running but the kind of running I like
the best is running long distance. I train every day.
Recently I ran a sub-three-hour time in the Edinburgh
Marathon. It wasn't a personal best but it was close to
a personal best. I train pretty much every day. I run to
work. I run home from work. Sometimes when I run to
work there's haar. Running in the fog I feel like I'm
completely alone. That's a good feeling. I also like
winning a race.

Are you married?

No.

What are you doing here?

I don't understand?

*This website is for married people who want to have
affairs.*

Oh – ha ha. I see.
  I'm married to running. I have found that women who
want to have sex with me also want to have a relationship
with me. They want to see me at weekends or evenings
when I train. They want to go to clubs with me and
drink, but I don't drink. They want to have children or

talk about having children which doesn't fit in with my goals right now. One day a girl said to me, 'Anthony – I will always be the other woman in your life because you are married to running.' She was crying but she was right. Since then I have had six affairs. They've been good, I think.

Why did you pick me?

I liked your smile.

: –)

Send me another picture. Here's my number. Text me.

TEN

Tell me about before.

Before the house was new. The car was new. There was Tesco. Before Tesco was like a palace. Tesco was open for twenty-four hours a day. I got an allowance of a hundred pounds a month. There was snow. People went sledging on new sledges we bought from Tesco. We drove to the cinema. I sat in the back of the car. Mum and Dad would talk in low voices. They used to put the music on so I couldn't hear what they said. They used to put on Rihanna singing 'Umbrella'. The engine was quiet because we had a good car. I put my head on the window. I remember seeing myself look back at myself. That's what it was like before.

What happened?

They took it away.

ELEVEN

Imagine a forest.

Snow
  Pine
  Sun
  Breath

Imagine running

Eleven miles
  One hour, seventeen minutes, thirty-six seconds,
  Seven-minute miles.
  Seven-minute miles.

Imagine Anthony running through a forest like a deer.

Glenrothes
  West Lomond
  East Lomond
  Glenrothes.

Sweat
  Heat
  Pain
  Cold.

Twelve miles
  One hou, twenty-four minutes, twenty-two seconds.

TWELVE

They?

Someone.

Who?

I don't know.

A person?

The bank.

The bank?

It turned out it didn't belong to us.

What?

It.

It?

Fields
    Birds
    Cars
    Tesco's
    Money
    Snow
    Love.
    It turned out it didn't belong to us.
    So they took it away.

It sounds like you're grieving for lost things, Christine.

Yes.
    I
    You need to grieve.
    Grieving is your unmet need.

THIRTEEN

Anthony,
    Are you there?

Hi, Elaine.
    Where are you?

In the bath.

That's sexy.

I was imagining you.

What was I doing?

Running.

I am running.

In the woods

I am in the woods.

Naked.

I am naked.

I want you.

You'll have to catch me.

I'll catch you.

My legs are fast.

My imagination is faster.

You caught me.

Anthony.

Yes.

Are you really naked?

Yes.

I don't believe you.

Re: Thinking of you. Send.

FOURTEEN

Now that we have an 'I need', let's see if we can
formulate that into a reasonable request. Yeah? A
reasonable request is one which is practical, which is
specific, and to which you are prepared to hear the
answer no.

 . . .

   I want sex equals I need emotional security equals so
a reasonable request would be – would you be willing to
hold me and touch me in a reassuring way when I am
doing the dishes?
   Yeah?

 . . .

   So I need to grieve equals –
   How can we make that a reasonable request?
   Would you be willing to –
   Would you be willing to –

Give me back my things.

We can't physically turn back time and get back those
things you've lost so maybe if we try to focus on now.
Let's think about now and how you're grieving for a
future that you once imagined but now you have to
imagine a different future and that's making you sad and
so what is going to help you with that?

I want to hurt them.

Something practical.

Revenge.

FIFTEEN

A good place to arrange a first meeting is

The Brewers Fayre, South Queensferry just off the A90.

Brewers Fayre is always easy to get to and has plenty of parking. Also, if your meeting goes well, there is usually a reasonably priced Premier Inn next door where you can retire for more intimate fun. What better way to end your evening!

Elaine.

SIXTEEN

Elaine?

Hmmm?

There's no fish.

There is fish.

There's no fish left.

In the freezer there's fish.

In the sea. In the sea there's no fish. That fish in the freezer is called icefish which is basically an invented name for some Antarctic bottom-dwelling species which has never had a name before because never before in human history has anyone ever needed to try and catch it. We have fished the sea dry.
    Elaine.

Ian.

I have fished the sea dry.

I'm going out.

Oh.

The Christmas party.

What Christmas party?

I told you.

I must have forgot.

I'll probably be late.
    I might even stay in town.
    If I have a drink, you know.

OK.

Will you be OK?

I'll be fine.
    I've got the computer.
    I've got the radio.
    I'll be fine.

Good.

SEVENTEEN

Do you mind if I sit here?

I . . .
    I'm meeting someone.

OK – so –

Well, it's just –

Should I go?
    Do you want me to go?

No.

OK.

It's OK. The person I'm waiting for. They're not here.
So –

Don't worry, I'll go when your friend arrives.

OK.

Only there's no seats

No.

It's busy.

Christmas.

Christmas.

People like karaoke at Christmas.

Yeah.

This is not normally the sort of place I go. I'm only here
because I'm staying here. I'm staying in the hotel. Nothing
else to do. Nowhere to go. Television. So I thought I'd
come down here and see what's happening to what. Only
it's dead. Everybody's dead. Never seen a room full of
people look so fucking grey. You can practically smell it
coming off the carpet.
     What's your name?

Anthony.

Anthony.
     At least you're alive, Anthony.
     I'll say that for you.
     You've got a pulse.

I – yes – I –

I'm Christine.
     Nice to meet you.

Nice to meet you.

What's wrong.
    Ants in your pants?
    Anthony?

Nothing's wrong.

You seem nervous.

Well I – it's –

You're bound to be nervous, I suppose,

Am I?

You're on a date.

How did you know I was on a date?

Aftershave.

Oh.

Relax, Anthony.
    You look like you want to run away.

Sorry.

Is it a blind date?

Not exactly.

Not exactly?

I've seen her photo.

Oh. It's an internet thing. No wonder you're nervous.
Photos probably fake. She'll probably look like a troll.
An old troll with a witchy head. You're embarrassed.
    She does look like a troll!

No.

She does.

No.

Show me the photo.

No.

Come on.

 . . .

 . . .

 Oh, Anthony.

What?

Be careful

Why?

She'll eat you for breakfast, Anthony.
 Believe me.
 She's old.
 She'll eat you up.
 She'll suck your bones.

I don't think that's likely.

Believe me.
 I know.
 What are you doing with witches, anyway?
 You look hot.
 You should be with a girl.

I don't know how to talk to girls.

You're talking to me.

You're talking to me.

You're very tanned.
 Anthony.
 Do you surf?

No.

My skin is practically translucent you can actually see the blood moving about in my veins I'm like a blank sheet of paper, my mother says.

You look like you surf.

I run.

You run.

Where do you run?

In the hills.

Hills in Scotland?

Yes.

OMG.
That's amazing.

Is it?

Yes.
Because
I run too.

EIGHTEEN

Administrator
Office Administrator
Seeking Office Administrator
Seeking Admin Jobs Dunfermline
Seeking Jobs Dunfermline
Jobs Dunfermline
Lion tamer
Lion tamer Dunfermline
How to become a lion tamer
Bums
Pictures of women's bums
Free pictures of women's bums

Free bum pics.
Why am I so useless?
Why is Ian Morrison so useless?
Ian Morrison is a cunt.
What's the point?
What's the fucking point?
What's the fucking point if we're all going to die?
We're all going to die?
Are we all going to die?

NINETEEN

I knew it!
I knew we would both be runners!

Did you?

Your body.

What sort of running do you do?

Fast.

What distance.

All of them.

Wow.

Look at us talking.
Do you want a drink?
I always drink soft drinks.

OK.

Are you sure?

I think so.
Yes.
Yes I'm sure.

TWENTY

Is this the end of the world?

One to ten of about two hundred and twenty-three thousand for is this the end of the world?

Is this the end of the world?
  Wikipedia.

TWENTY-ONE

I was going great up to the second split but then the heat got to me. I faded. I'll give it a miss next year, I think. It's too early in the season.

Yeah.

Do you want another sparkling mineral water?

Yeah.

It's amazing. Usually when I'm with a girl I never know what to say. I sit. They look at me. Older women are good at talking. But girls usually just look at you.

Not me, though.

No.
  You're different.

Do you want to kiss me?

What?
  I don't . . . I'm not . . .
  Yes.

Some advice, Anthony. If you're with a girl and you want to kiss her – take control. Look into her eyes. Let her speak. Ignore what she's saying to you. Listen to the sound of the words but not to the words themselves. Listen to her speak and then you just slowly you reach out and

Take her hand?

Take her wrist. Take her wrist into your hand. Hold your hand over her wrist with just a small amount of grip. Like this. You're tanned. You surf. You know what to do.

I don't surf.

No. No. Forget that, Anthony. Forget what you don't know. You're a man. You know everything. She wants you to know everything. Take her wrist with just enough grip to show you're in control and then

Kiss her.

Pull her face towards you.

What?

Pull her face towards you. Do it.

Like this.

Yes.

Pull her face towards you and say to her –

I want you.

No. Say to her. You want me.

You want me.

That's it.

Then –

Kiss her –

No, look into her eyes and say –

You're not a runner, are you?

No.

You lied.

Eyes – grip – look –

I don't know if I should –

Trust me, Anthony.

They kiss.

Sing:

> *Sleigh bells ring, are you listening,*
> *In the lane, snow is glistening*
> *A beautiful sight,*
> *We're happy tonight,*
> *Walking in a winter wonderland.*

TWENTY-TWO

There was a bang.
   There was smoke.
   And that's when I knew it was all over.

I told Ian to fix the bloody car I told him the car was broken because I'd been hearing a noise when I'd been going to work it's so much money when you take it to the garage and Ian knows about cars he knows what to do with a car so he should have fixed it but he can't – not while he won't leave the house – and so I'm just coming up to the Forth road bridge and I'm nervous my heart's thumping and I feel ridiculous but I also feel excited and then there's a bang and a thump and smoke coming from the engine and I pull over onto the hard

*shoulder and it's snowing and the car's just totally dead
it's finished and the snow's building up on the road and
I think if I call the rescue people I could be here all night
and it's going to cost us an arm and a leg and I'll be here
all night waiting because of the snow and suddenly that
feels like the end of the world because I just want to do
this I've built up to this I don't want to stand beside this
motorway in the snow watching the possibilities slipping
away and so I look out at the long arc of lights over the
water and I decide to walk it fuck it I'll walk it's only
over the bridge and so I do I walk over the Forth road
bridge in the darkness with the snow falling about me
and I can't quite believe the world I'm in is the real one
and I'm thinking –*

Am I going to do this?

Am I really going to do this?

*And halfway across I have a very distinct feeling of how
it would be like to hold him and to be held and kiss him
and to have him want me and to feel it I have a very
distinct feeling of that and I feel like I might actually fall
over it's so strong and I think 'Elaine you idiot' and then
I think 'No I'm not an idiot, it's not stupid to want it's
not stupid to want to be wanted, it's not stupid it's
human' and so I walk on over the water feeling like I'm
at the end of a wonderful film and choirs are singing and
the credits rolling and then on the right-hand side and
at a slight elevation I see the sign 'Brewers Fayre' and
I notice that it's got a missing apostrophe and suddenly
I feel very very guilty and I wonder whether I am feeling
guilty because of Ian and because I told a lie or if I'm
feeling guilty because I suddenly have a visceral feeling
of how sad it is that I'm walking across the Forth road
bridge in my little black dress on my way to meet a boy
I met on the internet to do that to Ian to do that to Ian*

*when he's so depressed to do it when he's so depressed
he can't even get out of the bedroom to do that and to
do it in a place so cheap they can't even punctuate their
own name what sort of a pass have I come to how low
can I fall and then I wonder 'But what if the chain is
owned by a man called Brewers or refers to an imagined
character called Mr Brewers in which case the apostrophe
wouldn't be necessary and then it's just a place to meet
and it's neutral and I suddenly want him so much and
suddenly I'm nearly dead because I'm not thinking and
a lorry swerves to avoid me*

You fucking idiotic bitch!

Fucking idiotic bitch.

*I'm crossing the slip road and the lorry swerves and
sounds its horn and a cold tingle of anxiety pours itself
over me like cold water and I'm suddenly wet with sweat
and scared.*

You could have died, Elaine.

*I could have died on a motorway slip road in my black
dress nowhere near a Christmas party and it would all
be found out I'd be found out but now I'm in the
Premier Inn car park and I'm surrounded by night and
the snow's laid across the tarmac like a fresh white
carpet and my footprints on it and the strangeness of the
place and I realise that he's in there that boy that boy
I've arranged to meet over the internet and suddenly
I feel nauseous so I lean over the grass verge into the
bushes and I vomit and then I sit a moment and then
I don't know what to do so I take some fresh snow up
in my hand and put it in my mouth to take away the
taste and with the cold newness of the snow the thought
of the lightness of touching him and the lightness of
holding him and being held by him and knowing he*

*wants me and feeling he wants me finally I know is that
I don't want to die without once just once having once
just felt the feeling of standing with a boy in a hotel
room and taking off my dress and here is the door of the
Brewers Fayre no apostrophe and here is the restaurant
and here are the people singing on the karaoke –*

> *Sleigh bells ring are you listening,*
> *In the lane, snow is glistening*
> *A beautiful sight,*
> *We're happy tonight,*
> *Walking in a winter wonderland.*

And here is Anthony.
*   And here is a girl.*

Kissing him

*Wearing the tiniest of skirts – a slash of red across her
waist and all the rest of her pale and young as milk –
and she looks at me and she smiles.*

Christine.

Mum.

And Anthony turns
*   And Anthony sees me.*
*   And Anthony runs.*

TWENTY-THREE

What?
    What you looking at?

What are you doing here Christine?

What do you think I'm doing here?

I don't know.

What are you doing here?

I came for a drink.

Don't lie to me.

I came here to see him.

Who?

Anthony.

Don't lie to me.

I'm not lying.

You came here to fuck him.

No.

No?

I was never going to do that.
    That was just . . . imaginary.

That's not what you wrote.

You read what I wrote.

Yes.

I wanted him.

Why?

You wouldn't understand.

Why?

I don't know.

Why not Dad?

Christine.

Why?

He seemed happy.

He is happy.
    As long as you talk about running.
    Christ, he's boring.

You should have stayed.

He didn't want me. He wanted you.

You were kissing.

I made him.

What?

He didn't kiss me back.

Oh.

He's not happy.
    He wants you.
    He has an unmet need for you.

I'm sorry.

Jut another thing you took.
    You win.
    You always win.

You're angry.

    . . .
    Would you be willing to formulate your anger into
a request?

I want to kill you.

That is not a reasonable request, Christine.

TWENTY-FOUR

Imagine a car park covered in snow.
  Imagine you're sitting on a wall with Christine,
  Pale as milk and young with a red slash of a dress
across her waist,
  And imagine she's crying.
  And imagine you hold her.
  And imagine she says –

I just want things to go back to how they were before.

And imagine you say –

I know.
  I know.
  I know.

TWENTY-FIVE

The distribution of population in any civilisation follows
a bell curve. Population is low at the start of the
civilisation, high in the middle of the civilisation, and
low again at the end. If we could take a position at the
end of time and look back over the entirety of human
history we would find that seventy per cent of all humans
who ever lived were alive during a middle period: what
we might call the 'heydays' of human existence. Now it's
not possible to look at history from the perspective of its
end, but from this we can infer a probability that – if we
are alive – there is a seventy per cent chance we are alive
during humanity's middle period. So what means is – if
we are alive, the world is probably not coming to an end.

You know things.

Wikipedia.

You know how to fix a car.

I should have done it before.

I didn't know if you'd come or if I'd need to get a mechanic.
      I couldn't leave you.

I know but.

There are bad days and there are good days.

What made it good?

The snow.

      . . .

      The world always seems new when snow's fresh.

Where did you find her?

She called.
      She was lost.
      I picked her up.
      We were driving back.
      That's when we broke down.

Is she OK?

She's OK.

She's asleep.

Look at her.

Has she been crying?

Yes.

Things have been so shit recently.

They have.
      They have.

But we're alive.
Elaine.
Aren't we?

We're alive.
We're alive.
We're alive and the world seems new.
These are our good days.
These are our heydays.

Music: Rihanna, 'Umbrella'.